# Sun-Up to Sun-Down

## The Lives of Golf Course Owners

*Tom Franklin*

Blue River Press
Indianapolis, IN

Cover designed by Phil Velikan
Cover photo © Joann Dost.
Packaged by Wish Publishing

Printed in the United States of America
10 9 8 7 6 5 4 3 2 1

Published by Blue River Press
Distributed by Cardinal Publishers Group
Tom Doherty Company, Inc.
www.cardinalpub.com

*This book is dedicated to my wife, Sharon, daughter Morgan, son John and all members of family and my friends who have loved and supported me.*

*It is also for the people in the golf industry who have been so gracious in sharing their stories and their expertise.*

# Table of Contents

*vi*

# Foreword

## A Brief Profile of the Typical Golf Course Owner

*Provided by Mike Hughes, CEO of the National Golf Course Owners Association since 1990*

The men and women who own golf courses are responsible for all areas of the business. While some course owners limit their involvement as investors or partners, the great majority of owners are intimately involved in the day-to-day operations of the golf facility.

To the layperson, the business of golf course operations may seem relatively simple — grow grass, cook some hot dogs, and sell golf balls — but the business is multifaceted and ever-changing due to elements such as market changes, weather unpredictability and government regulations, to name just a few. Owners realize they are competing not only against other leisure activities, but also against the facets of the game which seem to prohibit many people from playing on a regular basis — such as perceived difficulty and an investment of time and money.

Owners are investing in more-sophisticated assets to adapt today's golf business to today's consumer, such as better operations and customer relationship software, more-sophisticated machinery and on-course technology (such as GPS) and more-qualified people to execute the operation from top to bottom. Moreover, many golf course owners are forging alliances with organizations and companies, such as hotels and visitors bureaus, to help market golf to tourists and meeting planners.

Golfers are the lifeblood of the golf business. Owners realize that a comprehensive plan must be developed and executed at the facility to offer consumers a quality product commensurate with the price offered. The product typically includes friendly interaction with staff from bag drop to restaurant, an attractive selection of merchandise, good food and beverage and a "meet-or-exceeds expectations" golf course experience — including conditioning and reasonable pace of play. In order to make all of this happen seven days a week, from sun-up to sun-down, a golf course owner must let it be known to new and prospective customers that the product is available (marketing), get golfers committed to playing (sales), deliver the promise (service, merchandise, food and play) in a safe environment (risk management) and get them committed to come back again (retention).

Owners must contend with many forces impacting the way they run the business, including but not limited to federal and local safety standards, nearby or contiguous property owners, heavy taxation burdens, human resource policies, rising operational costs and increases in competition. They must contend with the financial pressures of financing, several types of insurance and all kinds of employment situations, including full-salaried, part-time and seasonal.

Nevertheless, the men and women who own and operate golf courses are up for the challenge each day they open the doors, because they love the business. Whether the owner is a multinational, publicly traded company or a family which converted the old farm to a golf course 30 years ago, there is passion among all course owners. Most people who step foot onto the first tee would rather be nowhere else but at that place at that time, and golf course owners receive great satisfaction from providing pleasurable experiences to millions of people each year — and an enjoyable working experience for hundreds of thousands of employees.

# Introduction

I still like Ike. President Dwight D. Eisenhower is considered one of the greatest American presidents. It may not be scholarly, but here is a reason why I like Ike. Ike was an avid golfer who was instrumental in the construction of golf courses on military installations across the United States. My youth was spent on a Navy base in Virginia, where my best friend Wayne and I played one of Ike's nine-hole courses almost daily during summers from age 12 through high school. The course was simple, beautiful, accessible and most importantly, free. In the 300-yard walk from my parent's house, I would meet with Wayne and be on the eighth tee. Now it's 50-some years later, and I can go to sleep at night rehearsing each and every hole in vivid detail. Golf is indelible like that. I couldn't tell you what scores I posted. What I remember is the occasional miracle shot, the day our buddy John drove a tee shot through the windshield of a moving security guard truck, how Wayne and I avoided those security guards one night when we raided the pond of two pillowcases of balls, finding a bit of shade under Mimosa trees, and my pride in the ragtag set of clubs I carried. Sure, we thought of ourselves as athletes and we loved to compete, but that wasn't the source of our joy. We loved the carefree hours and the company of friends.

Now I'm retired from a 33-year career as a college psychology professor. At last, I can play the game I love anytime I want. Not really. I live in Wisconsin, and more of the year is winter than golf season. I've often played in a stocking cap and several times in snow, but by November golf is done until spring. My golfing buddies and I spend our time in winter talking about golf, remembering miracle shots, miracle rounds, the wildlife we encountered while playing, and times we literally rolled on the ground in laughter. I should add that some of those roll-on-the-ground laughs have to do with my putting stroke. My pal Dave just told me that he can't wait until next season to see me miss another short putt. Out of love and pity, Dave and Doug chipped in to buy me a new putter as a retirement gift. We'll see who has the last laugh next season.

In the middle of winter, surrounded by my clubs and lots of golf memorabilia, I began this book on golf. Briefly, here is how this book evolved.

As mentioned, I'm a psychologist. Some say that's the perfect preparation for writing about golf. Some days I'm sure they are right. During the last five years of my career, I was part of a team from the University of Wisconsin-Stout that worked with the National Golf Course Owners Association (NGCOA) to develop a new academic program, the Bachelor of Science in Golf Enterprise Management. I was asked to be part of the team because I knew the academic bureaucracies, I had done several research studies on the golf industry, and everyone knew I was an avid golfer. I was involved in discussions with golf industry leaders from across the nation on the goals of the new academic program, and I helped write the proposal for UW-system approval that was unanimously supported in 2005. When I developed the first three classes in the curriculum, I became quite knowledgeable about the industry. This work got me to a PGA merchandise show and seven (and counting) golf industry shows that combine the NGCOA, the Golf Course Superintendents of America Association (GCSAA), and the Club Managers Association of America (CMAA).

In preparing the academic curriculum and participating in these industry-wide events, I was struck by two observations. Firstly, there are no books on golf facility management or ownership. There are numerous books on golf history, agronomy and the responsibilities of golf course superintendents, golf course architecture, playing the game, tourism, and the entertainment side of the industry. However, publications on ownership and management seem limited to articles from the National Golf Foundation (NGF) and NGCOA publications, particularly *Golf Business* magazine. These are excellent resources, but one must search through many individual articles to develop a composite understanding of ownership and management. I began to conceive of a book project that could address this apparent void.

Secondly, my inspiration for the project developed from the opportunities I had to meet so many interesting and successful business men and women in the industry. From mom-and-pop family owners, to multiple-generational owners, to multiple course owners, to corporate owners, I am continually impressed by the diversity of businesses and the people who own and operate them. My belief is that each has a story to tell that would interest and educate others.

Lastly, I want to add that I was inspired by the writing of the late Studs Terkel. His 10 books are oral histories in which people's stories are told in their own words. His work moves me.

My plan was to conduct face-to-face interviews with golf course owners across the United States. Audio recordings of the interviews were transcribed to text and edited as necessary to address the breadth of the industry, the diversity of personalities, and perspectives on past, present and future trends in ownership and management. Furthermore, it seemed positively brilliant that with my contacts in the golf industry, I could travel, meet interesting people, possibly get some free rounds of golf, write a book, and maybe even do some keynote addresses at golf business conferences based on my new fame. My positively brilliant idea was thoroughly supported by my golfing buddies, who assumed I could include them on the "Mooch Tour."

The book is a compilation of the personal stories of a diverse set of American entrepreneurs who, by one path or another, own golf courses. Big dreams, wild successes and dismal failures, realities and delusions are all part of the industry. The book should be of particular interest to owners and operators, but I hope it will be of interest to others in the golf industry, as well as those who love the game and want an insider's perspective.

# A Brief History of Golf

There is a thrill in hitting a roundish object with a stick to propel it to some distant target that has fascinated people around the world throughout history. That thrill is so universal that nearly every area of the world has some claim to the origination of the game of golf. Ball, stick and target games have been noted by historians as early as B.C. in the Roman Empire and China and in a variety of countries throughout Europe in the 1300s. Shepherds passing time by knocking pebbles with their shafts probably led to eventual competitions. In Rome pebbles or rocks were replaced by leather balls stuffed with hair. One can easily imagine the evolution of the playing fields, the technologies and the rules of competition from those early origins of the game.

While many countries have some claim to the origins of golf, it is the Scots who are largely credited with the game we know today. Their noteworthy contribution was a hole. Targets elsewhere had been gates, trees or stakes in the ground. The Scots used holes in the ground burrowed by rabbits as the targets in their early stick-and-ball games. The runs made by sheep, rabbits and other wildlife created "fairways," an ancient sailing term for the easiest direction to navigate. "Bunkers," or hazards, were created by animals seeking shelter from the coastal winds. Mother Nature played a huge role in constructing the first playing fields in Scotland.

Evidence suggests that in Scotland, "gowf" was played in some form by 1300. The game was played at St. Andrews prior to the establishment of the university there in 1403. By 1457 the game had become so popular that King James II had an Act of Scottish Parliament to ban it on Sundays so as to preserve the skills of archery in case of war. That edict was the first documented reference to today's game. Two more attempts were made to restrict the playing of "gowf." James III banned it again in 1470 and 1493, although the game was so popular by then that people largely ignored those edicts. King James IV (King James I of England), the grandson of the king who originally tried to ban "gowf," tried to prevent his subjects from playing the game, as well. But he, too, found it hopeless and gave up, eventually beginning to play the game himself.

By the 1500s the game "golfe," as it was known in the British Isles, had spread to England, and land grants were provided for "links," narrow strips of land only a couple of hundred yards wide that connected the sea to the villages. The landscapes and vegetation made for ideal golf courses and prestigious memberships to clubs and golfing societies flourished. Supported by royalty who enjoyed and even competed at golf, the game was primarily played by those of some wealth. Even today, golf is known as a game for those with money.

Golf competitions became so prevalent that the first written rules began to appear.

The first known rules for golf were written for a match at the Royal Burgess Golfing Society of Edinburgh in 1744. That club has made a claim to be the first formal golf club, but their evidence is not substantiated.

When the Society of St. Andrews Golfers held an open competition for all golfers, whether they were a member of the society or not, St. Andrews became the premier golfing town. In 1764, when the St. Andrews course finally settled on 18 holes (down from its previous 22), 18 became the traditional number of holes for golf courses.

In 1834 King William IV permitted the Society of St. Andrews Golfers to rename itself The Royal and Ancient Golf Club of St. Andrews. St. Andrews has since become known as the "Home of Golf," and the "Royal and Ancient" has been the undisputed authority on golf, with the exception of the United States Golf Association in America.

When golf first came to America is not known. There is evidence that in 1659 government officials in Albany, New York, issued a law prohibiting people from playing golf in the streets because of injury risks to people and windows. However, it is more likely that the game being played was similar to the Dutch game known as "kolven" because it was played on ice, not turf. There is also evidence of golf clubs and balls being shipped to the colonies in 1743, but again, whether they were used for the game of golf as we know it today is uncertain. The same is true for historical references to golfing societies in the 1700s in Charleston, South Carolina, and Savannah, Georgia.

A very short golf course, probably two holes, was founded in 1884 in Pittsburgh, Pennsylvania, and another in 1910 in Sarasota, Florida. Neither of these survived. However, in 1888 a New Yorker originally from Scotland, John Reid, had clubs and balls shipped from Scotland, and he and some of his friends constructed a six-hole course in Yonkers, New York. Their St. Andrews Golf Club became the first surviving club in America.

Shinnecock Hills Golf Club on Long Island, New York, lays claim to being the oldest formal organized golf club in the United States (1891). It also claims to have the oldest golf clubhouse in the United States (1892) and was the first club to admit women, which it did from the start. Shinnecock Hills has hosted the U.S. Open four times in three different centuries and is in the National Register of Historic Places. Even though Shinnecock has a proud heritage, the first 18-hole course in America was the Chicago Golf Club, built in 1893.

Just as the origins of golf in the world are debated, the origins in America are debated, as well. For a detailed history of the game of golf, the premiere source is *A History of Golf* by Robert Browning. Whether that history is told from the perspective of the playing fields, the implements or technologies of the game, the major tournament competitions, or the golfing legends throughout time, it is clear that golf as recreation, sport and business is global. Even though today's golf industry is truly global, the United States is home to roughly one-half of all the golf courses in the world, as well as roughly one-half of all the golfers in the world.

# The Golf Industry

The interviews for this book were collected between 2007 and 2012. This was during "The Great Recession" that began in 2007, and which some economists believe has had negative impacts that have only been exceeded by "The Great Depression" of the 1930s.

Because of its immense popularity, some once considered golf as "recession proof" or "too big to fail," to use another catch-phrase of this era. Economies are cyclical. They rise and fall. The golf industry is no different. This latest decline in golf prosperity follows a time of unprecedented economic and cultural heights for golf and has been painful for those in the industry. Those who love to play the game and those who make their livelihood from the game are typically optimists. Golf business people who understand the realities of the current economic times are fond of saying, "Flat is the new up." Be patient and persist. The swing will come back. Time will tell.

Here is a perspective on how high golf has been. According to the National Golf Foundation (Golf 20/20 Report, 2002), between 1986 and 2002 the number of U.S. golfers grew from 19.9 million to 26.7 million. That was an increase in golfers of 34 percent in only 16 years. The total number of U.S. golf courses during that time frame grew 28 percent to an all-time total of 17,120 courses. New golf course construction grew from an average of 150 per year to over 500 per year by 2002. The golf industry was booming.

The 2005 Golf Economy Report conducted by Stanford Research International showed that the golf industry provided some 2 million jobs and generated $76 billion in direct economic impact, with a total impact on the U.S. economy in 2005 of $195 billion, including $3.5 billion in charitable contributions. At that time, according to Joe Steranka, CEO of the PGA of America, those numbers made golf "bigger than the motion picture industry, bigger than the newspaper publishing industry, bigger than all of the spectator sports, professional sports and semi-pro sports combined." Clearly golf is more than just a game. It is a huge industry making significant contributions to the American economy.

With the economic downturn, things changed. According to the NGF (2010 Golf Industry Overview), there has been a steady decline in the number of golfers on U.S. courses. The number of golfers dropped by 1.5 million, or about 5 percent, from 28.6 million in 2008 to 27.1 million in 2009. The number of golfers is down about 9 percent (2.7 million) since 2005. However, the NGF suggests that the current demand for golf should remain relatively stable in the foreseeable future, leading to the phrase "flat is the new up."

The National Golf Foundation currently reports 15,890 U.S. golf courses in 2011, down from the 17,120 courses of 2002. In 2009 new golf course construction was the lowest in the last 25 years, at 49 new courses. New residential or real estate golf course developments are relatively rare during a time when there is an excess of residential inventory. Golf course closures continue to outpace openings, with an estimated 100-150 course closures per year expected over the next five years. Some argue that this decline in golf course supply is part of a gradual correction in a national market which experienced an overbuild of courses in relation to golf demand in the 1990s and early 2000s. The net closures should eventually help make existing courses healthier, as golf's supply and demand balance seeks equilibrium.

For the most current perspective on golf course supply provided by the NGF in 2010, see the table on the following page.

Until some equilibrium between course supply and golfer demand is established, the statistics and trends reflect the struggle currently faced by those in the golf industry. Not only are course closures outpacing course openings, but private golf clubs with initiation fees, annual membership fees and monthly minimum expenses have suffered during the recession. With fewer entertainment dollars to spend, golfers have looked for less expensive options. Consequently, private courses have been converting to public courses in three out of every four conversions, further adding to golf course competition in the public sector.

| Facility Supply 2010 | | | | |
|---|---|---|---|---|
| | Daily Fee | Municipal | Private | Total |
| 9 Holes | 2,922 | 701 | 759 | 4,382 |
| 18 Holes | 5,533 | 1,442 | 3,058 | 10,033 |
| 27 Holes | 458 | 152 | 208 | 818 |
| 36 Holes | 254 | 87 | 196 | 537 |
| 45 or More Holes | 66 | 13 | 41 | 120 |
| Total | 9,233 | 2,395 | 4,262 | 15,890 |

The NGF reports that roughly half of all U.S. courses are suffering as businesses. A loss of an estimated 20 percent of rounds played at a golf course makes a huge impact on the bottom line. Those experiencing the greatest operating losses are caught in a downward spiral, with fewer dollars for personnel, course maintenance and new capital expenditures. In these kinds of spirals, quality suffers and golfers will look elsewhere.

Throughout the golf industry, the recession has impacted manufacturing, construction, retail, service and other broad sectors of the economy. Specific declines have occurred in rounds of golf played, equipment sales, technology sales, clothing and other soft goods sales, magazine and book sales, golf travel and tourism revenues, tournament purses, sponsorships for professional tournaments, and the list goes on.

When golf course owners get together during tough times such as those experienced following the terrorist attack of 2001 and the recession that began in 2007, they talk about survival as businesses. More than any time in history, golf course owners have begun to cooperate by sharing business strategies and information. The personal stories of golf course owners told in this book attest to their perseverance, breadth of skills, and passion for the business and game of golf. These are stories of American entrepreneurship that are as varied as the personalities of the people themselves. Each story provides insight into the golf industry and the people who love the game. The thrill in hitting a roundish object with a stick to propel it to some distant location continues to fascinate people and will continue to drive the golf industry.

# The Philanthropist

Jay Miller, Owner of Hidden Valley Golf Club in Norco, California

ℬ    ℭ

*I interviewed Jay S. Miller, "Jaybird" to his friends, on February 11, 2011 at the Golf Industry Show in Orlando, Florida. Hidden Valley is the second golf course Jay has owned. He previously owned Cresta Verde Golf Club in Corona, California. Hidden Valley is an 18-hole public course designed by Casey O'Callaghan in 1997. The course ambles among natural valleys and ravines and features the natural vegetation of Southern California. Jay took over as president and managing partner on January 1, 2007.*

### www.hiddenvalleygolf.com

*In 1999 Jay and his close friend Bob Hoff cofounded Get a Grip Foundation to introduce all facets of the game to children (ages 7-18) with a special emphasis on academic improvement and life skills. "Golf is our Hook and Education is our Mission."*

### www.getagripfoundation.org/

*The California Golf Course Owners Association voted Hidden Valley Golf Club the 2010 Public Golf Course of the Year. The day following our interview, Hidden Valley was named the 2011 Public Course of the Year by the National Golf Course Owners Association.*

*Editor's note: What a fun interview. "Jaybird" suits him. Read an exclamation point at the end of each sentence. He is bursting with enthusiasm and ideas.*

ℬ    ℭ

I was born and raised in Springfield, Illinois. My mother played seven musical instruments and had a doctorate degree in education. My father had two degrees: one in mechanical engineering and the other in hotel and restaurant management. He rode the rodeo and put himself through Louisiana State University as a bull rider and a cow milker. He grew up in the bayous of Louisiana, and my mother grew up in New York, so they were from totally contrasting families, but they both loved to play golf.

I can remember it to this day. It was a Sunday, August 1st or 2nd in 1963, and my sister and I are watching my mom and dad play golf. I had this little golf club. It was a real golf club, but it was a miniature club. I never swung it or anything. I just had it. My dad had about an 80-yard shot over water on a par four, and he chunked it in the water. I'm sitting in the cart with my mom and sister and I said, "You know, Dad's not very good." Dad jokingly told me that if I thought I could do better, to step up and do it. So, I went all the way to the edge of the pond with a ball, took a swing with my little club, and sure enough the ball went over the water and landed about eight feet from the pin on the green. My sister said she thought she could do it too. We soon left the golf course and went straight to Fishman's Sporting Goods in Springfield, and my parents bought two sets of junior golf clubs.

My dad knew how much I loved sports. As a kid I played all sports–basketball, baseball, ice hockey, everything. My dad, with a degree in mechanical engineering, thought differently about things. What he would do was spoil you with money– but you had to earn it. So he called around central Illinois to find the best golf instruction for me. He called nine golf courses to ask who the best PGA pro was to give me lessons. Everyone told him the best was Dale Schofield. Dad went to Dale, who is still alive at 77 years of age. I see Dale once a year, and we play golf together. I give him one stroke per nine holes and I have to play the back tees. From the forward tees he still shoots par.

Dale started teaching me golf, and before long I was in my first junior tournament. I played during the week with Mr. Steele and his son, our neighbors across the street. We went to the course to play one weekend and there were lots of kids all over the place. I asked Mr. Steele what was going on and he told me, "Well, Jay, you're going to play in your first junior golf tournament today." I was seven or eight years old, and I won the seven-to-eleven age group tournament. My picture was in the paper the next day. I had been in the paper before with team sports, but this was the first time for just me, by myself, in the paper. I thought, "I like this!"

I got my first job in the golf industry at Bunn Park in Springfield, Illinois, working for Dale Schofield and the other pro at the course, Chuck Roland. I worked in the cart barn and I was almost 11 years old. By 13 I was working in the cart barn and in the pro shop and snack shop that were combined. People laughed at it, but those two pros owned the carts as well as the pro shop and snack shop. They were making in the six figures as pros back in the late 1960s. The course had no irrigation except around the tees and greens. It was basic, but the course was a hustler's hangout. By the time I was 14, I would bet you any amount of money that I could shoot even par and hit every shot off a beer can except for putts. I became one of those golfers who could really play and I sometimes played for money. When I was 15 or 16 my father found almost six thousand dollars in cash in my drawer, and he hit me in the back with a golf club. He told me he didn't want me ever hustling at golf again. To this day I play for $2 or $5, maybe $10 if it's somebody I know really well and we're not going to hurt each other with the bet. That was a lesson learned.

At that time I was still playing four sports. At 15 I gave up baseball, which I shouldn't have, but I did. I was a high school all-American in 1977 in golf. I got my name in *Sporting News* the first time they published high school all-Americans. Then I went to Purdue University on a golf scholarship. I was a member of the 1981 Big Ten championship team. I was a pretty darned good junior golfer, a real good high school golfer, and I was a decent to pretty good college golfer. I wouldn't embarrass your team and I wouldn't embarrass myself, but I wasn't destined to play on the PGA Tour. You know, I thought about it. I graduated from Purdue in four years, and I lettered in golf all four years.

I had a guy, Larry Wells, who owned a company named Metal Decor, who was going to sponsor me on tour. His company was the largest custom plaque manufacturer in the world. They specialized in donor walls recognizing people who gave money to charities, churches, colleges, hospitals and so forth. Mr. Wells gave me a little money to try to play mini-tour professional golf. But I knew I just wasn't good enough to make it where I wanted to go, so I told Mr. Wells I'd like to take on that franchise territory for his business that we had talked about. Those franchises could be bought from him, but I was his boy and he gave me the franchise and I went to work for him. In 1982 I was 22 years old, and I had my own business selling friggin' plaques. I thought that if this business fails, I'll just go play golf again. Well, people started buying the product. In 1984 I did the Betty Ford Drug and Alcohol Rehabilitation Center in Palm Springs. I sold them $140,000 worth of plaques at 25 percent commission. Mrs. Ford goes on the "Good Morning America" TV show and announces my name and where I'm located, and then I become the donor wall king. I got to play golf with President Ford and President Bush. Then I did the Barbara Sinatra Center and got to meet Frank Sinatra. All of a sudden, I'm selling up to $800,000 a year in plaques.

Then I started representing an emblematic jewelry company. The products were things like rings for sales awards, safety rings, lapel pins with diamonds representing so many years of service, and so on. Then I started selling trash trinkets, things like coffee mugs, friggin' Bic pens, and other things with logos on them. At first I thought it was way beneath me. My wife and I had sales in five states, I was playing 92 rounds a year of entertainment golf, and we were selling something like 2.8 million dollars of these products. We were having a blast!

In 1986 my wife and I were in Hawaii on our second anniversary. We won a trip through our church raffle drawing and then we got an upgrade. *(With even more excitement in his voice)* This is where God comes back into play. You're going to see this full circle by the time we're done here. So, we're in Hawaii, and as you can tell, I got ADD. I mean I got ideas floating in my head 24/7. Even though I can sleep perfectly, I'm just one of those kinds of people. I was 26 and my wife was 25. I just kept telling her that someday when I'm rich, I'm going to open up a foundation for children that will change their lives through golf and education. I might have to win the lottery, but someday I'm going to do this. Well, we were on our third day of vacation, and I have to have every minute planned, even when I have happy hour, sex, or whatever. It drives my wife nuts, but she's used to it now. We played golf in the morning and we were done at 11:00. Then I did scuba certification. I was Jacque Cousteau in the pool, but in the ocean it was different. I'm claustrophobic as hell and I almost drowned, even though I had been a competitive junior swimmer. So now that scuba is out, there go two hours that I'd planned in twenty minutes. So, then I go for my surfing lesson three hours early. No problem, they said they could fit me in right away. I fall off the board, cut my head open, and now my whole day is gone. I don't have any activities planned.

Well, I found my wife, who loves to read. She is a very intelligent, beautiful lady, and funny as hell. I just love that woman! I find her reading in a cabana. She sees me and right away says, "No, you're not going to ruin my afternoon. I told you to plan out your day. Oh, by the way, what happened to your head?" I told her I fell off the board, blah, blah, blah. She told me she was concerned, but she would see me at sunset as planned and other than that she didn't want to see me again. She said, "Why don't you go get yourself a pencil and paper, sit down and write this dream of yours about your foundation." So I got two big drinks, a pad of paper and a mechanical pencil, and I rented my own damned cabana at the other end of the beach.

Four-and-a-half hours later, I had written a 72-page thesis called Tee It High Foundation. That original thesis is the exact blueprint that we use to this day at Get a Grip Foundation. Well, I showed my wife my thesis at sunset and she said, "Oh my God, Jay, that's unbelievable!" We put it in the luggage, we go home, and we put it in our desk at home. At that time we had a five-bedroom home, no kids, and we were selling all those plaques, mugs and shit. For the next 13 years it sat in the desk, not to be seen or heard from.

In 1994 I won the member-guest tournament at Merion Golf Club with a former college teammate. I had a hole-in-one on number 13 on the last day of the tournament. That was a significant part of my life, because I met a guy named John Blackburn who was a member at Merion. He's also a member at Olympic and Pine Valley. He's my age and he lives in Southern California. We became very good friends. I was a bad Catholic and he was a mature Christian. With him and a best friend who is a pastor to this day, I accepted the Lord in 1996. Now I'm seeking to learn everything I can about my Savior and Heavenly Father.

In that process, John Blackburn introduced me to a guy named Bob Hoff– Robert A. Hoff. Bob was a partner in Cross Point Venture Partners. He was a Bucknell graduate and a Harvard M.B.A., born and raised in Chicago. Bob and I really hit it off. At that time I had no idea how much money Bob had. I could care less. We'd play golf every couple of weeks, have a few beers, and maybe go to a ball game. He's just a regular guy, very intelligent.

In 1999, on September 22, I'm turning 40 years old. My father's cancer came back and he died. A few days before he died, I visited him in the hospice and he had accepted the Lord. I wear a chain that I had given him to celebrate his acceptance of the Lord. At 4:56 in the morning he dies. My beautiful wife takes the phone call with the news, and then she goes to the refrigerator where I keep the names and numbers of all of my golf friends. She calls the first one listed – Robert A. Hoff. She tells him, "Bobby, Jay's dad died. Is there any chance you can get him out of this house, take him golfing and to dinner, and I can get the kids ready for us to all fly back to Springfield for the funeral?" At about 7:30 in the morning Barb woke me up, telling me she didn't want to wake me but my father had passed away. I just felt, "Praise God." It had gotten pretty bad for my dad at the end. Barb then told me, "Get ready, you're going to play golf with Bob at Santa Anna Country Club, and then you two are going to dinner. By then I'll have everything packed and ready to go to Springfield. I just need you out of this house. We'll fly out tomorrow morning."

So I called my mom, blah, blah, blah, and off I go. Bob and I played 18 holes and then we went down to Fashion Island at Newport Beach to Flemming's Restaurant. Well, we're sitting at the table and talking about my dad, who was an avid but terrible golfer, a 19 handicap. Bob turns to me and he says, "Jaybird, we've been awfully good friends. How much money do you think I'm worth?" I said, "You just got that timeshare thing and a jet, so I'll say 20 million." Bobby said, "Times that by 15." I told him he had to be shitting me! Well I fell out of my chair, laughing my ass off. I get back up and he asks me what I would do with that kind of money if I had it. I told him I knew exactly what I would do with it. I would buy a run-down golf course with a practice center, put up an education center, and open up a foundation to change kids' lives through golf and education. He looked at me and said it was the best idea he'd heard in his life. I told him, "Well, you know, I've got a 72-page thesis that I wrote about this 13 years ago. It's at home somewhere."

The next day I dropped off the thesis at his office, right across the street from the airport, just before we flew off to my dad's funeral. In the meantime I take a book on the plane with me. I don't read all that much. The book is *Purpose Driven Life* by Pastor Rick Warren, the pastor at Saddleback Church, where I serve as lead usher for the 11:15 service. I've been doing that for 12 years. Well, I'm reading this book, and it's like runway lights pointing me to change kids' lives through the game of golf. The message of the book and my dream of a foundation were right in line with each other, and I was so motivated.

Three months later Bob's wife, who is best friends with my wife, called the house and asked to speak with Barb privately. They asked me to go outside. It turned out Bob wanted to talk with Barb. Bob told Barb that I had given him the foundation thesis I wrote in Hawaii to look over. Bob said he wanted to talk specifically with Barb because what he had to say would affect her life directly. Bob and his wife wanted to give us three and a half million dollars to start the foundation. They wanted to do the whole blueprint I had prepared in Hawaii *with us*. "If you want to do this with us," Bob said, "Jay's got to sell the business and we have to buy a golf course. Let's have dinner to talk about it. Well, Barb gets off the phone and tells me, "Jay, you won't believe this, but that thing you wrote in Hawaii, it's pretty good work, but it's not detailed. You've never run a foundation, and they want to fund a full foundation to change kids' lives. We've got to retire from our business and buy a golf course." That's what we did. Now I have a purpose-driven life. I wake up every morning and know exactly what I'm supposed to be doing!

So, we have 3.5 million dollars, and in 2001 I found a golf course that was selling the lease-hold. It was the worst golf course in America, and there wasn't a close second-worst. It was called Cresta Verde Golf Club in Corona, California. It was designed by the actor Randolph Scott in 1927, and I think it was originally called Parkridge Country Club. The first member was Clark Gable. All the stars had farm estates out there and they'd escape out there. They had a clubhouse with a brothel on the top floor. When the depression hit, the course went through bad times. In the '30s the clubhouse was turned into a mental institution, but the course stayed open through most of the bad times.

Long story short, we started the foundation in 2001. Bob and I were playing Augusta National while our attorneys are in Sacramento getting the foundation registered and everything made official. The name, Tee It High Foundation, was taken and not available. The lawyers called Barb because they couldn't get a hold of me. They asked if we had a backup name for the foundation, and Barb, bright as she is, said, "Yeah, Get a Grip." The lawyers said they loved the name. I'll never forget this. Bob and I are flying in on Bob's private jet from playing Augusta National, I've played Augusta 118 times now, and Bob tells me to call Barb on his new phone to set up dinner. I get Barb on the phone and she's all excited wanting to talk with us. She tells us that Tee It High was taken and she had to come up with a new name on the spot. She told us the name she used was Get a Grip, for getting a grip on your life, your education and your golf club. Bob and I just loved the new name.

When we bought Cresta Verde, the course was doing 25,000 rounds a year. By the time we left the course in 2007, it was doing 46,000 paid rounds a year. We really turned the course around, and by then we had 400 kids in Get a Grip Foundation. The foundation was housed in a rented 1,800-square-foot modular building at the course. I was one of the first instructors in the program. I did everything, including changing the toilet paper.

Then I started getting courted by the landowners at Hidden Valley Golf Club. They still to this day own the land and I own the golf course. I run the course, pay the bills, including a small percentage that goes to the landowners. I'm the managing partner who owns the golf course, but not the land. It's a very modern, unique arrangement that's safe for both the landowners and me. The better I do, the better they do. Including the restaurant and banquet center and the golf course revenues, the landowners get about $350,000 a year for their property without an employee or worry. The landowners also donated one acre for us to build a 5,000-square-foot education center for the foundation.

Right now we have 300 kids in the program, with a two-and-half-year waiting list for other kids. Each week every child receives one hour of mandatory, serious homework tutoring, a forty-five minute mandatory, semi-private golf lesson, and a half hour of mandatory life skills training with a clinical psychologist. Then the kids can hang out at the golf course whenever they want during the week. They can get extra homework tutoring or SAT training, be on the traveling golf team, access our clinical psychologist for additional life skills training, participate in Bible study on Thursday nights that I lead, and play some golf. Some of the bragging rights are that we've had 3,800 kids go through the program and stay at least a year. We've never had a school dropout, never had a teenage arrest, and we've never had a teenage pregnancy. We've had 100 percent college placement and 88 percent either have graduated or are still in college.

This year, between the girls and the boys, we have 26 students playing on high school golf teams. Because of the foundation and me playing hardball, we helped establish girls' golf teams at every surrounding high school four years ago. At one of the high schools, Centennial Corona, the girl's team is all Get a Grip girls, and they have won the league championship for three years in a row. I used to say our model was not to produce Tiger Woods-type players, but Tiger Woods-type human beings, but that doesn't work anymore with what we know about Tiger. The point is, we aren't helping to create golfers, we're helping to create good and successful people.

When Bob and I bought the first golf course – he's not involved in Hidden Valley, he asked me, "Jaybird, do you know how to run a golf course?" I told him I have a business degree and I've played golf and worked at a golf course since I was a kid, so I thought I could run a golf course. I certainly knew all there was to know about carts, about pro shops and snack shops. Other than that, I told him I would figure it out. I did. I was at the course every day except Sunday from 6:30 until dark. I would open up and lock the gates at the end of the day. My general manager at the first course had 22 years in the golf business and he sure helped. He's anal as hell and I'm wild as hell, so we're a great combination. I've never had to fire any golf professional. I encourage them to learn my way of customer service — that it's about relationships and you should treat everybody like it's their first visit. I encourage them to move up in the PGA and then if they want, to go get a better job at a bigger place. A couple of my pros left the business and became great salesmen and make four times the money. I do like to compete and get my golf course as good as I can, bring in more players and make more money, and share profits with employees. My goal is not to buy another course. If it's God's will, then yes, I might buy another course.

What I really want is to see families playing golf again, and to get women on the course. Now we have 24 women in our Monday ladies' league. I want to see repeat customers. I'm now the starter on the first tee on Saturdays now. I'll have 190 players on a Saturday and I'll meet 120 of them. It's amazing. Some of them will say, "Where's the fucking starter?" Then I tell them, "I'm not only the fucking starter, but I'm the fucking owner! My name is Jay Miller. It's really nice to meet you." Most say they've never met an owner of a golf course before. I usually tell them I've never met a guy that calls a starter a fucking starter before. Then I'll give them my business card and ask them to send me an email in the next few days to tell me what they liked and didn't like, anything they want to bring up. They usually can't believe it. I always return their emails within 24 hours. If they suggest something positive and constructive, I tell them to come back and bring one other player at full price and they will be my guest.

The reason I own a golf course is because it makes the foundation completely successful. My foundation would not work at any golf course unless the foundation leader was the leader of the golf course. All of our kids can play Hidden Valley Monday through Thursday after 11:30 for $1. Average price is $55. Their parents, if playing golf with their Get a Gripper, can play for $15 with a cart. A family of four with a Get a Gripper can play for $32, where it would normally be up to $240. Then after 1:30 on Friday, Saturday and Sunday, they get the same deals. The kids get to hit all the balls they want on the public side of our range every day of the year. Last year they hit 1.7 million golf balls and were on the property a cumulative 144,000 hours.

Through total hands-on operation at the course, I've learned a lot. Then in 2003 I joined the California Golf Course Owners Association and I've been heavily involved in the organization. I became a board member in 2005 and an officer in 2009. The value of the California association and the NGCOA (National Golf Course Owners Association) is that I get to hang out with and learn from other owners who've been doing it twice as long as me. These owners are willing to take you under their wings and I can call them for any information I need. Ted Horton, the famous superintendent, is the one who recruited me into the NGCOA and the California Golf Course Owners Association. He's maybe the number one superintendent in the USA, and he took a liking to me and helped me get my golf course back in better shape.

Next, I hired Valley Crest Golf Course Maintenance Company. They were with me for two years at Cresta Verde. We remodeled the clubhouse, moved 500,000 cubic yards of dirt, and I redesigned the golf course. I even operated heavy machinery, busted a main waterline, and it was a friggin' blast. We really turned that course into something special, and Cresta Verde was named by *California Golf Magazine* among the top eighteen places to play for the value in the state. Bob and I owned Cresta Verde until March 2007, and then we walked. The court awarded us back our money from the land owners. I had discovered an environmental breach of contract and some dishonesty with the original contract with the land owners . It's a long story, but at one time I owned both courses at the same time. When we left Cresta Verde, Hidden Valley became my only golf course.

I met a superintendent through Valley Crest who had been to Hidden Valley before, and I decided to go hire him as my superintendent at Hidden Valley, without Valley Crest. It was amazing. In his first full year on his own, Iain Sturge from England was so talented, we were named the 2010 Public Golf Course of the Year by the California Golf Course Owner's

Association. That year I saved something like $80,000 in maintenance costs and put in $30,000 in bunkering and other improvements.

At Hidden Valley, that's where they had the prostitutes nine years ago. Other courses were opening in the area, and Hidden Valley's sales and reputation were going downhill. The owner at that time decided to close nine holes and make it a nine-hole course and then build 270 homes. That owner, Chuck Cox, started courting me in 2006 about buying the course. He was thinking, here's this Jay Miller and he turned Cresta Verde around. Chuck had three courses and I was taking his business with Cresta Verde. Plus, I had the foundation that was getting into the paper all the time. Kids were playing for nearly nothing. I was teaching golf and physical education at local schools in the summer. I was running a program for prisoners and golf. I had the reputation. People thought I was like Jesus. So, that owner courted me on a three year ownership deal, beginning January 1, 2007. We became friends and played golf together. We worked through the original contract and just kept doing more contracts. Right now he's 78 years old, and he has two partners who are the same age. Now, as owner of Hidden Valley, I've taken their worries away from them. Any repair over $5,000 for the course, clubhouse, restaurant, or whatever, we split 50/50. He calls me twice a month to see how we did at the course and cheerleads me on. He's got more money than God, but he loves being involved. It just keeps him going.

When Hidden Valley first opened under Chuck Cox's ownership and was managed by Kemper Sports, it was considered one of the best courses in the country. It won a *Golf Digest* Five-Star Award. But then in 2002 things changed. There was a prostitution ring out of Newport Beach working three western states. They'd operate a phony charity tournament at golf courses. With a $200 entry, there were all kinds of sex acts à la carte. The problem was that Hidden Valley and Kemper Sports knew what was going on after the first outing with prostitutes. At first they just thought it was a great charity event, but then they discovered what was really going on with the prostitutes. They held that same kind of event another three times anyway, and they got caught. The tournament got busted. Seventy-two golfers were arrested and taken away, but not booked. Twelve prostitutes, three of whom were transvestites, were arrested. I'll never forget it. I had just gotten done playing golf on a Friday at Cresta Verde, went into my clubhouse with my brand new plasma TVs – that was the day they got installed – we're having a couple of pitchers of beer and playing some gin, and then on the TV there's breaking news. One of the old guys knew right away it was Hidden Valley, and there on TV are 72 golfers in plastic cuffs and these girls getting led away by the police. Next thing I knew, my business started really booming. Your wife's going to say, "Tommy, you can go play golf, but you're not playing that Hidden Valley!" Mr. Cox told me all about it a year later. He and his partners considered who could successfully run their golf course. Who can we bring in as a managing partner and give a piece of the action? He told me I was the one they wanted because of my Get a Grip Foundation.

I'm in such a competitive market. There are 15 golf courses in a 12-mile radius, in a population that doesn't really support golf. There is so much traffic. When I took over at Hidden Valley, we were doing 27,000 rounds a year. Last year we did 36,700 paid rounds in a bad economy. Then I give away golf. I have four high schools playing the course in addition to the Get a Grip kids. That's another 5,000 rounds that aren't paid for. I'm one of the first people who started "Youth on Course" with the SCGA, the Southern California Golf Association. There are seven other courses around us who participate. Kids play our courses for $4.

In 2004 I started working with 90 homeless kids from The Dream Center in Los Angeles. I would close Get a Grip on Wednesday afternoons so we could work with the homeless kids. They would be bused to the course for golf, dinner and Bible study. I did that for about a year and a half, but the drive got to be too much, and they found another, closer activity for the kids. Doing the program with those kids did get me to reach out further to improve lives through golf.

I had three prison guards that were members at Cresta Verde, and I thought I should start teaching prison kids to play golf. Lots of people thought I couldn't teach prison kids to play golf because they just wouldn't pay attention. I thought

I could, so I went to three different youth prisons to see what would happen. At first I tried to call the prisons on the phone, but they were government entities and I couldn't get to the right people, so I went personally to the prisons. I just went to their gates and introduced myself, telling them that I owned a golf course that operated a foundation for children to improve their lives through golf. I told them I wanted to do an experiment teaching prison kids to play golf.

At the first prison I got escorted to the director's office. He had about an eight-foot-long rattlesnake skin on the wall behind his desk. I asked him if that snake was from the prison property. He told me, "No, I bought it online, but I tell every single kid here, go ahead and escape, that's what's waiting for you!" Well, I told him my idea, and we started talking right away about how many kids we could handle at the course. We started with six prison kids. Every Wednesday six kids came with a prison guard, and my pro and I would teach them how to play golf. These guards don't carry guns. They just have handcuffs, and they all have MBAs. The guards are educated. About 90 percent of the kids are gangbangers.

Well, the first guard told the director of another youth prison about what we were doing. This second prison had both girls and boys, and before I knew it I had 18 youth prisoners at a time in the program. We had four guards and three golf professionals and me to make it work. Then word got out to a third youth prison, and we got up to 24 kids at the same time. This went on for three years.

However, when I was building my education center at Hidden Valley I ran into a permitting problem where I couldn't get the education center permit if I brought prison kids to the golf course anymore. In the meantime, the prison with both girls and boys closed, another of the prisons formed a baseball league and they were out too, and then I was back to the original Joplin Youth Center I started working with. I had to sign a document that Get a Grip would not have the prison program that I had started at the course. My lawyer told me that this ruling might apply to Get a Grip, but not to my public golf course, which was open to any paying customer.

So, every Saturday my pastor friend, two of his golf studs I had taught to play golf, and I taught eight youth prisoners on a soccer field with "almost balls." A drive won't go more than 120 yards. Also, I bring about 100 real golf balls that aren't of any use, even at the driving range. We take those balls to the top of Saddleback Mountain on the prison property, and each kid gets to hit 15 balls off the top of the mountain. Once they get the balls into the air, they fly. We do that every Saturday. Then on the last Monday of each month, the kids come to the course in a van with guards and they pay me $1, making them official customers, not violating my education center permit. My teaching pros at Get a Grip volunteer, and we play with the kids in scramble events for two hours, then we go to a back section of the clubhouse, my wife and I buy dinner, and we rap with the kids for 45 minutes to an hour. These kids had to be on their best behavior in prison in order to continue in our golf program, or they would be replaced by other kids. Believe me, the chance to be outside playing golf for hours, drive a golf cart, and get a dinner was an opportunity those kids didn't want to lose. In fact, our golfing prisoners got the best behavior scores and academic grades at their facilities.

With all these programs I have going at the golf course, everyone in the community knows that the owner at Hidden Valley not only started a foundation for kids, but every day he's in town, he's there working at the foundation. He personally teaches these kids, then he has a youth ministry for prisoners where he personally teaches these kids, and then he serves on boards for other associations. Wow! They must think that guy is special. I do it because I like to and I know I can help. But just imagine what the person who doesn't really know me must think. They must think I'm a saint. Even if those people in the community only play golf twice a year, they're going to play at my place. Some people think I'm a marketing genius, but I'm really not. I presented a workshop on marketing at a conference about how we market at Hidden Valley. All of our decision-making processes for our golf and restaurant operations are based on principles right out of the Bible. My business life is based on my principles taken from the Bible and my spiritual beliefs.

At my church there is another pastor, other than Rick Warren, who has been speaking at the church for 18 years. He is the Billy Graham of youth ministers. At any Christian church in America, you can find his books and instructional tapes. He is Pastor Doug Fields. After trying for 10 years, I finally got Pastor Fields and his son to play golf with me. Now we are very close friends and I have a deal with him. I supply him with golf equipment, lessons and a course for free, but he's got to play with me, and he has to try to better me as a Christian man, father and boss. It's a perfect arrangement.

At Hidden Valley you get a great value for golf. It's a challenging golf course, and we warn new guests how hard it is. On the weekends, it will take you four-and-half to five hours to play the course. I try to make the course play easier by shaving the hills and slopes and making collection areas around all of the greens and so on, but it's a golf course with 600 feet of elevation change! The greens are fast as kitchen tile. On U.S. Open weeks I advertise in magazines, "I know what you're thinking in your Lazy Boy, drinking your beer and watching the U.S. Open: How could that guy miss that downhill three-and-half footer? How could they do that? Come out to Hidden Valley and find out. For the week of the U.S. Open, our greens will be running U.S. Open speed. If you can play 18-holes without a 3-putt, I'll give you free rounds of golf for a foursome." All they have to tell me after their round is if they didn't three-putt. Well, I get about one person a year who can do it. For the quality and challenge of the course, you get a great value.

I take my team leaders at the course and give them different leadership responsibilities on each project. For example, when we needed to market our course after winning the California Public Golf Course of the Year, I might have picked a few people from the golf side of the operation that I thought had the right personalities for the project. It could be a cart boy with some artistic ability on that marketing team. That's about keeping their work interesting with variety and matching projects with employees' abilities.

In June last year I was complaining to my superintendent about how his employees weren't cutting the cups on the greens correctly. I told him the only time the cups are right is when he cuts them on Saturdays and Sundays. I was really bitching at him. So what I decided to do was to teach all of the Hispanic workers in groundskeeping to play golf. We formed a league for them. I brought out the *Get a Grip* pros the next Tuesday for a two-hour teaching session. We got a club in each of the grounds workers' hands. The next week I taught them, and the following week they started their league. The maximum score they could take on any hole is double the par to keep pace of play moving. Now, when they play they can see and understand as a golfer. If a putt doesn't go in and they think the hole was cut terribly, they understand. Now I've got waiters in the restaurant playing golf. All of my bartenders, who are mostly females, have now gone through at least a one-hour class with me about how to talk to a golfer. I tell them that if they are at a loss of what to say, just drop a golf ball on the bar and let it roll. Then ask the guest if our greens were as fast as the bar countertop. Don't worry; the golfers will pick up the conversation from there. Everybody in the foundation, including the receptionist, plays golf now. All of these processes with employees help them to provide the best service to our customers and they all use golf as a vehicle for learning.

I also started a golf mentoring program for Get a Grip. Thirteen-year-old kids in America get an average of 50 minutes of outside exercise a week. It's not enough. So I started raising money outside the Get a Grip budget just for a program called Get a Grip Golf Mentoring. I put one of my older golf professionals, Cal Pierce, in charge of the program. We got 14 volunteers from men's clubs to help. Every Monday, Tuesday and Wednesday with the volunteers and our staff, 20 kids from Get a Grip get to play nine holes. That's 60 kids a week playing nine holes. Then, we went even further by making it mandatory. Get a Grip is run in sessions that are seven weeks long, then one week off, then another seven-week session. Every child has to play nine holes every quarter, except in the winter. I'm just always thinking about ways to grow the game of golf. Getting young people to play is critical to that goal.

Last year we had a "Grow the Game Summit" for the California Golf Course Owners Association and I was the keynote speaker. My presentation and thesis was called "If I was the czar of golf, how would I grow the game?". I have the solution to growing the game of golf. My idea is to raise 10 million dollars from throughout the golf industry to use with 1,000 preschools, geographically spread across middle-class neighborhoods across the country. I'm not trying to save anybody's soul here. This is about Jay Miller's plan to get youth on a golf course and grow the game of golf. This is about golf business. We've got an LPGA member who is an artist, and she's designed posters and books to get three-year-old children to pull a little sling and make a golf club swing. It's all made of Styrofoam. The little kids see this and they want to do it. That's their introduction, and by the time they are five years old, they're on a golf course for real. I've seen it work. So, you get 1,000 preschools where about 60 kids get 45 minutes a week of golf education fun by swinging this device. Then by kindergarten they get to hit balls behind their schools. That could be 60,000 kids every year, who by six years old are ready to go to a golf course. Well guess what? Their moms and dads will learn and go to play with them. We have to make golf accessible and attractive to little kids.

Of course, I want a loyal customer base at my golf course, but I got so frustrated with how few kids came to the course to learn the game. So I started $10 clinics. That includes 50 minutes of instruction with two pros, the balls, with eight learners per clinic. Imagine if 1,000 golf clubs offered these kinds of clinics. The industry could bring in 40 or 50 thousand new players a year. It ain't that difficult! The last part is taking people who are cool, these eight to 22-year-olds who are celebrities, and get them on the covers of popular magazines for their age groups, or get them on YouTube, with golf clubs in their hands. Use those role models to promote the excitement of golf. Let's face it: Advertising "First Tee," the USGA's plan to grow the game with youth, on TV advertisements for a PGA Tour event is just not reaching the youth you want to attract. Adults who already play golf watch PGA events on TV, not kids. Have Snoopy playing golf. Have Sponge Bob playing golf on the media the kids actually watch.

These are hard times for the future of the golf industry. But even in death and destruction, somebody always make money. I think we have 1,550 too many golf courses in America. Unless we take some extreme measures in a real hurry to grow the game of golf, we're going to be in worse shape in two years. The economy hurt everybody last year. It hurt your business, everybody's business. I actually grew my business in a bad economy. I grew my food and beverage profits by 9%, and I brought more players to my course. I did OK last year. I think it's because of the relationships I have in the community. People know me and my product. But as an industry, we're in trouble.

It scares me that 100 million people in America are playing golf with their thumbs. We could buy a really cool golf game that we would like to play inside my living room. That might cost $750 now, but by next year it will be $450 and the game will be even more special. It scares me that people under age 30 are addicted to something electronic that doesn't connect them to other real people. It scares me that human interactions continually get reduced. How to talk to somebody or how to write a letter are becoming lost skills. Golf is a lot about fellowship, about being paired with other people you don't know. Nowadays when three people show up to play golf and a single player asks to join their group, that single is likely to be denied. Back in my day as a kid, people always got together with people they didn't yet know to play golf.

It doesn't scare me that we have to relax the dress code on the course. If you really want the formality and tradition of golf, there are courses, private clubs, where you can go to get that. Golf was invented around exclusivity. There was a hierarchy of the wealthy who didn't want to be around the so-called public. That tradition is OK at some facilities, but we need to make people understand that golf is accessible and fun for everyone.

Another thing that scares me is the separation of ability from the touring golf professional to the average amateur. Back in the old days, a touring player was a plus 3 handicap (averaged three strokes under par per round). Now the best touring pros are plus 8 or 9 handicaps, and the average amateur's handicap is 19.2. That's like an average difference of 27 strokes between the best pros and amateurs, and it makes amateurs feel inadequate. It bothers me that golf manufacturers can sell a new set of clubs to some guys every six months. We get sold on the idea that if Davis Love plays the new clubs, he will play better. People don't understand that Davis Love could hit the ball 300 yards with a broom stick. We get convinced that we can buy a good game.

It also kills me where our culture is going with instant gratification. I see this every seven weeks when new kids come into the Get a Grip program. They will tell us before we start that they already play golf. Then when we go to the range with the teaching pros, the kids don't even know how to hold the golf club. We say to the kids that they told us they played golf. They might say, "Yeah, I could shoot 54 on Tiger Woods EA Golf, the electronic game, right now." They think they are playing golf. Then the frustration sets in when they can't get a real golf ball in the air on their first five tries.

Now, here's what excites me about the future of the industry. I would say that in three to four years maximum there's going to be a connection between real golf and electronics. We already have golf carts that play music. I think that pretty soon the GPS units in golf carts are going to have virtual golf games. The GPS will still tell us how far to the green and all of that, but you and I will also be able to play real golf and at the same time play virtual golf in between real golf shots. Then we can check our Facebook pages or emails too, all while playing golf. That scares me, but it also excites me. If it grows the game, that's where we have to go.

There are more and more owners talking about encouraging "alternative golf." Every golf club manufacturer has warehouses full of clubs that are now considered illegal by the USGA. What's the problem with people playing with so-called illegal clubs if they play better with them and want to play more golf? Suppose golf courses could get another 25 members who played illegal clubs. Who cares! That's 25 more members! Here's a thesis I'm promoting. How about if all professional golf tour players used persimmon woods and all amateurs can play with whatever sets of clubs they want to use. Create a new handicap system for amateurs. Allow mulligans on number 1 and 10 tees. Create a system for awarding gimmie putts for amateurs. I call it the Tee Party Golf Movement. I was in conversations with others at a conference to actually form a board to promote these kinds of alternative golf games. Golf should be fun. If it's fun, people will play.

Another thing that bothers me is the lack of nine-hole golf courses. It reminds me of drive-in movie theaters going by the wayside. It's not just about nostalgia. Nine-hole courses created more options and opportunities for golfers. I'm also concerned about big corporations buying golf courses and then hiring big management companies to run them. Many of those corporate-owned courses are impersonal, and small businesses have a hard time competing with that kind of operation. Any golf course built after 1985 or so is to really sell homes and require the use of golf carts. Now, my highest net-profit line-item is golf carts, but I really like to walk. Lots of other golfers want to walk, too, but it's getting more and more difficult to do at too many golf courses. If you walk a golf course, you walk seven miles and you play better. You really have the out-of-doors experience.

Overall, I'm both optimistic and I'm scared for the industry. My heart goes through my back when I see a golf course closed, but we have to weed our garden. Some of those courses that are closing probably should be closed. When we let developers take over the building of golf courses and focus on home development, we let the industry get away from us. Now we're starting to take the industry back. It's like whats happened with third-party tee sheets. We gave up revenue to third parties to try to fill tee sheets and get more golfers on the course. That trend is changing, and we're starting to take charge of our own tee sheets again. Those of us who really love the game of golf and our industry are starting to step up again to make golf more accessible and more fun.

As you can see, I have lots of opinions. The bottom line, though, is that I own a golf course so that I can improve kids' lives with my foundation. That's my purpose. But, you know what, that purpose has been very good for my golf business, too.

## Miller's Lessons

- Have a dream about what you want to accomplish. Live a purpose-driven life.
- Golf is more than just a game. Golf is a vehicle for learning life skills. Owning a golf course can be a vehicle for teaching life skills and at the same time promote business objectives.
- Customer service is about relationships. Treat every customer like it's their first visit.
- Talk to your customers and encourage their feedback.
- Paid customers are great, but give it away, too. The benefits will follow.
- Keep employees' work interesting and challenging. Match projects at the course with employees' abilities, regardless of their typical job assignments.
- All employees should learn to play golf, even the receptionist. That helps them to provide the best customer service, and they will use golf as a vehicle to learn their industry and improve their skills.
- Find ways to "grow the game" by getting youth to play golf.
- "Even in death and destruction, somebody makes money."
- Encourage "alternative golf" in which the rules of golf are altered to allow mulligans, gimmie putts and other breaks. The more fun you make the game to play, the more people will play.
- "The bottom line, though, is that I own a golf course so that I can improve kids' lives with my foundation. That's my purpose. But, you know what, that purpose has been very good for my golf business, too."

# Bootstrap Entrepreneurs

## Mike and Linda Rogers, Owners of Juday Creek Golf Course in Granger, Indiana

ℰ℧ ℭℬ

*I interviewed Mike and Linda Rogers and their daughter Michelle Wittig, who is the course's general manager, at the Golf Industry Show in Las Vegas on March 1, 2012. Juday Creek (pronounced "Judy") is a public 18-hole course with an active banquet and golf outing business, as well as men's, women's and beginner golf leagues. The course was selected as the 2010 National Player Development Award Winner by the National Golf Course Owners Association for the outstanding quality of their educational programs. This is a beginner- friendly course with junior golf instruction, junior golf camps, junior golf leagues, and a program called "Mom and Me on the Tee" for moms and their children to learn golf together.*

*In addition to other businesses, the Rogers family owned five restaurants in the Michigan/Indiana area, sometimes called Michiana, prior to developing and opening Juday Creek in 1989. In addition to the golf course, they are currently operating their business, Nugent Builders, that specializes in building high-end custom homes. This is one active and productive family. Linda became the first female president of the National Golf Course Owners Association at this 2011 conference event.*

www.judaycreek.com

ℰ℧ ℭℬ

**Linda:** Mike and I got married when we were very, very young. Our daughter Michelle came along right away. When we left our little town of Bad Axe, Michigan, we went to Mt. Pleasant, Michigan where I was going to go to college. Michelle was four months old when I started college. Mike was working as assistant produce manager in a supermarket, and I was also working in a restaurant. We were busy people.

One day Mike was talking with a gas station owner where we bought our gas and the guy told Mike that he wouldn't be seeing much more of us because he was getting a bigger service station in another town an hour away. Mike's wheels started turning, and he asked what was going to happen to the station we used. The guy told Mike that he was looking for someone to take it over. Lo and behold, we got a little money together for a gas station.

**Mike:** It was all the money we had. We didn't have any money. Linda was 20 years old and I was 21 or 22. All we had was a car that was half paid off, and we ended up selling it to get some money.

**Linda:** We were fortunate because I had a full trustee scholarship, so my entire education, including books, was paid for. I was able to save the money from an educational loan, and with the two of us working all the time we were doing OK, so we started in the service station business. During that time, I graduated and then went back for some graduate-level classes in business.

**Mike:** We owned the gas station for about three years. We worked hard at it, and we made some pretty good money, maybe $28,000 or $30,000 a year, and back then in the early 1970s that seemed like a lot of money. We bought a wrecker, and we were doing tune-ups and that sort of thing. But then the gas shortage came, so we didn't have any gas to sell and there wasn't much service work to do. That got pretty depressing. It got to be a real drag.

I got this idea that I wanted to own a business where people wanted to come there because they enjoyed it and didn't have to come there because they needed it, like at a gas station. So, we ended up looking into and buying a bar in southwest Michigan. The bar was in a rough area. When we started with the bar, we were coming from our comfortable town of Bad Axe, and we didn't really know much about blacks and hillbillies.

**Linda:** It was just such a different environment from what we knew. We adjusted and we fit in fine, but it was a challenge at first. We called the bar Fish Corners, and coming with the bar was a house for us to live in. As strange as the neighbourhood was to us, we thought we were in heaven because we had a bar with a liquor license and a house to live in. The house was actually an old school building built in the 1850s called The Fish School, so being at a four-corner intersection, we called the bar Fish Corners.

**Mike:** The house was an old block building and it had no heat. We didn't even have enough money to buy a refrigerator. The windows were built so that we could put our milk, vegetables or whatever between window panes to keep them cold. That house was pretty bad.

**Linda:** The house was terrible. We had an old furnace where we built wood fires. What we finally realized was that if we made the fire with coal, it would stay burning through the night.

**Mike:** We would be literally freezing in the mornings when we got up. Then the well went bad, and we didn't have any water. Linda had to drive 40 miles to one of the restaurants we eventually bought, and she would have to fill water jugs along the road just so we would have water in the house. That's how poor we were. It was just crazy. One time I caught a snapping turtle. That became our dinner that night.

**Michelle:** If you look at Michigan, it's kind of shaped like a hand. The bar was in the southwest corner of the state and Bad Axe was in the northeast part of the state, by the thumb. Mom and I would drive back and forth between the two places, the gas station and the bar, on the weekends.

**Linda:** We knew it would be a while before we could open the bar. So in the meantime, I took a job teaching school in Flynn. Every weekend, Michelle and I would drive down to help with the bar and then drive back the four hours to teach by Monday.

**Mike:** One time Linda didn't have any money to drive back or get anything to eat on the way.

**Michelle:** I remember that time because we had bought a frozen pizza. Since we didn't have a refrigerator we left the pizza out in the snow before cooking it. A dog ate our pizza. That was tough.

**Mike:** It's true. It was so freaky. We had no money, but I had a check I was going to cash on Monday. Typically they would leave about 4 P.M. on Sunday and I couldn't cash the check. So we continued to work on the bar, and I was going to get up early on Monday to cash that check. We could eat the pizza and then they could drive back. Well, I went to get the pizza, and all we could see were dog tracks. I had tears in my eyes. It was crazy. We were starved. Then Linda went through the car seats and found enough spare change so that when Linda and Michelle left, they could stop for some food.

**Linda and Michelle in perfect harmony:** We stopped at McDonalds and *split* a cheeseburger.

**Linda:** We knew there was food in the refrigerator in Flynn, but we didn't have credit cards or money at the time.

**Mike:** By the time we had made the bar ready to open, we didn't even have money to stock the place with beer or liquor. We had a junky old truck. I mean, that thing was JUNK. We went down to the bank and got a loan for $500 with that old truck as collateral to buy our inventory. That got us started.

**Linda:** With my salary from teaching, we had a little money to fix up the bar. People had been watching us work on the bar all along, so when we opened the doors to business, we had customers.

**Mike:** The clientele was like right out of the movie *Deliverance*. Some of our customers' cousins must have been in that movie.

**Michelle:** In that school system, I was one of two white kids in my class in second and third grades. Our location was where the Underground Railroad from the Civil War ended. It was a combination of poor whites and poor blacks. There was a nuclear plant nearby, so there was some money in the area, and the school itself was pretty nice. When Mom and Dad asked me about my teacher and whether she was black or white, I honestly didn't even know. At that age those kinds of things just don't matter.

**Linda:** The people were really wonderful people, and we got along just fine. Lots of them were involved with blueberry farming. It was just different from what we had known. It was so different that if we hadn't lived that experience, we would never have believed it.

**Mike:** If you could ever see our photo album from that time, it would make your beard stand on end. I'm just telling you. At the bar we had built a softball field complex, and we had all these softball teams coming in. We would get 700 to 1,000 people coming in for tournaments. We would roast pigs, and people would bring a dish to pass. One time we roasted a full pig, and we had to butcher the pig inside our house. I'll never forget seeing our little Michelle holding the pig's tail up so I could make another cut.

This was a rough area and it was a rough bar. The previous owner had been shot and killed in the house we were living in. He had been running the bar, which at that time also had a gas station and a convenience store. People knew he had money, so someone broke into the house, killed him, and robbed him. When we bought the bar, we didn't know anything about that.

After we owned the bar for a couple of years, one of the customers flicked a lit cigarette into the face of one of the young guys in the bar that I played basketball with. He called the kid a nigger to his face. The kid went home and got a gun. He was a friend of mine, so when he left the bar we kept watching for him to return. He ended up sneaking into the front door and shot the guy in the leg. Everything went so quiet after that gunshot. It was like someone unplugged the jukebox. Then someone said that his gun was only a single shot. "Let's get him!" So the kid runs out the front door into the parking lot. He had one of those sweatshirts with a hand pouch, and he had other bullets in that pouch and he reloaded the gun. When those guys went out after him they soon came back in when they saw he had reloaded. I locked the door behind them, and then I went out the back door and found Arnold shaking in the parking lot. He was pointing the gun at me and I said, "Arnold, put the gun down. You know me." So he put the gun down, but he was shaking so much that the gun went off. It almost blew his foot off. He was shaking that much. It was so scary. His dad came and picked him up. He was sentenced to two years in prison.

**Linda:** It was so sad. He was such a good young man. Not that the other guy should have been shot, but he was trash. He was the instigator. He said things that should have never been said.

**Mike:** There are so many stories with the bar. Some guy threw a pool cue ball at Linda when she was behind the bar. The cue ball just missed her head. It would have killed her if it had hit her. We called the police and they caught him. He ended up going to prison for that. But how scary is that? Linda was about 23 years old, and some guy fires a cue ball at her. That's a rough place!

**Linda:** I'm a pretty small person. I had to be very straightforward and strict with bar patrons. If they acted up, I told them that one more time and they will never be able to come back to the bar again. That's how we had to run it.

**Mike:** One day a 15-year old kid came running into the bar and he said, "Mike, I think there's somebody dead over there in the yard." So I got my gun, and then I started literally sneaking from tree to tree where the kid said he thought somebody was dead. I didn't know if somebody was going to shoot me. I saw a disheveled black guy standing there and I said, "What's going on?" The guy said he shot his wife. He shot his wife with a 12-gauge shotgun from only 10 feet away. She had been chasing him with a .357 handgun, but he had the shotgun and he shot her right in the face. I've seen quite a few dead people, and I knew immediately that she was dead. So the guy goes into shock. Then the cop we called "Stretch," about a six-foot-nine-inch black guy, shows up. He sees what's going on, and then he goes into shock. He didn't know what to do. I had to take the guy's gun and then help put the guy in the cop car. He'd been drinking and was pretty messed up. After he was in the car, a group of maybe 20 black people showed up and started chanting and pretending to faint. It was something. That was a rough place.

Every day around 2 P.M. I had the same two hillbillies come into the bar. They were the greatest guys. They came in *every* day. They'd have a beer before they went to work at Whirlpool. They were in there one day when a guy came in wearing a suit. Nobody ever wore a suit in that bar. This guy had to be lost and just wandered in. He ordered a beer, and we got to talking. He was from Detroit. All of a sudden I look out the plate glass window and see a rabbit on the other side of the street. I told my regular customers, "See that rabbit. Let's get it!" I always kept a 12-gauge shotgun behind the bar, so I grabbed the gun, kicked open the door, and shot the rabbit from the bar doorway. This guy from Detroit must have been wondering where the heck he was. I told the regular guy Dick, "Go get that rabbit. I'm going to the house to get the frying pan." Within five minutes, the rabbit was butchered and cooking in the electric skillet behind the bar. We ate it. The guy from Detroit didn't know where he was at, but I'm betting he is still telling that story.

**Linda:** The realtor who had sold us the bar had seen us take a place that was really terrible and make it so much better, including a great softball complex. Teams came from all around to play at our fields. We had tournaments almost every weekend during summers. We held six softball league games every night. At age seven, Michelle was helping out. She had a concession stand that sold hotdogs, candy bars and that sort of thing. If you gave her a $100, bill she could make change. She ran it.

**Michelle:** I'll never forget the day that Elvis died. I was crying in the parking lot as I was picking up the cans and candy bar wrappers.

**Linda:** That realtor said we did such a good job with the place that we might be interested in another property he had about 45 minutes away. It was a closed up, dumpy bar, pretty rough, but we might want to take a look at it. So we went to take a look, and we ended up buying it. It was so bad that before we could get a liquor license, we had to meet with the sheriff to assure him that we would make the place much better than it had previously been. We told him about our expertise based on Fish Corners, and we got the license and then opened up, calling the place Lindys, after me. In the early 70s, nobody expected a woman to own a bar, and Mike used to always say that the next time we open a business, we're going to name it after you. So we named the new place Lindys, but people would still come in and ask if *Mr.* Lindy is in.

We took that old bar and restaurant and made it really nice. It's a family restaurant that is still in existence today. We were there 18 years.

**Mike:** We bought a pizza recipe from a young girl who used to come to play softball. She had worked at a place that had the best pizza you could imagine. That pizza is really amazing. I have that recipe locked in a safe today. It was a big start of that business for us.

**Linda:** We started out with pizza and sandwiches and then eventually expanded to a full menu, prime rib and so on. Mike had been running Fish Corners, and I was running the restaurant 45 miles away. Then we sold the bar with the softball complex, and we just had the one restaurant. Before long, Mike got antsy, just jumped in the car, drove to another town, and found another place to lease. So we opened up another restaurant. Before long, over about a 10-year period, we had opened five restaurants, all called Lindys.

**Michelle:** It was probably more like five-and-a-half restaurants. The five were spread out, and Dad would drive around to them and sometimes stop at a little place called Egg Roll Heaven that had great food.

**Mike:** It was just a little place, about the size of a room in a house. This little Asian lady would make egg rolls and really excellent food.

**Michelle:** The owner said she was looking to sell out, so we bought that, too. We owned it for about a year.

**Mike:** It was a spur-of-the-moment decision, and we didn't really make money on that one. It's interesting, though, that now, 30 years later, one of the realtors who sold one of the houses we built remembers us from when she used to eat at Egg Roll Heaven.

From that gas station to the bar to the five-and-a-half restaurants, we moved fast. We operated each business thin. We really watched our budgets, and people got confidence in us because we were being successful. We basically borrowed money for each of the businesses.

**Linda:** We did everything we possibly could to make those businesses successful. We worked 10 to 12 hours a day, seven days a week. To give you an idea of how hard we worked, two of our restaurants were full menu restaurants, and I ran those. One was in Michigan and one was in Indiana, about half an hour away. Because one state observed daylight savings time and the other state didn't, I could work lunch in Michigan and then drive half an hour to Indiana to work lunch at the other restaurant.

Michelle worked at every one of our businesses, beginning as a child, and now she runs the golf course. We all kind of grew up running our businesses. By our early 30s, Mike and I owned over five businesses. Michelle was a part of all of it, and I sometimes tell people she's my sister because we all kind of grew up together.

**Mike:** We're like the Three Musketeers. We are tight. But we like to argue and have our own ways. If there is a disagreement, then the one of us that can persuade the third one of us will usually have their way.

**Linda:** In one year we ended up selling four of our five restaurants. We were left with our original restaurant. I was pretty much running that one, and Mike started playing a lot of golf. It was hard to have us both running the same place, so he had the time to play lots of golf. He was in his early 30s and was starting to get bored, so he said maybe we should get into the golf business. We could play a lot of golf, and we could take the winters off. Of course, that never happens in the golf business, but we didn't know that at the time. It is how most people think about the golf business, though.

So we looked all over to find a place where we could have a golf business that we could afford and in a location we wanted to be. We couldn't find anything, but Mike found a 200-and-some-acre property that was right where we are today. We decided to develop part of the property into a housing development and the rest into a golf course.

**Michelle:** I was already living in that place, Granger, Indiana. I was going to college at St. Mary's College there, and I always like to say that they followed me.

**Mike:** To build the golf course, we hired Ken Killian out of Chicago as our architect. He had built Kemper Lakes. He was a mid- to high-range-expense architect which was all we could afford. We probably spent maybe a half a million less than we should have to build the course. There is always something more you could do with your golf course, but we had a limited budget and it was tough. By the time it was built, we were out of money again.

**Linda:** We bought the property in 1986 and started the housing development that year. Then in '87 and '88 we built the golf course. We opened the course in the spring of 1989. We kept the restaurant for six years after we opened the golf course. I would work all day at the golf course and then would drive the half hour to work at the restaurant.

**Mike:** It probably seems strange to build a golf course with the little golf experience I had, but I am antsy. I need to keep moving. Sitting here for this interview is killing me.

**Linda:** Mike is a true entrepreneur and a visionary. His mind is always working, and he comes up with these ideas. He's come up with lots of ideas that we've never pursued in business. Once we start something and get it going, he gets bored again and wants to move on to the next idea. That usually leaves me running the business. And, of course, Michelle has been right in the mix, running the businesses.

**Michelle:** Right after college, I worked the restaurant and the golf course, and I was teaching some college, but then I moved to Chicago to get my master's degree in marketing.

**Mike:** When we were building the course, we hired a union crew that worked with rented equipment, but I did lots of the work myself. I ran bulldozers, everything except the drag line. The builders wouldn't let me near that. At night after the crew left, I would go out and run the equipment. As union workers they didn't really want me running that equipment, but I was always able to get someone to tell me where the keys were. Those workers would come back to the site in the morning and see what I had done during the night and say, "Somebody's been out here running our equipment." I would just tell them that whoever it was shouldn't do that.

**Linda:** To market the course for our grand opening, we rented an airplane with a banner that said, "Juday Creek is now open!" We flew that banner over all of the other golf courses in the area.

**Michelle:** It takes a while to build a golf course, and we had people watching us build for almost two years. They knew we were ready to open.

**Linda:** When I look back at our opening, there is one thing that could have been better. We had hired the National Golf Foundation to do a market study to help us determine what to charge our customers. We took their advice on how much to charge. The advice was way off base. We ended up looking at what our nearest competitors were charging and based our prices accordingly.

Even though I didn't know much about running a golf course, I had lots of other business experience that served us well. Golf is a great game, but people have to remember that foremost for the owners, it is a business and has to be managed and operated with sound business principles.

**Michelle:** When we started with Juday Creek, golf outings were very popular. We were so strong in the food and beverage area because of our restaurant experience that we had an advantage. Some golf courses struggle with food and beverage, but we could knock out a banquet with no problems and provide really great food.

**Linda:** One day we had a few of our staff call in sick. Michelle and I were the only ones working, and we had a big outing event. There were like a hundred-and-some people. Michelle and I were getting all of the players out to the golf course with our usual system, then we were back into the kitchen, and the two of us cooked all the food. When the golfers came in, we collected their score cards and then began serving them and waiting on them. People were stopping us and asking us if we had twins. We were everywhere. We got it done.

Managing food and beverage costs and staffing costs is much more accurate with outings and banquets than it is operating a full-time restaurant. When you know how many guests to expect and when to expect them, you have control over food costs.

**Mike:** Our location wasn't really conducive to a full restaurant. Michelle runs fish fries and that sort of thing and people really like our food, but it isn't a restaurant that's always open.

**Michelle:** We also do some golf cart catering. People in our neighborhood call the course and order food that we deliver by golf cart. That's a bit unusual, I suppose.

**Linda:** We have so much restaurant experience that we are very strong in the area of food. Michelle has been a part of all that experience, and now she expands on her knowledge. You probably wouldn't call her a chef, but her food is as good as or better than most chefs. Juday Creek really does have a great reputation for food.

**Michelle:** Our kitchen is staffed mostly by high school students, but the food is from my recipes. Our guests sometimes just can't believe we don't have a fancy chef preparing their food.

I train those kitchen employees, and I also teach during the winters at St. Mary's College. During the warmer months I'm too busy at the golf course to teach. When I put my kids to bed at 10 each night, that's when I have the time to prepare for my classes. We all stay busy.

**Mike:** You can probably tell how intense we are. Right now we have three businesses. You can imagine how many phone calls we get in a day. I, all of us, return those calls immediately, as soon as we can. We don't want to wait until tomorrow. When we call back immediately, then that problem or concern isn't there for us tomorrow. It's handled and done with.

We each do our best to exceed customers' expectations, whether it's hosting a golf outing, one of Michelle's salads, or how we build houses. That goal of exceeding expectations is really important to us. In over 40 years, in all of our businesses I don't think we have ever had a dissatisfied customer. That's real! That's the truth! I've now built over 200 houses, and I don't have any dissatisfied customers.

**Michelle:** When Dad builds houses, he calculates all the costs up front so the customer knows just what their costs will be. There are no surprises. That's the same way we do golf outings, weddings, or whatever we do. People know we are up front and that we are going to deliver what we say. That kind of honesty is appreciated.

**Linda:** In 1995 we sold the last Lindys restaurant, and that's when we started Nugent Builders and started building houses. We quickly realized that custom home building was the best business we have ever been in for Mike, because every project is finite. Building might take six months or nine months, it's done, and then Mike can move on to the next project. He's antsy, and it keeps him from being bored. The golf course is a long-term project, which Mike doesn't enjoy, so just Michelle and I run the golf course.

I stick my nose into the building business, but that's mostly Mike's business. I do all the bidding contracts, and I work a lot with the customers at the beginning and end of the builds, but Mike goes out with customers to pick out tile, carpets, cabinets and paint colors. He's so creative. He has that eye. Our houses are distinctive, and people recognize when they see a Nugent house. Michelle Obama's decorator actually went through one of our houses to get some decorating ideas. We had done a house in black and white, and they were looking for a black-and-white theme for a room in the White House. That's a compliment!

**Mike:** Our whole focus is not to just make money. The key to success for us is the friends you make and enjoying the work you do. Everybody has to have a job, and sometimes work isn't all that much fun, but generally you should really like what you do. Success isn't judged by the money you make, but by enjoying the people you work with and the friends you have. That's what makes you happy.

My mother had 14 kids, and we didn't have much money. That background gave me drive to make money when I was young, but now I am more focused on enjoying life and helping Michelle enjoy her life. That's what parents want for their children.

**Michelle:** I have two children. Our six-year-old son is coming to work this year. He has plans. He wants to be the boss. He keeps firing his sister when he doesn't like how she does something. He tells her, "You are fired!"

I guess all of us like to be in control. I have been a good employee for others, but I come from two parents who like to be in charge and I do, too.

**Mike:** If you ask me what the highest achievement for the golf course is, my first answer is that it is still coming. That's what improving is all about. We will soon be celebrating our 25th anniversary, so we're doing some things right. The governor has been there, as well as Chicago politicians. The lieutenant governor has been there, who Linda knows very well.

Through the golf course business we got invited to a fund-raising speech by President Bush for a local congressman. There were about 7,000 people there. When we got there, a friend of ours had arranged special seats for us. The Secret Service escorted us from the bleachers to seats on the stage just behind the President's podium. That was so amazing!

**Linda:** I got to actually talk with the president and get pictures with him.

**Mike:** It was so funny. Our best friend's brother paid $4,000 to have his picture taken with the president. When Linda got into the reception line, she handed her camera to the guy who just laid out the four grand and had him take Linda's picture with the president. You should see her pictures!

**Linda:** I felt so comfortable with him. We had a real conversation. It must have lasted five minutes. I asked if he would sign my badge, which he did. The pictures were real natural of us having the conversation.

**Mike:** We made CNN that night. The footage showed all of these war heroes on stage with the president, and then there was me in this orange sweatshirt that looked like a Halloween costume. My friend Joe, who also owns a golf course, called me that night from Florida, wondering how I managed to be on stage with the president. Of course, I teased him for all it was worth and fibbed to him that I was on Air Force One too. I don't care all that much about politics, but it was hilarious.

Linda is always on TV or radio and Michelle is, too. That really gets to our friend Joe, because he wonders how we get so much publicity and he doesn't. One time close to April Fools' Day I got one of our staff to practice for half a day calling Joe up to say, "Hi, this is Maureen McFadden calling from WGwhatever. I would like to speak with you about your golf course for our broadcast." Well, we did it and really played up our interest in his course, and we taped the whole conversation. He was so excited. "Oh, please come out and see my course!" We just let him go on and on. It was so hilarious! Later that night, we went out to dinner with Joe, and he couldn't wait to tell us he was on the radio. He said, "You are not going to believe what happened to me today!" Then I said, "Oh, could it be this?" Then I pushed the play button on the recorder. He stewed a little bit, but it was just great fun. I suppose I have some history playing April Fools' jokes.

**Linda:** You asked about our best day at the golf course, and for me there isn't one particular day that stands out most. I love the days when there is lots of activity and people are around. Michelle has done an awesome job of bringing kids to the course. We have junior golf instruction and camps for kids 7 through 17, and team leagues for kids in fifth to 12th grades. When kids are at that golf course, they add real excitement. We have Junior Team Golf Leagues where the different teams have their own team golf shirts.

**Michelle:** They get to pick out their own team names and shirts. We have the Golden Dragons, the Muskrat Ninjas and that sort of thing. It's amazing the energy they have brought to the other golfers on the course. The other golfers follow different kid teams and ask how *my* team is doing. The kids can practice at the course while we are open for play for other golfers. It has really brought new energy to the course.

**Linda:** It's hard to say there is one really special day. When there is stuff going on, that's exciting and what I like the best. Our two golf course dogs, Mulligan and Sandy, are always there, and that adds to the excitement, too.

**Mike:** For me, here is what I really love. Imagine this: Linda and I are in a bar one night at a restaurant and three different people came up to us. I get tears when I tell this story. They said to us that we changed their lives. These were all people who had previously worked for us at the golf course. It was so emotional for me. Two of those three people we had fired. Linda had fired them, and they still were telling us how we changed their lives.

**Linda:** I have a way of firing people. I hate it. I hate it. But, I have a way of doing it. I try to make them feel good about themselves. In one of the cases, Mike caught the guy drinking. He was one of my best friend's sons. In the other case, the guy was the son of a policeman and he got caught stealing. I knew his parents very well, and the guy asked if I was going to tell his dad what he had done. I just told him that I didn't hire his dad, that I hired him. I told him that if he wanted to tell his dad then that's up to him. I ask them how they would feel and act if they owned the business. Of course, they are always crying, but I try not to make them feel too bad. I give them a hug when they leave. I tell them that the important thing is that they know why they are leaving, and you can learn from the experience and you will be a better person for their next job.

Over the last 40 years, we have had literally thousands of people work for us. We still have people who worked for us 30 years ago keep in touch with us. We have had people who became doctors, attorneys, all kinds of successful people who worked for us. We get Christmas cards, visits, all kinds of communication. That feels good. When people come to work for us, they become family and they know that. Even now, our director of golf is like my son.

**Michelle:** With our event director, her first job was with us. Her dad was the director of the labor department for the state of Indiana. When she first started, she told me she went home and cried and told her dad that she had to clean toilets. "Can they make me do that?" He told her that, of course, we could ask her to do that kind of work and that she'd be going back there again tomorrow. She has been with us for 18 years now, on and off. Now she says that she is passionate about her work and really wants to be with us. She has had some other job offers that were attractive, but she just loves what she does with us.

*(I asked about the future for Juday Creek.)*

**Mike:** We are always wondering what's next for Juday Creek, and we all have differing opinions. Some of our property could be profitable for us to sell for commercial development. There is a hospital that was recently built right next to us, and some of that property sold for like $400,000 an acre. I'd like to sell about 20 acres of our golf property for commercial development. In my opinion, and Michelle doesn't necessarily agree with this, I believe that the time golf takes is too long. I want to build a 12-hole golf course. Everybody asks me, Why 12 holes? Most of our golfers aren't trying to go out and shoot 70 anymore. Most of them just want to go out and relax and have fun. Nine holes just don't seem like enough, but I think that 12 holes are just about right. You could play in less than three hours. You could charge one price, have less course maintenance, and reduce expenses in lots of ways. I think we would be packed.

**Linda:** It would be a different market. We wouldn't be looking for the traditional golfer, but we would be looking for the new golfer. There probably is a good market for the new golfer.

**Michelle:** I agree that the property is so valuable that from a business perspective, we have to consider that plan. But for our traditional golfers, our outings, leagues and junior golf programs, I think we need a full course. This idea opens a real can of worms for us. There are pluses and minuses for both points of view.

**Linda:** Mike and Michelle go back and forth on this debate. I'm right in the middle. Here's how I think about it. Timing is important. Someday we will sell that property, and then we will have to evaluate our options. Someday shorter golf courses are going to pop up, and we may have a 12-hole course at Juday Creek. Markets change. In five years, the 12-hole course may be the perfect idea. In some ways our debate about a traditional course or a 12-hole course to save time and money is just the kind of dilemma the golf industry faces on a larger scale. How do you maintain long-standing traditions and make golf less expensive and less time-consuming?

**Michelle:** Dad has lots of good ideas. On the other hand, we often say, "Right again, Mike!" But usually we say it with our fingers crossed behind our backs.

**Mike:** Someday Michelle might just take over everything, and if she can keep sending me enough money to live in Florida, I'll be happy. I can spend a lot of money.

Michelle and I are so much alike, but we don't always see eye to eye. Right now, it would turn my stomach to not have my hands in the business, but the day will come.

*(I asked for comments on the golf industry in general.)*

**Linda:** We all know that economic times have been tough, but I truly believe the golf industry will rebound. It's going to take a lot of work, and it's going to take the effort of every single person involved in the industry to bring it back. There is so much competition for people's time. We have to get into the heads of the young people we want to attract to golf. They may not answer the phone or respond to emails, but they will respond to social media like Facebook. We have to find ways to reach those young people. Also, you can't just open your door and expect them to walk in. You have to create opportunities for them to participate. I see many golf properties where the owners are crying the blues, but they aren't doing what's needed to create fun learning opportunities and events to create opportunities for participation.

Michelle not only has a degree in marketing, but she has great ideas. We have a program that we run at Easter that's called "Greens, Eggs and Ham." We feed the guests breakfast, host the golf event, and they get a ham. At Thanksgiving we do it and they get a turkey. The food really gets donated to the local food bank, but the program brings in golfers. We give away 80 to 100 hams or turkeys each year. Golfers get mulligans in the tournament when they bring in canned food. We donated about 1,000 pounds of food last year. The industry needs those kinds of creative ideas.

**Mike:** What I think is important for the industry is getting staff at our golf courses that don't just look at their jobs as work, but who have a real energy and passion for golf. Like I said earlier, it's important for people to really enjoy what they do. At the same time the staff needs the expertise to make the business profitable. Lots of owners are getting older and sometimes lose the energy. Getting younger people with the passion, personality and expertise involved in the industry is going to be key for the industry.

**Linda:** Right now the supply of golf courses exceeds player demand for golf. So, we have choices. We can reduce the supply of golf courses. Obviously that can be painful for the people involved with those courses. Or we can continue to look for creative, fresh ideas to increase player demand. We have to think outside the box with our ideas. Some of the ideas to increase demand may seem to reduce respect for some of the old traditions of the game. However, golf course owners are business people, and their missions are to maintain and improve their business successes.

Just this morning I walked on the stage for one of the keynote addresses for the Golf Industry Show conference. Key leaders throughout the golf industry were introduced. I was introduced as the new president of the National Golf Course Owners Association. Out of the one dozen or more leaders, I was the only woman on stage. For those new ways of thinking about the industry, it's a start.

## Mike and Linda Rogers' Lessons

- If you think that owning a golf course will mean that you can play a lot of golf and then take your winters off, you're wrong. That almost never happens in the golf business. You're too busy.

- To market the course for their grand opening, the Rogers family rented an airplane with a banner that said, "Juday Creek is now open!" They flew that banner over all the other golf courses in the area.

- To find the price to charge for golf in your market, base your judgement on the local competition. Using professional advice from marketing specialists who are not local can produce poor decisions.

- Golf is a great game, but people have to remember that foremost for the owners, it is a business and has to be managed and operated with sound business principles.

- Previous restaurant experience creates an advantage. Some golf courses struggle with food and beverage, but the Rogers family can produce a banquet with no problems and provide really great food.

- Managing food and beverage costs and staffing costs is much more accurate with outings and banquets than it is operating a full-time restaurant. When you know how many guests to expect and when to expect them, you have control over food costs.

- Always respond to inquiries and requests as soon as you can. Don't wait until tomorrow. When problems or concerns are dealt with immediately, they are handled and done with.

- Do your best to exceed customers' expectations in every service or product you provide.

- Calculate and communicate all costs up front, so the customer knows just what their costs will be. There are no surprises. That applies to golf outings, weddings, or whatever you do. That kind of honesty is appreciated.

- "Our whole focus is not to just make money. The key to success for us is the friends you make and enjoying the work you do. Everybody has to have a job, and sometimes work isn't all that much fun, but generally you should really like what you do. Success isn't judged by the money you make, but by enjoying the people you work with and the friends you have. That's what makes you happy."

- It's fun when there is lots of activity and people are around. Create opportunities to bring kids to the course. Juday Creek has junior golf instruction, camps for kids 7 through 17 and team leagues for kids in fifth to 12th grades where the different teams have their own team golf shirts. When kids are at the golf course, they add real excitement.

- "When people come to work for us, they become family and they know that."

- Terminating employees is painful, but it can be productive. Tell the terminated employee that the important thing is to know why they are leaving and to learn from the experience and be a better person for their next job.

- The Rogers family is considering transforming their 18-hole course into a 12-hole course. In some ways this debate to save time and money is just the kind of dilemma the golf industry faces on a larger scale. Maintaining long-standing golf traditions and making golf less expensive and less time consuming are current industry challenges.

- Find ways to reach young people. You can't just open your door and expect them to walk in. You have to create opportunities for them to participate. Do what's needed to create fun learning opportunities and events to encourage participation.

- Getting younger people on your staff with the passion, personality and expertise for golf business is going to be key for the industry.

- "Right now the supply of golf courses exceeds player demand for golf. So, we have choices. We can reduce the supply of golf courses. Obviously that can be painful for the people involved with those courses. Or we can continue to look for creative, fresh ideas to increase player demand. We have to think outside the box with our ideas. Some of the ideas to increase demand may seem to reduce respect for some of the old traditions of the game. However, golf course owners are business people, and their missions are to maintain and improve their business successes."
- Hard work pays dividends.

# Legacy

## Frank Jemsek, Owner of Cog Hill Golf and Country Club in Lemont, Illinois

ဆာ ဈ

*Cog Hill Golf and Country Club opened in 1927. It is in Lemont, Illinois, just southwest of Chicago. The family-owned complex of four public 18-hole courses includes the world-famous Course #4: Dubsdread. In addition, the Jemsek family owns the St. Andrews Golf Club, a 36-hole complex and leases Pine Meadow Golf Course, both in the Chicago area.*

*Of the four courses at Cog Hill, Dubsdread is by far the most famous. The course was designed by Dick Wilson and Joe Lee in 1964 and then redesigned by Rees Jones in 2008. Dubsdread hosted the PGA's Western Open Championship from 1991 to 2006 and the PGA's BMW Championship in 2007 and from 2009 to 2011. Dubsdread has hosted four USGA (Amateur) Championships. Among the numerous accolades for Dubsdread are ratings in the top 100 courses in America by* Golf Digest *and* Golf Magazine. *It was among* Golf World *readers' choice top 50 American public courses. It was selected as one of "America's Most Important Golf Courses by Decade" by* Golf Digest *and rated #1 in Illinois in* Golfweek's *"Best Courses You Can Play."*

*The "old world" clubhouse at Cog Hill Golf and Country Club contains three dining halls, with total indoor seating of up to 280 people, for fine dining, weddings, banquets and other special events.*

*Cog Hill and the Jemsek family have rich histories in American public golf. The reputations of the courses and the family are known around the world.*

*I interviewed Mr. Jemsek in his office at Cog Hill during the afternoon of December 9, 2008. This is a working office, not a showcase. Judith Mokelke (HR manager) and Marla Weeks (office manager), one of his two daughters who work at Cog Hill, share the space. Daughter Katherine, president of Cog Hill Golf & CC, was visiting Pine Meadow that day. His son Joe (golf course architect) and General Manager Nick Mokelke were in and out of the office throughout the interview. This is a busy office. Even on this winter day in Chicago, the parking lot had about 50 cars as at least 80 guests enjoyed a banquet luncheon.*

www.coghillgolf.com

ဆာ ဈ

Years ago before the golf cart, you needed a caddie. As soon as I was old enough to carry a bag, if there were no other caddies available, I would caddie. Any kid was better than no caddie at all, even if you had to put the bag on a pull cart. I started at age 11. Before that, I used to spend the summers at my aunt and uncle's house, because my parents were so busy at the golf course. I decided I wanted to spend summers with my parents. They said if you want to be here, you have to work. So I caddied and also worked as a parking lot attendant. My job was to greet each car and unload their bags. Years ago people didn't have tee times in advance; they just showed up to play. My job was to encourage them. I just told them, "Oh yeah, you can get out to play." At St. Andrews, where I started, working people expected a round to take five or six hours. Some people remember how slow it was.

I did those kinds of jobs through high school. Then I went to college. Loyola in New Orleans was the farthest south I could get on a basketball scholarship *(Frank is 6'8")*. I played collegiate golf there, too. I also went to a restaurant program at Cornell University. When I graduated and came back to Chicago, my dad told others, "Everything will be all right now. Frank is back." You know, a prejudiced father. That's how family golf courses are. There are lots of relatives involved. All of our courses were connected when my father was alive *(Joe Jemsek died in 2002 at age 89)*. It was a family act. My sister was involved, even though she didn't like it as much. And, in our family with a Russian background, the first-born son was the one who basically inherited the family property or business. That was me. I knew I would be in the golf business, and I loved it. My uncle was in charge at St. Andrews, and I worked with him right after college to help keep the course running well. I kind of assumed that I would take over at Cog Hill.

But you know, reality sets in. When my dad decided to replace a retiring manager, he told me I wasn't going to manage Cog Hill. He wanted Nick Mokelke, who had already been working with my dad, to be general manager. Dad said that Nick was more organized than I was. At first I was really disappointed. I was the family member and I was older than Nick. However, having someone who is really smart, organized and efficient on your team to help run the business was and is the way to go. Nick is still our GM today. That experience helped drive me to become a better leader and realize that leading is about making the hard decisions. Not necessarily making the most popular decision, but doing what is best. That's how I got started in the business, and gradually my roles evolved until I was running the businesses and not my dad.

*(Nick Mokelke popped in and out of Frank's office several times during the interview. Their exchanges took only moments on each decision needing Frank's approval. Clearly Nick was efficient and organized. While Frank wore a polo shirt and a Cog Hill sweater vest, Nick was dressed in a business suit and completely looked and acted the part of corporate management.)*

Of course, it was my dad, Joe, who got the family into the golf business. Back in the 1920s, as a young kid Dad started hitching rides to Cog Hill to caddy. When he was 16, he started entering golf tournaments and played on the winter tour. He was a very good player and won the World Long Drive Championship in 1934. But he felt like his future was in golf business. It was very hard to make a living playing golf, and he felt he could be more successful running courses. So he kept working with Marty Coghill and his brothers, the original owners of Cog Hill, in order to learn as much about running a golf course as he could. Eventually he became the head pro at Cog Hill and took over the pro shop.

One of my favorite stories about my dad is when he was still a caddie. The Coghill brothers were playing golf. My dad was caddying for Marty, who said to my dad, "Son, what do you think of this place?" My dad replied, "It is the most beautiful place I have ever seen, and someday I am going to own it." All the brothers laughed, but my dad felt like with hard work, you could accomplish anything.

In 1938, when Dad was only 25 years old, he took the position of head pro and club manager at St. Andrews Golf Club in West Chicago. St. Andrews started as a private club *(built in 1925)* but changed ownership a few times. The depression made it tough on businesses. The Hough sisters *(Grace and Alice)* were struggling to make ends meet with the golf course when they contacted Dad. They were unable to sell the business for more than they owed on the property.

Just a year later, Dad married Mom, Grace Hough. Things happened fast. When Aunt Alice and Mom decided to split up their inheritance, Mom and Dad took over ownership of St. Andrews with a $50,000 note, and Aunt Alice took the subdivision. That was 1940. They made some bold moves investing in the course. Mom stopped teaching school so she could help run the course. Financially it was a tough time. New golfers had to be found, so Dad started going out into local communities to give free golf lessons and started golf leagues at the course. When the courses started doing better, they put the profits back into the course and clubhouse for needed improvements. In 1947 St. Andrews became the first public course in the United States to host a U.S. Open qualifying round. The course got national acclaim as one of the best daily fee courses in the country. Mom and Dad brought family relatives into the business and before long, Mom went back to teaching, which she loved.

Dad didn't just excel at promoting St. Andrews. He promoted golf. In '49 he originated television golf with the weekly program, "Pars, Birdies, and Eagles" in Chicago. With tour pros and amateurs, the show focused on golf instruction and rules. The show ran for 14 years. During this time, "All Star Bowling" was a successful TV show. He convinced "All Star Bowling" to make the first-ever made-for-TV golf matches. Up until then TV cameras had to be pretty stationary. You could shoot boxing, bowling or other sports with a stationary camera. Then when TV technology got better, you could track a golf shot. In 1956, my dad was involved with the TV show "All Star Golf" that televised golf matches. Sam Snead and Cary Middlecoff played the first match at Cog Hill. First prize in those events was $2,000, so the best pros of the day wanted to participate. First prize in a professional tournament was about that same amount. That made my father very popular with the tour. At first people didn't think viewers would watch golf on TV. Today we know otherwise!

In 1951 Dad bought Cog Hill, where he had caddied as a kid. He made Cog Hill a public course, too. Some have called my dad the patriarch of Chicago golf, and some have called him the patriarch of public golf. In the early days, the best golf courses were private. Even people who were making money were having trouble getting into private clubs. They might have a two-year waiting list to join a private club. During the 1949 U.S. Open at Medinah Country Club, my dad overheard some of his customers talking about how they wished they could have the chance to play at Medinah which was private. My dad knew they, like many others, would probably not ever get the chance. This was when he decided to try to bring a championship course to them. Dad wanted everyone to have the opportunity to enjoy the quality of golf courses and the quality of clubhouse and customer service that private club members enjoyed. What he did here at Cog Hill started a national trend of improving the standards of public golf.

Of the four courses at Cog Hill, Course #4, Dubsdread, is the most famous. *(Dubsdread implies the course inspires dread in "dubs," or novice golfers.)* Dubsdread has been nationally ranked since it opened in 1964. People around the world know about Dubsdread. We've hosted major championships like the Western Open *(1990-2006)* and the BMW Championship *(2007, 2009-2011)*. In '07 Tiger Woods won the BMW here with a final round 63. That pretty much sealed the deal for him for that first FedEx Cup Championship. Right now we are doing renovations on #4, Dubsdread. We are fortunate to have Rees Jones as our architect and Wadsworth Construction Company for the course work. Rees and Wadsworth are the best in the business; in the end, you know it will be done right. An added bonus is that my son Joe, a budding golf course architect, gets to closely observe the best in the world. We've held a variety of USGA events here, too, including Men's and Women's Public Links Championships and a U.S. Amateur Championship. The fact that the courses are public means that anyone in the world can play where the best players in the world play. Long term, we would love to have a U.S. Open here. That was one of my dad's dreams.

My dad used to play golf at a golf course in Florida named Dubsdread. Florida's Dubsdread has a great history. Many great golfers used to spend their winters there, and there was always a game going on. Dad enjoyed the competition and the camaraderie at the course, and he always liked the name. So, when Dad built #4 he decided to use the name, too.

My dad had a great sense of humor. He used to put up signs deep, really deep, in the woods on the courses. The signs said, "If you are looking for your ball here, contact Joe Jemsek, Pro." It was funny, but it also promoted the business. Those guys needed lessons.

He was named Illinois PGA Golf Professional of the Year a couple of times. In 1988 *Golf Magazine* called him one of the "100 Heroes of Golf," and *Golf Digest Magazine* named him "One of the Most Powerful People in Golf" in 1991. That same year, he was named the national "Golf Professional of the Year" by the PGA of America at 77 years old.

Dad was a bit over six feet tall. People always thought he was 6'3" or 6'4." His presence filled a room. He created a legacy, not just for our family, but for people who love golf. You can see that I have had big shoes to fill!

I was terribly shy as a kid. I even took a Dale Carnegie course on public speaking as a young adult. I am still a little shy today, but I love the social aspect of being around golf. I really try to remember people's names. It is important to me to try to make people feel at home here. I keep index cards with foursome's names handwritten on the cards to try to remember as many as I can. It's part of the customer service we want to provide, but mostly it is important to me and lets our customers know how much I appreciate them.

The biggest challenge in the golf business is to keep up with the times. We need new players. Players can't spend five or six hours playing a round these days. We love the golfer who plays three times a week, but we understand that takes time away from family and children. If we can get kids out with their parents and they have fun, then we know we have a golfer for life. Developing tomorrow's players is important to the industry. Right now we have high schools that use our courses as their home courses for matches and practice. We also donated the use of the land for the Chicago District Golf Association to help them build the Sunshine through Golf Course, a three-hole course used for special needs golfers and juniors. My son Joe designed the course.

Part of keeping up with the times involves finances. My property taxes just went up over $400,000 a year here at Cog Hill. I was already paying $8 or $9 dollars a player in taxes.

This new increase adds another $3 to $4 per golfer. The taxes, combined with payroll, leave little margin for privately owned facilities. We have to be extra careful when making decisions. Not only do we hope to make a profit, but we need to continually reinvest in the property. In addition to the course renovations for Dubsdread I already mentioned, we were in need of updating and repairs in the clubhouse. I tell Nick *(Mokelke, GM)* that what we do should last 100 years. Our family is in this business for the long haul.

A while ago we went to foursome's greens fees on all of our courses. It benefits us because we collect the revenue for four golfers at a time, and the golfers have a guarantee they will have the same time every weekend. If one of the registered foursome doesn't show, then a single can join their group. We encourage singles to come to the course. When singles join new groups, they often make social networks that last. Golf is social, and the more we can promote those relationships, the better for our business.

All our courses have great practice facilities. We built state-of-the-art practice facilities at Cog Hill in order to make the golf experience better for the customer. When we saw that we could make a profit, we made it a practice to build great practice facilities at all of the courses. People riding down the highway might be drawn to the course just to use the driving range. People like to hit balls even if they are just beginning the game. That gets them in the door and helps our bottom line.

We have always done well with corporate, charity and social golf outings. Those events not only mean greens fees to play, but banquets and other food and beverage sales, pro shop sales, and potential customers. My dad was one of the first people to market corporate golf outings. The staff at Cog Hill is experienced in handling these events. They see and resolve problems before they happen. It may be the first outing for a chairperson, but that's OK. We take the time to help them with organization and make sure that when they arrive, everything is set up and ready to go. I always do my best to be here for every outing. Because we are so well equipped to manage big outings, we have hosted some major charity events at Cog Hill. Celebrities like Michael Jordan, Tiger Woods,

Walter Peyton, Mike Ditka and Dave Duerson have hosted those charity events. That's good marketing for us. Right now, we are looking into some new marketing directions. You have to keep pace with the times.

Obviously the economy is in trouble right now, but I'm optimistic about my businesses and about the future of golf. My dad was just getting started in the depression era, and he struggled but did well. The industry has seen some decline in customers, but I believe that will pick up again. We'll be open when customers come back in bigger numbers. People need to be outside to enjoy life. You know, factory workers absolutely love to play golf. They need to get outside. Kids need to get outside. I think it's healthy to have fresh air and the exercise. History shows there are downturns and positive swings in industry. The game itself is too great to not survive economic hard times.

In peak season we have about 332 employees at Cog Hill. There are 80 full-time year-around employees. Our staff understands the importance of representing our business to our customers. We're fortunate to have staff with long histories here.

There have only been two head superintendents at Cog Hill since 1927, when it was opened. Ken Lapp, our Head Superintendent, worked for my dad beginning in 1949. He started washing glasses in the bar when he was 11 years old. In '55 he became superintendent at Fresh Meadow Golf Course, where he built all 18 greens and tee boxes. For a while that was the most popular course in Chicago. It was the closest 18-hole course to the city and had some infamous mobster-types as customers. He's been with us for 60 years now. Kenny's dad, Amos Lapp, was hired by my dad just after World War II as the superintendent at St. Andrews. My dad said that hiring Amos was the best personnel decision he ever made. With Amos came his son Ken, and that ended our greens-keeping needs for history. Our first superintendent, before Ken, was George Dahlman. When George died, Kenny took the job. He must have turned down 20 job offers to work at Cog Hill. The #2 course is his favorite golf course in the world. Kenny is a firm but fair superintendent. He gives our employees responsibility with good guidance, and they respect him.

Superintendents across the United States know and respect Kenny. His son Tom and his sister have worked with us for about 50 years. It's a family package for the Lapp family, too.

Nick Mokelke, our GM, started working for my dad in 1963. When Nick was in 7$^{th}$ or 8$^{th}$ grade, he rode his bicycle five miles to Cog Hill. He was a caddie, a dishwasher, a cook and a starter. He did everything. Nick ran Glenwoodie Golf Club for us for a while and came to Cog Hill permanently in '79. He finished college while working here, which made his dad very happy. For the past 25 years he's been our club manager. He's been president of the Club Managers Association of America and still serves on their board of directors. Nick is a very hands-on manager and is always focused on the quality of our food.

Right now we have two head chefs, Jose and Ricardo, who started with us as dishwashers. They share the head chef position. When our previous head chef took another position he recommended that we hire Jose and Ricardo to replace him. Usually head chefs came from France, Switzerland, or some noted city, certainly not from the kitchen crew. But the previous chef said he would stake his reputation on those dishwashers and we gave them the responsibility in 1984. It's a big job. Our banquet and dining services stay busy. We can seat over 300 guests in our three indoor dining halls and up to 700 guests in our Pavilion Tent. They have been great for us. Because they share the responsibility, it gives them the chance to have a life with family away from the course.

You're as good as the people who help you, and having committed staff with such longevity has been a blessing. I could go on. Our head waitress is 80 years old, and she's been with us for 50 years.

Our golf shop, driving range and restaurants are open every day of the year, except Christmas Day. The golf season in Chicago may be brief, but we are definitely a year-around business, and we appreciate the good people who help us.

I suppose the achievement I am most proud of so far was bringing the Western Open to Cog Hill. We hosted the Western Open at Dubsdread from 1991-2006. A lot of people don't know it, but the Western Open is the third-oldest professional golf tournament, after the British Open and the U.S. Open.

The Western Open brought professional golf to Cog Hill and showed we have the quality of services and golf course geography to host very large crowds. We hosted over 50,000 guests on the Sunday of the 1997 Western Open. Not only has the tournament brought an international reputation to Cog Hill, but we have donated our facility to the Western Golf Association for the event, which has enabled hundreds of thousands of dollars to stay in the Evans Scholars Foundation that provides college scholarships to caddies. Hundreds of caddies have gone to college with our assistance. The Western Open has been a win-win for lots of people, and I am quite proud of the accomplishment. (*In 2007 the Western Open was renamed to the BMW Championship, as part of the FedEx Cup Championship. Cog Hill hosted the BMW in '07 and again from 2009-2011.*)

My dad always dreamed of bringing a U.S. Open to Cog Hill. I share that dream. I believe that we have a great facility for the U.S. Open. I've been talking with the USGA about hosting a U.S. Open as soon as possible. We are already a big stadium for viewers, as we have proven, and some of our course renovations are focused on new spectator mounds and other changes for those big events.

Should golf become an Olympic sport and should the International Olympic Committee choose Chicago for the 2016 games, then I believe Cog Hill is the obvious site. Right now, we are under tough competition with great sites like Medinah Country Club and Olympia Fields Country Club. They have both hosted U.S. Opens in the past and are great courses. But I'm prejudiced. I believe that we have a good shot at it as well, because they are private clubs and we are a public facility. We have a course that the public can play. Who wouldn't want the opportunity to play a golf course where the Olympics were held? American tourists and international tourists to Chicago can play Cog Hill, and as a result, could bring more tourist dollars to Chicago and Cook County. I know people who have played here, and when they mention it to their friends, their friends are impressed. They played where the pros play. Besides, this is a course the American pros know well. There's nothing wrong with a home-field advantage for our American athletes. It would be terrific to host the Olympics. There are lots of unknowns, but I'm an optimist. *(In October 2009, the International Olympics Committee made golf an Olympic sport but decided on Rio de Janeiro as the location of the 2016 games.)*

In the meantime, we will continue to provide the best golf and the best customer service to our guests that we possibly can. Gandhi said, "A customer is the most important visitor on our premises, he is not dependent on us. We are dependent on him. He is not an interruption in our work. He is the purpose of it. He is not an outsider in our business. He is part of it. We are not doing him a favor by serving him. He is doing us a favor by giving us an opportunity to do so." That quote captures my dad's vision and it's a philosophy I live by.

*(As we were concluding our interview, I had to ask Frank, "Michael Jordan and Tiger Woods have been here many times. How well do you know them?")*

*(Frank responds with a laugh):* I know them just well enough to say hello. If I was wearing my name tag, they might call me by my name *(another laugh)*. They're busy people. I did know Earl Woods *(Tiger's father)* a bit. By mistake he got left behind at one of the Western Opens, and I gave Earl a ride into Chicago. I liked him a lot. Life's going pretty well for Tiger. It's pretty much the way Earl planned it out for him. My dad and Earl knew each other pretty well. They actually shared a hotel room during the '91 Master's tournament. They asked each other if they could sleep through someone else's snoring. Apparently, they could *(another laugh)*.

## Jemsek's Lessons

- "Leading is about making the hard decisions. Not necessarily making the most popular decision, but doing what is best."
- "Not only do we hope to make a profit, but we need to continually reinvest in the property.... What we do should last 100 years. Our family is in this business for the long haul."
- "Golf is social, and the more we can promote those (social) relationships, the better for our business."
- "You have to keep pace with the times."
- "You're as good as the people who help you...." Having loyal, committed staff is a blessing.
- Make sure your customers know how much you appreciate them.
- "A customer is the most important visitor on our premises; he is not dependent on us. We are dependent on him. He is not an interruption in our work. He is the purpose of it. He is not an outsider in our business. He is part of it. We are not doing him a favor by serving him. He is doing us a favor by giving us an opportunity to do so." (Gandhi)
- In a family business, one may inherit the responsibility of "big shoes to fill." One also has the responsibility of passing the legacy to those who follow.

# All In!

## Bill Aragona, Owner of Boulder Creek Golf and Country Club in Boulder Creek, California

ℬ ℭ

*I interviewed Bill Aragona on February 11, 2010, at the Golf Industry Show in San Diego, CA. Bill and I discussed his ownership story on the patio of the San Diego Convention Center. Boulder Creek Golf and Country Club is a resort facility among the redwoods of the Santa Cruz Mountains. The facility includes a challenging 18-hole executive golf course, a full-service restaurant and bar, conference and meeting facilities, condominium lodging for overnight rentals or vacation packages, and tennis. The golf course was designed by Jack Fleming and originally opened in 1961. Bill bought the resort in 1979.*

*Bill became the new president of the NGCOA (National Golf Course Owners Association) the day after our interview.*

www.bouldercreekgolf.com

ℬ ℭ

I am one of those legions of people who love the game of golf. When I was younger, I played competitively. I had a dream: I wanted to be a golf pro. However, even though I played golf in college, I wasn't good enough to go on the professional tour. I had to be content playing locally, the state amateur and that sort of thing. I qualified in a few national amateur tournaments, but nothing really big. I never really wanted to be a club pro, because at the courses where I played, I thought the local pros were treated quite poorly. There didn't seem to be much respect for them, so I didn't want to go in that direction. A few of the better amateurs I played with got what I thought were the good jobs. They became manufacturers' representatives for companies like Titleist. Those were the plum deals, and I never got one of those jobs.

In my mid-30s an opportunity came along to buy an existing golf course, Boulder Creek. Prior to that, my good friend and business partner Dan James and I were buying old Victorian homes in San Francisco. The homes were being sold at estate sales when people died without wills or successors. So we would show up on the courthouse steps and buy the houses at good prices. Then we would fix them up and rent them out. For us this was just a weekend deal, but we had a nice stable of rental homes. Dan sold stock quotation equipment to brokerage companies, and I was working for 3M selling microfilm equipment. One day Dan came to see me and told me that Tom Culligan, the owner of Boulder Creek Golf and Country Club, wanted to sell the property. Dan said we should sell all of our rental units and buy the golf course. I thought about the idea for a while, and then I decided, "Why not. What the heck!" So we started selling our rental units, but we still didn't have enough money to buy the course. We hocked everything and put up a $100,000 nonrefundable deposit to show our commitment. We were total neophytes. We didn't really know what we were doing. We went to all of our friends to see if they wanted to invest in the golf course. Almost every one of them told us we were crazy. We did get one guy, Marshall Gleason, to put up some money, and then Dan and I got second mortgages on our houses, and we put all of our resources together. It was like the poker card game, Texas Hold'em. We went all in! There we were. All of a sudden, we were in the golf business. That was March 20, 1979.

When we moved to Boulder Creek, I was married with a young daughter, and Dan was married with two children. We just uprooted our families and moved. It was a huge lifestyle change. I had left a good job with a big company, a good income and a new car every two years. My wife couldn't stand the change, and after a couple of years she left Boulder Creek and me to move back to the city.

At first running the course was pretty easy, because it was in the spring and people were coming to play golf. We thought it was great. There was a lot of money coming in. Then came winter, and all of a sudden, there was nobody playing golf. There was no revenue, and we had to get a loan to get by. It got tough. The first year, we barely got through it. We quickly realized it wasn't what we thought, where you just stand in the proshop and collect money. We thought that if you treat people decently they will come in droves. We soon realized this is heavy-duty stuff. You have to make payroll, pay the bills, and pay the taxes. There was a whole gamut of things that neither Dan nor I were prepared for. We made it through the first year and then spring came again, the golfers returned and we had money again. We were determined that we would save money this time so we would have money for the winter.

We were so short of staff that Dan and I would trade off being at the course. One day he'd come in to the proshop at six in the morning and stay until nine at night to run the golf course. The next day I would do it. On the days he worked the golf course, I would come in at night and run the restaurant. The next night he would do the restaurant. That's how hard we worked.

One particularly cold August night in 1980, in our second year, we had a crisis. After people finished their rounds of golf, they had a habit of coming into the clubhouse and tossing their scorecards into the fireplace. We hadn't had a fire in the fireplace since the winter. At the end of a long day, at about 2 a.m., I was closing the place up for the night, and I didn't clean out the fireplace. I just tossed a match into the fireplace to burn up the scorecards. There was a lot of paper in there. Evidently, the fire went up the chimney and a spark got though a crack in the chimney and started a fire in the ceiling of the clubhouse. The fire caused the air-conditioning to go on and that blew the air around and fueled the fire even more. So I got a telephone call at about four in the morning to tell me my building was on fire. I stumbled down there and sure enough, half of the building was gone. We felt like we were in the old movie with Jimmy Stewart and Betty Hutton where there was a big fire, but at the end of the movie they are hopeful about surviving.

The next day we opened anyway and barbecued for our guests on the outdoor grill. We tried to be positive, but reality hit and we thought the business was dead. We had to let nearly all of our employees go. Dan and I were running the whole business out of the little proshop. We had condos that we were renting, groups coming for events and outings, and we were doing it with a bare-bones staff. Looking back, it may have been the best thing to ever happen. Between my partner and me, we had to do every single job in the resort. We did the cooking, the housekeeping, everything. It gave us the opportunity to really learn the business from the ground up. And it taught us a lot about how business works. We had a daily battle with the insurance company. They didn't want to pay for anything. Insurance is great until you need to use it. We learned how to go to war and fight for ourselves. It took about a year, but the insurance came through and the clubhouse was rebuilt. By that time, we had become savvy operators, and we started doing very well. We learned a lot in a short period of time.

We had started doing a good business, but in a couple of years, in 1982, we had a tremendous El Niño rainy period — we had over 100 inches of rain. We have two dams that are sources of water for the golf course. Well, one of the dams got wiped out by half of the mountain in a mudslide. It was going to cost a fortune to get it cleaned out and to repair the dam. We tried to get an SBA *(Small Business Administration)* loan, but it kind of stumbled. At that time, Leon Panetta, who now runs the CIA, was in Congress as our representative. I went to Washington D.C., and I camped out in his office. I brought all of the paperwork and met with his staff. They were great. They walked that loan through for us. So we got to a point where we had a commitment of $350,000 to clean out the dam. At that time, there were three partners and we had formed a corporation. For my original partner and me, we had everything we had invested in the resort. For the third partner, it was more of an investment of money. He got a legal opinion saying that even though we had become a corporation, the responsibility for the loan to repair the dam could go back to the individual owners of the property, should there be any problems satisfying the loan. Our third partner decided he wasn't going to sign it. He said, "You guys have nothing. If we tank and can't pay the loan, then they are going to come and take everything I have. I'm done. I'm out."

There was a gentleman named John DeNault, who had property right alongside the golf course. During our very first week there, he came over and said to me that he felt really bad that he didn't help out the last guys who owned our resort. It had sold once before, and the people had gone under and the original owner took it back. We were kind of like the second guys in to buy from the original owner. The property had been pretty run down, and he didn't want to have to deal with it again. Well, Mr. DeNault had said he felt bad about not being more help to the owners before us and to please come to see him if we ever got into any trouble. The first time I met him, I thought he was the Mafia. *(Bill made his imitation of a grumbling Mafia voice as he repeated, "Come to see me if you need anything.")* At that time, I thought he would be the last guy I'd go to for help. But now we were up against it. We can't get the SBA loan unless all three guys sign for the loan, and one of the guys won't sign. The other two of us don't have anything else to put up as collateral.

So, I go and knock on this Mr. DeNault's door and I tell him my sad story. I bring all of our financials and any documentation I have for our business. He said he didn't want to see all of that. He asked me how many loans we had on the place and I told him we had about six. He asked me if we didn't have any loans, would the resort make any money. I told him, "Yeah." Then he just said, "OK, how much do you need?" I told him we needed about $20,000 to make the payroll this month, and then I needed some way to deal with our partner who wanted out so that we could get this SBA loan. So, I swear to God, he pulls out his checkbook and writes me a check for $20,000. He tells me he's going to Hawaii for two weeks and that when he gets back, we'll talk some more, but that this money will keep me going until then.

When Mr. DeNault returned, I told him more about our loan problem and the third partner. He told me he had been very successful in his life betting on people. He told me his father had been one of the principle founders of Farmer's Insurance, and he himself was on the board of Farmer's. He personally had founded Twentieth Century Insurance with a partner he trusted. And he had a savings-and-loan business that he had started. So he said, "I have plenty of money, but I bet on people." He asked to speak with our third partner and they did talk. Mr. DeNault told him who he was and what he was, and then he signed a note to our partner that he would cover any losses on the loan. "Go sign the loan." The partner signed the loan, and we used the money to fix the dam, fix the proshop — we fixed everything that needed attention.

Mr. DeNault watched us through this process. There's no such thing as a free lunch. He started advising us on this and that. Eventually the third partner realized he wasn't ever going to make much money on the deal, and he sold most of his stock to Mr. DeNault who became a partner with Dan and me. In effect, Mr. DeNault became our bank. When we needed money, we went to him. Then we had some really good years. Mr. DeNault is over 90 years old now, and God bless him, he's still there to lend us money to keep us going. If it weren't for him, I'd be gone. I'm not one of those owners with a lot of personal wealth. I'm kind of "the face of golf." I'm just a little operator chasing a dream, who by hook or by crook has been able to survive.

Around 1984 or '85, Dan moved back to the San Francisco Bay area because his son had a serious allergy to the redwoods. From that time on, he did our sales and other work from the bay area, and I ran the resort on site.

In the 80s and early 90s we used our extra money to buy condos that surrounded our golf course. We rented those condos from their owners as a mini-resort when we could. As property values went up, the people who owned those condos either lived in them fulltime, put full-time renters in them or sold them. It was too expensive to keep them as second homes. So we started buying condos as they came up, and we had a small resort going. At one point, we had about 20 condo units that were on a rental plan, plus the 16 that we already owned. We had a nice pool of close to 40 condos, and that worked great. Then, as golf started to turn in the direction it's going now, we started selling off the condos one by one to help make money. Looking back now, that was a mistake. I wish I had found ways to keep the condos, because right now we are struggling. We only have about 20 units in our rental pool. That's not enough to do the corporate business we used to do. Now we have to live on the people who come for vacation packages and short getaways.

In 1989 we had a huge earthquake. It was the one where they were just getting ready to start the World Series in San Francisco and Al Michaels was on TV saying, "I think we're having an earthquake." All the power went out. That was unbelievable, but it was actually one of our finest hours. We had a generator for power and we had a satellite dish. We were virtually the link to the outside world. We stayed open 24 hours a day. People in the homes around us had no power and couldn't cook, so they came to the resort and we cooked for them. We became Emergency Central for our neighbors. We had some minor structural damage. Some chimneys went down and that sort of thing, but the clubhouse was able to function, and people were able to come in and talk to their neighbors, and we helped them get through it.

You know, I love golf, and I hoped I would be financially successful and make money at golf. But what you learn is that you are the source of income and livelihood for a lot of people. You become City Hall for the people living around you in a rural area. It's an important responsibility, but it's not necessarily one you are ever going to get rich off of.

The golf course is a short layout of about 4,300 yards. It's beautiful, in the Santa Cruz Mountains, carved out of the redwoods. You could never build something like this among the redwoods in California today. Never, never, never, ever. We have local people who enjoy the course, including a men's club with over 100 golfers. We have lots of guests from the Santa Cruz area, which isn't too far away. For many years our core golfers drove about 45 minutes to come and play. They came from San Jose, Sunnyvale and areas like that. But that's changed. Now there are so many golf courses in the area that I have lost some of that core clientele. We first started to see a downturn around the year 2000 as more courses opened. We still had golfers who wanted to come into the mountains, but we started losing about 2,000 golfers a year when the other courses began to open. I've been keeping good records since 1982. Last year, which was our worst year, we dropped to 29,000 rounds. That was the worst we've ever done. In the late 80s and early 90s, we were at maximum capacity on our little golf course: We were doing 60,000 rounds a year with six-minute intervals between tee times. It was like Beirut out there! There were golf balls flying all over the place. You know, it's a tiny, little golf course. The fairways are pretty close together. So then we went to eight-minute tee times and then we went to ten minute tee times. We raised our rates and tried to focus on a better quality experience for the guests. Now with the downturn, we are back to eight-minute tee times and we are thrilled to fill them. We're just like most other courses; we're doing discounting, two-for-ones, and using a third-party retailer to sell tee times. Now it's not "build it and they will come," now it's "build it and beg them to come."

Honestly, these days it's tough to own a golf business. We have had to scrimp and save a lot. Overall, though, we have a beautiful golf course, and we've had great people working for us who would go through walls for us. It's frustrating and it drives you nuts and you don't know if you'll ever get it right, but all in all when I talk with other owners, I believe that we've been doing a pretty darned good job of it. I have to take some pride in that. I'm kind of the hub that makes that happen. I don't want to be cocky about it, but my people count on me. What makes me proud is what makes me frustrated, in reverse. The golf course needs work, I have trouble making payroll, I can't get people the raises they deserve, and I'm losing employees. Sometimes I have to sit down with an employee I really respect and tell them they need to go somewhere else to make the money they really deserve. That part is really hard.

Up until a couple of years ago, I had employees who had been with me a long time. A year and a half ago I brought in a management company *(Touchstone Golf, a management firm headed by former American Golf executive Steve Harker)*. We were to the point where we were just losing, losing, losing. I was worn out. I was beat. I knew what we had to do. We had to retool, and we had to get people to do things differently. We had to get some employees to leave and I said, "I can't do it." So we brought a management company in, and now I act as an in-house consultant. I keep my office at the course, but the management company is responsible for the day-to-day operation. I gathered everybody together and told them we have a new company coming in and they have new ways of doing things. "There is an opportunity for all of you, but you have to decide if you want to work with what they are offering." I had some key people leave.

In California all employees have to go through social security and that kind of thing. We had a lot of Hispanics working for us. They gave me all the right kind of documentation. I got a legal opinion about the legal status of those employees, and the attorney told me they were OK. These Hispanic employees were wonderful, wonderful workers. They always welcomed me. They always laughed at my attempts to speak Spanish. If they had a barbecue with a wild pig caught on the course, then they would prepare them, make carnitas or some other wonderful dish, and invite me. They were all great cooks. Many of them had second jobs working in restaurants. They were the American Dream. I respected them so much. Half of every dollar they made they sent home to Mexico. God bless them. We paid them as much as we could. The average guy in town wouldn't do their work for 10 bucks an hour. When the new management company came in they had to check everybody's documentation. Since they manage multiple courses, they have very strict standards for the letter of the law. So the Hispanics quit en masse. My superintendent of 20 years said he wasn't going to train all new guys, and he left too.

The woman who was my bookkeeper for 25 years left. She was old-school in how she did much of her work. She wasn't real computer-literate. The new company wanted her to learn new software, so she retired. Prior to that, the woman who had been my assistant general manager and was just fantastic at her job went to the University of California at Santa Cruz and doubled her salary. I just couldn't pay her like that. Another woman who took her place and worked for us for a few years did the same thing. Really, those are good things. They went off for bigger and better lives.

Of the core group of employees who had been with me for 20 or so years, there are only a couple still with us. Sometimes in a meeting with the new management I'll see one of that core group kind of roll their eyes at some new policy, and I have to tell them that I did it the wrong way. We had better times previously and mistakes could be covered. The new company is by-the-book, and it has to be that way now. It's a business. I wanted it both ways. I wanted it to be a big family, and I wanted to make money, too. We had Christmas parties and in good years I gave everybody bonuses. I believed in the Japanese principle that the head of the company shouldn't make that much more than their best-paid people. Really, I was just a golf bum at heart. I went into the business so I could get it organized so I could play more golf. Of course, that never happened. I had played more golf as a salesman in San Francisco. I always wanted my employees to feel that I worked every bit as hard as they did. Then if I went away to play golf or do something else, I believed they would work just as hard as if I was there. That was my style, but now looking back on it, other owners I know with similar styles have gone away. Now I believe you have to be tougher. Knowing that is why I brought in the management company. Those former employees are all still my friends. Those who left don't hold it against me. They understand what was needed. Now with my appointment as president of NGCOA, I know I can do it, because at my golf course there is management doing the best job possible.

Along with changes in management and staff, there were other changes, too. Two years ago we filled in the swimming pool. It was such a drain on the profits to maintain the pool. We are in the process of converting the old pool area into a wedding garden. Other golf courses in our area that are doing well as businesses have created an additional source of income from weddings. Our property is a natural for those kinds of events. We have the mountains and the redwoods and condos to rent for the entire wedding party. With the condo associations in Boulder Creek, five of the six have their own pools, so our guests still have access to swimming pools. Along with the golf operation we had a small tennis club. There wasn't that much money coming in from the tennis so we've had to let that go, too. It costs five to six grand to fix up a single tennis court. With six courts, we would never get back any new investment in the courts. We still have the six courts, but they are in various levels of disrepair. We'll figure out what we'll do with the courts.

The restaurant has been downsized. We used to be open Friday, Saturday, Sunday and Monday nights, four nights a week. Again, with fewer and fewer golfers and vacationers, the restaurant started to become a negative. On good years the food would break even, or maybe lose just a little bit, but the bar made a bundle. So our decision was to downsize the restaurant and keep the bar going. Now we are breakfast and lunch daily, and we do a monthly spaghetti night for local guests. During football season we also have a Monday night dinner for Monday night football games on TV. In the spring when the golfers return, we'll start regular Monday night dinners again.

The course is open year-around, but this winter we've had 50 inches of rain already. When I first got into the business and I would meet somebody from Wisconsin, I thought it was too bad they had to close their golf course for so many months of the year. Now I think, "That would be great!" We're open in the winter, but it's wet, and very few come out to play golf. Still, the grass grows and the course has to be maintained. That means we have to keep a grounds crew and do regular maintenance year-around, but without year-around revenue. A good January or a good February would be about 1,500 rounds. That's like 50 rounds a day and it's not enough. If the weather is good, about the middle of March is when the golfers start coming back in some decent numbers. Then through the summer until mid- or late-September it's pretty good.

With the management company, I'm kind of working myself out of a job. Each day I get asked for less and less advice by our general manager. I like to make sure I'm around when the older, core groups come in, so they can see the continuity. I still take care of the state requirements and reports for water use, because that's pretty technical. I also keep up to date on what's going on in the county in case we need any permits or requirements change. Right now I'm moving my office of 30 years and throwing away paperwork we don't need anymore. I guess I'm downsizing there, too, trying to get it down to just those records and documents we have to keep. I'm just clearing the decks to get organized for the next couple of years to be the next president of NGCOA. If I continue to work myself out of a job at Boulder Creek, then great. In two years I'll be 70. I will have done it for over 30 years, and I still get to play golf. Really, I'm getting to do now what I thought I was going to do 30 years ago. I get to play golf.

I've never been very good at predicting the future. For the industry, I'm hoping we've already hit bottom, like we were when I started in '79, and that things are going to start creeping up again. Some golf courses in my area in Northern California have started to close. It's really a good thing. There are too many golf courses. Not too many people are bidding on those courses that are for sale. Maybe they just have to return to being bare land again.

Mr. DeNault always gets mad at me. He tells me I should have been a priest because I'm always trying to give stuff to people. That's not how businesses operate. The way I've always thought about our prices is that we don't want to be the lowest or the highest. I've always shot for rates somewhere in the middle. When the management company first came in, they bumped our prices up. Now the company and I have come to a meeting of the minds, and our prices have gone back down again. They are running the business mean and lean. That makes me hopeful that when people start playing again, we will be in a good spot. We'll be back in our little niche. I always thought that at times when golf was on the way up, people would play us because the course is so pretty. We look like a more expensive course than we are. And then, when times got bad, the golfers would quit going to the upscale country-club-for-a-day courses and come back to us because of our value. In 30 years I saw two or three recessions, and we always hung in there. We got by. We would always just get different customers, but his time around that just hasn't happened. We just lost them. So now our prices are back down again and we don't want to run so many special deals that those customers expect those deals to be normal. Hopefully, the strategies will work again.

I love the business. I really do. You're around people that are mostly happy. I've always taken delight in finding guys who were miserable and just turning their attitudes around. When I was younger and guys would come in all grumpy, I'd tell them, "You know what? I don't think you are going to have a very good day today. Are you sure you want to play today? Let me just buy you a drink, and you can just sit in the clubhouse a while before you go home." Of course, they would go out and play, usually with a different attitude to appreciate their day. I love that stuff. Running the proshop at the golf course is control central. I don't do the proshop check-in now. It's all computerized. Times are changing.

In some ways, I'm glad I didn't make more money. It might have changed me. I loved going out on the course and being with my employees every day. They always knew they could come to me and yell if they wanted to. Sometimes I yelled right back. If I thought I hurt their feelings, I would apologize. I'd tell them I'm Italian, and I'm not "touchy-feely." In my family if you got yelled at, you yelled back, and then it's all over.

When my dad retired, he and my mom bought a condo at the golf course, and Dad worked part-time as a bartender in town. Sometimes Dad's Italian temper would just go off on people and nearly send them off crying. I'd have to tell him, "Dad, this is my time. You've got to play by my rules." It was the greatest thing to be able to give my dad, who loved golf as much or more than me, the opportunity to be at Boulder Creek. When he was working, he worked six days a week and then got to play golf on Sunday. Mom would get so mad at him for staying at the golf course too long. Then I was able to give him the gift of golf every day. Lots of our guests called him The Mayor, and they always asked him questions about the course. He'd just tell them, "Ask my kid. He's the smart-ass college kid. Ask him." It was so much fun! Dad died about five years ago, and some of the fun went out of it for me. Mom is over 90 now. She just recently moved from the golf course to a rest home. Now she's the Queen of the Rest Home. Every day after work, I stop to visit her. Even if you're an adult, you always want to make your parents proud of you. Mom still tells me she is proud of me.

I'm very, very happy. I live about 40 minutes from the resort, near Santa Cruz, by the ocean, which I love. In the mornings, I leave my home and it's foggy and raining by the ocean, and then when I get to work in the mountains, it's sunny and 75 degrees. The microclimates in our area are unbelievable. Then by the time I get home at night, the fog has lifted and it's clear, and I can take a nice walk on the beach. I have the ocean and the mountains, my two favorite things.

I've got the greatest wife in the world. She runs our county convention and visitor's bureau, and she is deeply involved in tourism. I've always believed you have to give back. So 15 years ago I was on the board of the convention and visitor's bureau, and I was on the board of the restaurant association. We had to hire a new director for the bureau, and I was on the hiring committee, so I interviewed Maggie, my eventual wife. For years she and I worked together on the bureau until one day she told me that my term on the board was over. I had served all of the terms allowed. A few weeks after that, she called me up and said, "Now that you are off the board, I can ask you out." She had been named Woman of the Year and asked me to be her escort. That was the beginning of our relationship. We were married four years ago, after I had been single for 20 years. For all of those years working together I never imagined. Duhhh!

Now I get to actually play golf. My current golf buddies are so irreverent and so much fun. Early on, being a top-notch golfer was so important to me, and sometimes it was too important. I could be a real son-of-a-b. Not long ago I attended a seminar with a local golf instructor who focuses on the mental side of the game. He said, "Why should the enjoyment of the greatest game ever be tied to a number?" Bells rang for me. Now it's full circle, and I can play golf for fun and really love it.

## Aragona's Lessons

- Sometimes you have to take big risks. Sometimes you just have to go "All In."
- Learning your business from the ground up, by doing all the different jobs that are needed, enables you to manage your business effectively.
- A crisis can become an opportunity.
- "You know, I love golf, and I hoped I would be financially successful and make money at golf. But what you learn is that you are the source of income and livelihood for a lot of people. You become City Hall for the people living around you in a rural area. It's an important responsibility, but it's not necessarily one you are ever going to get rich off of."
- There are times when downsizing or even eliminating some staff positions, services and facilities is required to keep your business viable. These are tough decisions but may be needed.
- Outsourcing business services to specialists means that management practices and personal styles will change, but those sacrifices can preserve the business.
- Courses open during the summer season envy those courses open year-around. Courses open year-around envy those open only during summers. Each has liabilities and assets. Appreciate what you have.
- Even as adults, make your parents proud of you.
- "Why should the enjoyment of the greatest game ever be tied to a number?" Play for fun!

# I Did It My Way

James Oliff, Owner of Mattaponi Springs Golf Club in
Ruther Glen, Virginia

ℰ⟩　℧

*I interviewed James A. Oliff, sole owner of Mattaponi Springs Golf Club in
Ruther Glen, Virginia, at his Oliff and Berridge, PLC law firm in
Alexandria, Virginia at 7 a.m. on October 15, 2009. Oliff and Berridge, PLC
routinely ranks among the top five U.S. intellectual property law firms based
on number of issued U.S. patents, has been recognized among the top 10 U.S.
firms for chemical, electrical and mechanical patent quality, and has ranked
at the top of intellectual property firms in the United States representing the
world's 50 largest companies in terms of prosecution and litigation counsel.
The firm employs 80 attorneys, with a total staff of well over 200.*

*Mattaponi Springs (pronounced "matta-pone-aye") Golf Club is an 18-hole
public facility on 330 acres of natural, dramatic countryside in Caroline
County, Virginia. The course was designed by Bob Lohmann, who also
designed the Merit Club, site of the 2000 U.S. Women's Open. Mattaponi
Springs was ranked #1 on the East Coast and #2 in the United States by Golf
Digest for "Best New Upscale Public Golf Courses for 2005-2006," ranked
#3 by Golfweek for "Top Courses in Virginia," and in 2009 was rated
among "America's 100 Greatest Public Golf Courses" by Golf Digest.*

*Mr. Oliff was preparing for a business trip to Japan and told me he only had
up to an hour to give me. Once he began talking about his golf course, his
passion was obvious. I reminded him of the time after an hour and a half.*

www.mattaponisprings.com

ℰ⟩　℧

I grew up in a fairly low-income area of East Baltimore.
Golf was not something that I was exposed to while growing
up. I got exposed to golf by sheer accident much later in life.
After I finished undergraduate engineering school (*B.S. in
aerospace engineering at the University of Maryland*), I went into
the Navy. After I got out of the Navy at the end of the Vietnam
War, I helped a neighbor who was a writer for *National
Geographic*. He was moving from Washington D.C. back to
California to be a professor teaching creative writing

somewhere. As we were loading his U-Haul truck, he had a set of left-handed golf clubs (*Jim is left-handed*) that he no longer wanted, and he gave them to me. That was my first reason to strike a golf ball, and I did. I really enjoyed the game. Like most people, I was never a good golfer and I'm still not a very good golfer, but I enjoy it nevertheless. As I'm trying to teach my son-in-law, you can enjoy golf even if you don't play it very well.

After the Navy, I went to work at the U.S. Patent Office while I was going to law school at Georgetown University at night. After graduate school I went to another firm and I was there about eight years during which time I made partner. Way back then in the early '70s, I tried to get a group of people that I worked with to do a project like Mattaponi Springs. The one lesson I came away with from that experience was that getting a committee to do anything is very difficult. You spend more time trying to schedule the meeting than substantively getting anything done. The experience did give me the opportunity to do a lot of research on golf course construction, financing and other topics. This was all very preliminary, but it did give me some introduction to golf course ownership. I got my toe in the water a little bit. Since then the thoughts were always there in the background as something I wanted to do. My nature is that I like to do things differently and uniquely. Then at the end of 1982, I decided to start my own law firm. We started January 1983 with four attorneys and a total staff of 13 people. We are now among the top 10 intellectual property law firms in the United States.

Throughout these experiences, I continued to play golf, not seriously, just now and then, but always enjoying it. Also during that time, we were raising our children at our home here in Northern Virginia, and we bought an abandoned farm in central Virginia, south of Fredericksburg in Caroline County. From 1980 to '86, we spent much of our time renovating a big, old farm house that we moved into in 1986. I didn't really have culture shock from being the Fairfax (*northern Virginia*) hillbillies moving down there. The people down there were very, very welcoming and very friendly. It was a very nice introduction to the area. The people were different and unique, and we very much liked that we were so welcomed there.

While my children were in elementary school and high school and even in university, that was our weekend and holiday place. Any time we had time off, we went down there. At one time my wife pointed out that during one year we had spent a total of five months in Caroline County at our farm. Virtually every moment we could arrange we were there. Also, I bought another small business in that area, and I had some people working for me in that business. At the time I bought it, it was a small farm store, and I converted it to a farm and hardware store. The store is still going. I have some people who manage it for me. It was just a hobby for me. I was never seriously involved in running the store, and that's still true today. It was another link into the area.

That area didn't really have a quality golf facility at that time and lots of things were coming together for me there. I had the time and the energy and the financial resources to seriously look at developing a golf course. I had a young man then who was working for me who was quite athletic and certainly sort of a hard-charger, a high-energy person. So I asked the young man and another very close friend and confidant, my brother-in-law Larry Wagner, to start looking around and thinking about location parameters. We defined our geographic region we were interested in, and I asked them to go and look for actual sites for a golf course. We looked at five, six or seven sites before we settled on our current site. My goal was to create a nice course, what some people would refer to as upscale daily fee or elite daily fee. Even though I didn't have this terminology then, what I wanted was a country-club-for-a-day experience. I'm not a country club kind of person. It's not my nature. But I wanted to create an experience for somebody who perhaps didn't have the interest or financial resources to become a member at a country club to play a very nice golf course, receive some very nice services, bring some friends in and truly enjoy a round of golf. That was around 1996 to '98 that we were looking for sites, and at the latter part of that time frame, we found our site and we wanted some architects to look at it.

Larry and I spent a couple weeks traveling around the country interviewing architects. I intentionally wanted to go to their facilities. I didn't initially want them to come to my property. I wanted to see what their internal operation looked like, because I knew, just like my law firm, when new clients come in, I typically bring into the room everybody who will be involved. I don't pretend that Jim Oliff will be doing all of this great work for them by himself, because they know that's just not possible. And so we spent a couple weeks meeting with architects, and among that group were Bob Lohmann (*Lohmann Golf Designs in the Chicago area*) and his team. We visited his facilities, and I was so impressed that within five minutes of the time we arrived he had his entire team in the room with us and in very great detail described the role each person would have in the process. That way of doing business was certainly one of the reasons we selected Bob as our architect. One of his assistants who did the nuts and bolts of the design was a gentleman named Mike Benkusky. Bob and Mike turned out to be exactly what I was hoping for, just good solid Midwestern people, honest as the day is long. They knew better than me what I didn't know and they helped me in every conceivable way they could to make sure things were done properly. Even though we thought we had a fantastic site, I think in looking back that the selection of Bob and his team was critical. I knew the architect would be important, but I don't believe we would have the successes we have if we selected someone other than Bob and Mike. They were extraordinarily accommodating to us and the kinds of things we were trying to do.

One of Bob's accolades comes from designing the Merit Club, where the 2000 U.S. Women's Open was held. While I haven't actually seen the Merit Club, I did travel around to some of his other courses to see those sites, to talk to owners and superintendents. I wanted to learn more about design, but I also wanted to know about how maintainable the courses were.

Bob and Mike made several visits to study our site, including a fly-over topographical survey. That "topo" survey is a tool I would recommend to anyone building a golf course. The site was completely wooded, and that seemed a little problematic for me. But they could walk that site with the "topo" survey in hand and get a really good flavor for landing areas and routing. It's a big site at 330 acres, and they walked it maybe four to six times. I remember challenging them a couple times on original plans and telling them they were dead wrong in what they thought. But once we began clearing woods and saw landing areas and green sites open up, I called them to tell them how impressed I was that they could see the beauty of that area for a golf course when it was fully wooded. That's one of the areas where their experience really showed up. The final design was a fourth or fifth generation of the routing.

At the beginning of the process, I read every conceivable book I could find on golf course design and construction, particularly since I wanted to build the course as much as possible by myself. We bought our own construction equipment and hired our own people. Larry was instrumental in making that work. We had experienced people. Through Bob we hired a shaper from Mississippi, Roy Bullion. He was extraordinary, and he had worked with Bob and Mike before. They communicated really well, and he was another instrumental part of the project. For a lot of the construction I had my own local people, and through a friend of a friend I hired a guy, Kevin Patton, to install irrigation. He had experience with golf course irrigation at courses up in Pennsylvania. Kevin gave his all, not just to irrigation, but to every phase of construction.

There are many interesting side stories in the construction. We brought a young man in to do some of the rough clearing. He was 19 or 20 years old and didn't know how to run anything other than a farm tractor. Roy, our shaper, took a real liking to the young man, Eric Graudszus. Eric was a very diligent, hardworking young man who wouldn't even think of missing a day's work. By the time we were finished with construction, Eric, with Roy as his mentor, was a Class B shaper, and now he travels around the country shaping for golf course construction projects. I'm assuming he's a Class A shaper by now. Every time I talk to him he's in another part of the country shaping a golf course. He is a great side story for me.

And that brings me to my son, Adam. After engineering school and before starting a career in the U.S. Army, Adam came in and functioned as our construction manager, negotiating construction, construction equipment, and all other necessary agreements and supplies. He helped clear, shape, install irrigation and drainage, sod, repair equipment, and anything else that was needed. I could not have done it without him. Right now Adam is on his way to Afghanistan for a second tour there, following one in Iraq.

We had bought the property in late '97 or early '98 with the condition that we would get zoning approval. We made the purchase contract with that zoning contingency. In that area a golf course requires a special-use permit, and that process takes months. The process turned out to be more complicated than I expected. We had one particular person who objected to our use of the land. It was unfortunate that he objected, but others in the review were very supportive, and we got through that process. The local county government was very supportive, as they saw the golf course as an economic opportunity for the county.

After zoning approval, we had to do a soil and erosion control plan because of all of the clearing we were doing. We brought in another engineering company to do that plan, which was particularly important while the site was unseeded. Also, we had to do wetland delineation. We started out with the original USGS (*U.S. Geological Survey*) survey that suggested there were about eight acres of wetland on the site. But when our environmental scientist did his study, we found we had somewhere between 55 to 60 acres of wetland on the site. That was one of the reasons for a major rerouting. One of our goals was to not disturb any wetland, but also to take advantage of it from a visual standpoint. After that survey we had to have the Army Corps of Engineers come out to confirm it.

As part of the process in Virginia, at any time when you plan for disturbance of the land, a whole host of state and federal agencies are notified. The Virginia Department for Historical Preservation, which I'm not sure is the correct title, came out to be sure we wouldn't disturb any historic features, such as Civil War artifacts or battlegrounds. One border of the property is Polecat Creek, which feeds into the Mattaponi River, and at one time the Mattaponi Indian Tribe occupied that land. Although it never came up, we were always conscious there might be important historic features such as a burial ground that might be on the property. We didn't find any Civil War or Native American artifacts or relics.

One interesting thing, by sheer accident: My daughter was an undergrad at the College of William and Mary, and on one parents' weekend a professor in the geology department gave a lecture on the history of the Chesapeake Bay. I attended the lecture and discovered that millions of years ago the bay extended into the area of our golf course site. That's astonishing when you know how far away the Chesapeake Bay is today. Sure enough, one thing we did discover were the remains of an enormous number of different species of sharks. The site is very, very hilly, and my guess is that at one time the hills may have been sand dunes.

We really do have beach-style soils. They are really excellent soils for golf course construction. They naturally drain extraordinarily well, but they are highly erodible, if the soil isn't seeded properly. Some of the other properties I own in that area are only 20 miles west, and they are the more classic red clay soils. Now I know why the railroads were built where they were and why Highway 1 and Interstate 95 are built where they are. They are built along a fall line where west of I95 you get the typical Piedmont soils like red clay and east of I95 you get the sandy, loamy soils. I was astonished at the differences in soils in such a narrow area. The volume of topsoil and sand was much better than anyone imagined, as we got into it with construction. I can remember the shaper at one point was raving about some of the soils we were moving. He said that he just came from a construction site in Texas, where they would have paid any amount of money to get the kinds of soils we have.

It may sound like the construction process was relatively smooth and without challenges, but there were probably a thousand problems that had to be dealt with. At times I'm sure I had headaches and complaints, but when the problems come up, you get through them. For instance, we have a really nice downhill par-3 hole that had to be reshaped three times, because every time we thought we were finished with it, a major thunderstorm came in and blew the soils down the hill and we had to push them back up the hill and add more drainage. Little things like that seem quite amusing today, but at the time they brought tears to your eyes. When you are on site at 5:30 in the afternoon spreading seed and trying to stabilize the soil and then see an enormous storm come in and wash away your work, you can get pretty frustrated.

We have a beautiful lake at the very top of the site that we dug for water storage. We brought in thousands of tons of large landscape rocks to enhance the feeling of a mountainous course and to line the banks of the lake. After the lake was dug and then carefully lined with all of these large rocks, we discovered that the soil wouldn't hold water. So Eric, the excellent young man I mentioned before, came out with an extremely large excavator to renovate the lake. He individually numbered all of those rocks so they could be removed and then later replaced. There were hundreds if not thousands of rocks lining that lake. Each rock was removed and we installed a large rubber lining for the bottom of the lake so it would hold water. Then Eric replaced each rock in the exact locations they had previously been. I can tell you that the liner for the lake was very expensive and the labor involved was enormous. We brought in a subcontracted group from Texas to install the liner, but my local team did the majority of the work to make sure it was done right. Even though the liner required heavy equipment to put in place, my workers' hands were raw from working with it. Those kinds of challenges are time consuming and labor intensive.

I got involved in construction myself. I quite enjoyed it. I was born and raised in the city, but I have an engineering degree, so I have a bit of understanding about how things work. It wasn't until we bought the farm and I renovated the farmhouse that I found out how much I enjoy getting out on a tractor, cutting hay, and doing other outside work. Of course, with the farm it was relatively small construction equipment to move dirt and do other projects. I was quite comfortable with a backhoe, and I could use a dozer a bit, too. But when you see a golf course shaper at work you really realize how you can move dirt, and I could never pretend to do that. I probably couldn't shape a good, flat road with that equipment. I did have really good people doing that work.

Toward the end of construction at Mattaponi Springs when we got into building the greens, I had not previously looked at the green design drawings in great detail. When the green shaper told me we were about a month away from building the greens, I really started looking at those designs. Because my undergraduate degree is in engineering and I'm a patent attorney, I look at a lot of drawings and I can comprehend drawings. At first blush the green designs quite frankly looked awfully exotic. When I came to that conclusion I immediately called Mike Benkusky and asked him if he was creating some kind of new experiment with our design. I told him I was not interested in being part of an experiment. I asked him to show me examples of where he had built greens with those kinds of elevation changes. He told me about a course he had built in Danville, Indiana (*Twin Bridges*), with similar green designs. I had to make a business trip to that area, so I went to that course and met the people who ran the course and talked with some of their regular golfers. I found that the greens were one of the best assets for the course. That calmed me back down about green design.

If I remember correctly, I met the clubhouse architect when I interviewed him for construction of the golf course. His name is Jeff Timmons, with Timmons-Kelley Architects near Richmond. He and his family own a private club in Midlothian, Virginia, that he designed. I went to look at that course, and in the process Jeff showed me the design for the clubhouse he built for Kiawah Island. It's a magnificent clubhouse, and it was done in a style that I like. As we got near the end of course construction I had Jeff come in and design the clubhouse. Originally we planned to build the clubhouse on some lower ground, but we later moved the site to some higher ground between holes nine and 18. Now, coming in on 18 you play right into the clubhouse. I walked the site of the clubhouse countless times trying to envision what I wanted, but I just didn't think that knoll of higher ground would accommodate the building. In fact, I thought it might look a bit goofy. That's where professional experience comes in to help. After some initial resistance from me, Jeff convinced me to take the crown off that knoll and spread it out a bit to make a very nice site for our clubhouse.

On the original clubhouse site, we considered there was a building that had been a huge mess hall for a Boy's Camp. That was our construction office while we built the course.

Jeff was able to completely convert that building into an outings building where we host some of our golf outings. It gives those groups complete privacy away from the clubhouse. We do wedding receptions and other events there, too. That building sits adjacent to our lower lake, which we had to add. When the wells we were digging didn't produce the volume of water that everyone guaranteed they would, we decided we needed an extra storage lake at the bottom to capture some water. The lake next to our outing building makes a beautiful site, and thanks to Jeff, all of the buildings are architecturally compatible. It was astonishing how Jeff could blend the designs of the buildings and convert that old mess hall into the outings building at relatively small expense. Stylistically, the buildings all blend very well with the beautiful, natural landscape of the course. We wanted a lot of glass in the clubhouse so we could bring the outside to the inside with great views. We wanted earth tones and large porches so that guests could sit outside and enjoy the views of the course. Jeff achieved all of our goals. His experience really benefitted us.

Originally we planned for a fine-dining restaurant in the clubhouse. I suppose that could be seen as a mistake. We changed our plan for fine dining into a grill with a much more basic menu. We still have people come out to eat and enjoy the beauty of the views while they eat. Even some of the local people when they come in to eat are astonished with the beauty of the property. It feels like you have travelled to the mountains. Even though I thought I knew the local area very well, I was amazed the first time I saw the site of the course. The elevation changes are really dramatic.

Mattaponi Springs has benefitted from a lot of positive press. We were ranked #1 on the East Coast and #2 in the United States by *Golf Digest* for "Best New Upscale Public Golf Courses for 2005-2006." We were ranked #3 by *Golfweek* for "Top Courses in Virginia." *Pros and Hackers* magazine did a cover story on us. *Washington Golf Styles* did an article on us. Just recently in 2009 we were rated among "America's 100 Greatest Public Golf Courses" by *Golf Digest*. I don't fully understand the process for getting all of this recognition. We did a "soft" opening in the fall of 2004, and golf reviewers started coming out to see us. I don't even know how the reviewers find out about us. Sometimes they announced they were coming to play the course and evaluate us, but other times they just played the course and told us afterward who they were. Because they are looking for things like ambiance and service, they don't want us to know who they are until later so they can find you in your natural state. On leaving the course, they would typically introduce themselves and give a rough description of what they liked or didn't like. But you never really know what's coming from their visits until their articles are published. Honestly I always thought those kinds of rankings were political and based on connections people have with the golf industry or media. We had none of those connections at all. I was quite flattered with all of the accolades in the national and regional publications.

By today's standards, we have a fairly high daily rate of $89 on weekends and holidays. For the Washington area, that rate isn't so high, but for our remote location the rate is fairly high. We do get local players, but we live on a more upscale play coming north from Richmond or coming south from the Washington area. Our price squeaks some of the people from the Richmond area, but for many of the people from the Washington area our price is irrelevant. Also, we get a lot of interstate business. People going to Florida from Canada, for example, who follow golf course rankings will make a point to stop and play here. Groups of people going to Williamsburg as tourists will book tee times on their way. Now we are getting some annual groups from all over the country who fly into Washington on their way for golf in Myrtle Beach and play us on their way down or back. There is a couple who comes regularly from Pennsylvania. They will drive down for the day. She says the only reason they come to Virginia is to play Mattaponi. They say that some Saturdays, they get up without a plan and then decide to drive down here, get a bite to eat, and play the course. These kinds of guests are one of the reasons I built the golf course, and it's really gratifying to me.

One thing we did that's now catching on was to make the course very female friendly. One change in design was to move the forward tees up. From my own perspective, not being a very good golfer, we had a number of very challenging forced carries over hazards that made it hard for golfers like me and most females. Bob Lohmann and I agreed to widen some fairways for more generous landing areas and to move forward tees up to make the course more friendly, particularly for female golfers. The ladies quite enjoy playing at Mattaponi, and we are getting more and more couples and women's groups on the course. We wanted the golf course, to the extent reasonable, to be pretty low-level testosterone. I think it has worked. I have to admit when I am out there on weekends, typically playing with my son-in-law, it's very gratifying to me to see the couples and women's groups playing the course. That means our ambiance is right. Originally the front door of the clubhouse was to open to a small bar, and we had planned to put bar stools there. When we brought in an interior designer to consult with the clubhouse plans, she told us immediately that we should absolutely not have the clubhouse open up to bar stools. She told us that when women come into the building, the last thing in the world they want to see is men sitting at a bar and drinking. So we don't have bar stools at the bar. The clubhouse has a nice, warm feeling, and the women who come here feel comfortable. That's just one of those little things that you try to do right, and it appears to be working. The percentage of female play is on the rise.

Our general manager is a woman. I'm not so sure her gender helps bring women to the course, but I would like to have a female pro behind the counter. We get a very nice African American group at the course, and we also get a lot of Korean and Japanese golfers. To better serve them, I would love to have an Asian in the pro shop who speaks Japanese and/or Korean. I've been encouraging Brenda to help us hire a female, an African American and an Asian in the pro shop, along with our middle-aged white male pro shop staff. It's easy to say we'd like to get that kind of diversity in the pro shop, but because of our rural location we are geographically challenged and it's hard to find that kind of diversity. Right now we have some leads and we are working on it. I have many women employed in my law firm. I have to admit, I like female employees. We do have a bright young woman named Christine working for us at Mattaponi. She worked for us at my daughter's riding school at our farm. She's in high school and on her way to becoming a vet tech. We brought Christine to the course to work part-time. She is just a natural service-oriented young lady. For instance, when we had the Executive Women's Golf Association come to the course for an outing, Christine said that our mannequin in the pro shop should have on women's apparel, even though we had never done that before in our four years of operation. It took the female focus to see that opportunity. I had missed it, and now we dress the mannequin in women's apparel. I've never been behind the counter. I'm not a behind-the-counter person and I know that. I'm the last person for that job. I'm the guy that's behind the guy behind the counter.

My staff has lots of autonomy because I'm not usually at the golf course. My general manager, Brenda Simmons, is a very, very good manager. She comes from an accounting background, and she is very detail oriented. Right now we are the best staffed we have ever been with the quality of people we have. We have a really good food and beverage manager right now, who is female. We have a new pro in the pro shop. Right now he is transitioning from another job and is only parttime, but he keeps increasing his time with us week by week. We have the best superintendent we have ever had, and our course is in the best shape it's ever been in.

One thing I've learned from talking to many owners before building the course, when you get to the end of construction, several things happen. A year or two before the end of construction, the budget is gone and that typically means some things get left undone. Those other owners warned me that grassing, cart paths, clubhouse and driving range may not be completed before you want to open the course. We didn't do that. I was not going to let that happen. We opened with nine-foot wide concrete cart paths, a fully completed clubhouse and an additional building for events. The course was completely sodded, and we let the grasses grow for a year before we opened, which is unusual for most new courses. And, we have a huge seven-acre driving range and teaching facility that was also sodded. When we opened, we looked like we had been there for a long time. This preparation for opening was all done by design, but of course there is a positive and a negative to this preparation. The positive is that we opened the way we wanted, completely ready. The negative is that there is a lot of money sitting on the ground that's not bringing in any revenue. We didn't want to open with a bunch of warning signs and directional signs or erosion control problems that many new courses have to face because the bankers want them to start making revenue. We wanted to open with a course that was completely ready to be enjoyed.

As a business we are doing pretty well, particularly this year. We have really worked on service. This is something that has grown out of how we operate our law firm. I like to think we have a unique law firm that our clients see as very different. Those principles are applied to the golf course so that people who come to Mattaponi see us as something very special and different. In addition to good personalized service for our guests, there are some extra service steps we take. Any groups or outings that are on the course are assembled for group photographs, if they are interested. The groups that come through each year really appreciate the group photos with dates on them. The framed photos of the groups are really appreciated as an extra touch that we provide. This year is a really tough year for the golf industry, but we are beginning to see the benefits of our extra service efforts, particularly with repeat business.

Through Bob Lohmann, I met a gentleman named Tom Rodems who owns and manages about five or seven courses in the Midwest. Tom has come in and given me a lot of advice on golf course management. I really like Tom. Again, he is a good, straight-up, no-nonsense Midwesterner who knows how to run a business. In his words, "It's all about retention." Bringing guests in and then getting them back is really important, particularly for the kinds of golfers we're chasing. We are asking them to pay a little bit more money, and in return we want them to know they are getting value. There are a lot of good golf courses out there. Nationally, golfers are spoiled by the number of good courses they can play. We want our guests to know they have something special here in terms of quality of the facilities and quality of the services.

Our basic goal for the future is to continue to strive for perfection, which I know may be unachievable. I want to continue to improve our level of service by making it even more natural for our people to provide. I want to improve the kinds of demographic information we collect on our players. I don't mean a name and an email address; I mean information like what do they like to drink, what do they like to eat, what is their preferred playing time, and what are their interests. When they come we should be able to ask them how their new car, by make and model, is doing. We should be able to tell them we just got some of their favorite cigars in. Knowing their name and adding these kinds of small, extra touches is something I want to continue to perfect. A key component of these goals, as I mentioned before, is getting pro shop staff who can relate to them. Even if they are part-time employees, it would be great to have them available when Asian groups come, for example, to greet them personally in their language. So, our basic goal is to polish what we are already doing. There are so many good golf courses, but service is how you distinguish yourself.

When I'm at the course, I try to be very low profile. I go to my own golf course as a customer, and I give my comments, which are typically negative, to my staff. I'm an East German type of judge, and I'm pretty hard on my staff about what I see. I'll be the first to compliment anyone who is doing a good job, but I'm a tough grader. I'm always looking at how fast my food came, and whether I got what I asked for. American golfers tend to be very different from most Asian golfers. American golfers are in a rush, and I fit that profile perfectly. If I'm playing and making the turn after the front nine, I just want to get back out there. So, my staff will bring food and drinks out to the players on the course. The players know they can call the clubhouse at any time, and we will bring what they want out to them. Or they can call ahead, and we'll have what they want waiting for them at the turn. If people are unhappy, they typically won't express their criticisms, but I will. I want to continually push our level of service so customers recognize how special they are treated.

Another thing that's important is that maybe only 10 percent of golfers can differentiate a really well-designed golf course from a typical golf course. We all know greens are important and people appreciate good greens. What I love is when our golfers who understand good design talk about our course in terms of relationships between lengths and shapes of holes, locations of bunkers and shapes of the greens. All of the factors in the design of all 18 holes are important, and I love it when our golfers appreciate our design. One of our regular golfers, Joe Bickett, was an executive for Phillip Morris. He oversaw their manufacturing operations. He quite enjoys golf, and he has traveled the world playing it. When he first came here, he sought me out right away. It's his nature to see who was behind Mattaponi Springs. When we first talked, I told him how skillfully Bob Lohmann and Mike Benkusky envisioned and developed our site. Joe told me that, yeah, that's important, but that's not the end of it. He said that when he's out on our driving range and the railroad tracks are off in the distance and he hears a train coming with the whistle blowing, then he feels 16 years old again. He notices that there are no houses to be seen, the cart paths are all hidden from view from the tees and landing areas, that there are teak benches around tees, that the clubhouse is comfortable and airy, and that the pine straw in the pine woods is all very tidy. Most people will realize there is something different here, but most can't express it. Joe has been around enough, with enough experience in manufacturing and design, that he has an eye for it and can express what he appreciates. I have to admit it makes me feel really great when somebody like Joe, or other golfers I overhear and who don't know who I am, comment on how special Mattaponi is. It means we have achieved some of the qualities we wanted to achieve.

I mentioned it before, but I love the number of women who play the course. It's a great delight to me to see the women out there feeling very comfortable and very welcomed, not feeling like they are in the middle of a testosterone environment.

*(I asked Jim for his perspective on the future of the golf industry.)*

I can't talk for the industry, because I don't think in those terms. I don't care about the industry. I care about Mattaponi Springs. That sounds insulting and I don't mean it in that sense. I don't really understand the industry. You know, I read *Golf Business* magazine, and I have a sense for the industry, but what I find disturbing is that when I read about the industry, I see the same names over and over again. I feel like the industry and the publications need a fresh look. When we bring a new employee into our law firm, particularly when they have come from another firm, I ask them to look at everything we do. I tell them that everything we have done in the firm has been thought through, and we have a reason and purpose for it and believe it's the best, but they are coming fresh and we want them to take a good, hard look at us. If they see things that don't make sense to them, or they have a better way of doing things, then please put it on the table. We have been doing things our way for so long, we don't see things with fresh eyes. It's like when I take new, young attorneys with me to Japan for the first time. I've been there so many times, and I think I know it so well that I don't really see it anymore. So from what I read about the golf industry, I just don't see a lot of fresh minds and fresh thinking. There's a lot of talk about growing the game, but my sense is there's not a lot of doing. But again, I'm the last person to be setting goals for the industry at large. My thinking is not at that level. For me, job one is sitting here in my law firm being an integral part of it. My job two is to help Brenda Simmons and my other staff to bring Mattaponi Springs to its maximum. I do that only on a part-time basis, but I quite enjoy it. It's a great change of pace for me, but the law firm stays job one.

## Oliff's Lessons

- You can enjoy golf even if you don't play it very well.
- Selecting a consultant, such as a golf course architect, is done best by experiencing his or her existing work first-hand.
- Designing and building a new golf course is full of challenges. Choose an architect and construction personnel wisely, use a topographical map from an aerial perspective, and walk, walk, walk the land.
- Media accolades for a golf course are invaluable for recruiting golf customers.
- Creating a golf course ambiance that is appealing to women requires attention to course design, clubhouse design, including the bar and the pro shop, and staffing.
- When Mattaponi opened it looked like it had been there for a long time. The turf was grown in, the cart paths and the clubhouse were complete. This preparation for opening was all done by design, but of course there is a positive and a negative to this preparation. The positive is that the course opens to create the impression that was intended, completely ready. The negative is that there is usually a lot of money sitting on the ground that's not bringing in any revenue. Opt for the positive impressions that will soon generate revenue.
- Design golf course services in ways that enhance golfer retention. Customers need to recognize the quality of services that are provided. There are so many good golf courses, but service is how you distinguish yourself.

- "I want to improve the kinds of demographic information we collect on our players. I don't mean a name and an email address; I mean information like what do they like to drink, and what do they like to eat, what is their preferred playing time, what are their interests. When they come we should be able to ask them how their new car, by make and model, is doing. We should be able to tell them we just got some of their favorite cigars in. Knowing their name and adding these kinds of small, extra touches is something I want to continue to perfect."

- Concern for the golf industry in general is secondary to concern for the quality of the business you manage. That's job one!

# *Fun Is Good!*

George Kelley, Owner of Stevinson Ranch Golf Club in the
Central Valley of California

ଛ   ଓ

*I interviewed George Kelley on February 11, 2010, at the Golf Industry Show
in San Diego, CA. After three days of phone tag, George and I connected on
the patio of the San Diego Convention Center, overlooking San Diego Bay.*

*George is a fifth-generation descendant of a California pioneer family. His
family businesses include farming, a dairy operation, cattle, real estate
development, the upscale Stevinson Ranch Golf Club and Greenway Golf.
Greenway Golf specializes in golf course maintenance, golf course
management and golf course consulting and project management. Greenway
provides management and agronomy support for 21 courses worldwide and
has developed, marketed, or maintained golf courses for over 20 years.*

*After a three-year career as a touring golf professional, George was a real
estate broker specializing in golf-related ventures. In 1995 he developed and
co-designed the highly acclaimed Stevinson Ranch Golf Club. Among many
accolades,* Golf Digest *rated the course "Best New Upscale Public Course in
California" in 1996 and "Top 25" of all California courses in 1997. It is the
first golf course in California to attain "Signature" status with Audubon
International for its dedication to environmental excellence.*

*At the time of the interview, George was serving as president of the California
Golf Course Owners Association.*

www.stevinsonranch.com

ଛ   ଓ

The land my golf course is on has been in my family since
1852. My family's businesses have been ranching, farming and
dairy going back for generations. It's very unusual in California,
but we are a California pioneer family. I describe the golf course
as near the epicenter of nowhere. When you drive out there,
you're in the country. There is very little around it, although
within 30 miles there are 800,000 people.

*93*

My parents were very well educated. My dad went to Dartmouth and my mom went to Stanford. I was the oldest of four boys, and my parents wanted us to get a great education. The public schools in the rural area around our land were not good, so the decision was to send us to boarding school or to buy a second home in a location where we could go to private school. In 1962 when I was 12 years old, my dad asked his attorney about moving from the ranch to Pebble Beach. Dad said, "Hey, Ray, do you know any good real estate brokers? I'm thinking about moving over to Pebble Beach." Ray responded to Dad, "Well, why don't you just buy my home. I hardly ever use it." Dad bought it. So in 1962 my dad bought the home I mostly grew up in and where I learned to play golf. The house is literally on the first green at Pebble Beach Golf Links. At that time, the house cost $82,000. (*Current value is estimated at over $10 million.*) Unfortunately, we don't still own the house. That's a whole other story.

I didn't want to move. I just didn't want to go. I was playing Little League and basketball. I was very happy being out in the country. I was just kicking and screaming about having to move to Pebble Beach and leaving my friends. My dad said that if I would shut up he would buy me some golf lessons and that maybe I would like playing golf. Well, I took to golf like a duck takes to water.

In those days, Pebble Beach was privately owned, and we had a family membership for $450 for unlimited play for everyone in the family. Dad had his own golf cart stored under the house. People think I'm full of shit, but I used to go down in the evenings and dump my entire shag bag in the bunker on the first green and just hit bunker shots, chip, and putt. Or I would go down to the practice area at the beach club and tennis courts. You had to pick up your own balls. In those days, they didn't even have a real driving range at Pebble. In the evenings during summer I could hit perfect 4-woods from the practice area onto the first green at Pebble. Of course, I was very respectful of the course. I would very meticulously fix every divot and ball mark.

From the time I was 12, I lived and breathed golf with a complete passion. I became one of the better junior players in northern California. I was recruited to play golf in college, and I went to the University of Southern California on a partial golf scholarship in 1968. I went there for two years, but Los Angeles wasn't for me at the time. I had only known two places in my life, the ranch and Pebble Beach. I was immersed in this urban jungle and I wanted out, so I transferred to the University of Colorado. I missed a year of golf eligibility, but I played my senior year at CU. After graduation in 1973, I played golf professionally for three years. I played internationally on the European Tour, I played in Australia and New Zealand, and I played the Asian Tour. In three years I kind of got it out of my system. I describe my pro career as having flashes of brilliance. I played really well one day and not so well the next day. I played in the U.S. Open at Winged Foot, the British Open at Carnoustie, and the Australian Open. I had a reasonably good career, but in those days there wasn't a lot of money in pro golf. My best finish internationally was fourth in the Dutch Open.

While I played and traveled in Australia, the now-famous Australian golfer, Greg Norman, was a promising young pro who hung out with our group of guys on the Australian Tour. We became pretty good friends. In the fall of 1976, Greg took his first trip to the United States to represent Australia in the World Cup being played in Palm Springs. When I found out that Greg was coming to California, I invited him to stay with my family and me in our home at Pebble. Greg stayed with us for 30 days. It was great. We played golf at Pebble during the days and caroused at night. During that time, I was entered in my last pro tournament, the Spalding Pro-Am held on the Monterey Peninsula. There were lots of tour pros and mini-tour pros, like myself, in the tournament. Greg got an invitation to play the event. But when he contacted the Australian PGA about entering the tournament they told him he was not eligible under the rules of the Australian PGA to play outside of Australia with his apprentice status. He was not yet a Class A member. So, as it turned out, Greg Norman hauled my bag as my caddie for my last professional tournament. What a way to go!

After those three years, I went into commercial real estate brokering in San Francisco. About 1985 I got a call from a friend of mine who was also a friend of Hale Irwin. I casually knew Hale a bit. Hale was doing a design deal on a golf course up in Jackson, California, in the Mother Lode in Amador County. The guy was paying Hale for designing the course, but he didn't have enough money to do it himself, so he needed a joint-venture partner. He needed to sell it or find a partner. So I went up and met with him. It was a beautiful property. I told him I was in commercial real estate and I knew what he needed. I told him I was a former professional golfer and I had a lot of golf contacts, but he needed to give me an exclusive listing on this property. And he did. So I went to work. Dialing for dollars. I called everyone I could possibly find who was in golf development, or golf business or residential development. I really enjoyed being able to meld my real estate background with my golf background. From that point forward, as a commercial real estate broker, I specialized in golf-related real estate transactions.

That coincided with a time when the Japanese were buying everything in sight. I was living in San Francisco, I was a member of the Olympic Club, and I was meeting lots of Japanese businessmen. I ended up brokering several deals for Japanese clients in the late '80s. I had a bunch of high-end properties in escrow in 1990 when the Japanese market kind of collapsed. About that time, the National Golf Foundation (NGF) published their infamous report saying that we needed to build a new golf course a day for the next umpteen jillion years to meet golfer demands. People believed the report, and in hindsight it basically torpedoed the industry. The NGF identified the areas in the country that were most under-supplied, and in the top 10 areas identified was Merced, which is 20 miles east of Stevinson Ranch. It was the fourth-most-undersupplied public market in America. Modesto, which is 25 miles north and a little west of Stevinson Ranch, was the eighth-most-undersupplied public golf market in the country. So I thought, "Jeez, I'm doing all these golf deals for other people, and my family owns this land." My father had passed away, so I went to my mother and my brothers and I said I want to do a golf course on our property. There is a great opportunity. To make a long story short, the family said they didn't have the capital to build the course, but they would put the land in, and I would need to find a partner to build the course. So I started getting the entitlements to build and looking for a partner to build the course. Then in 1992 or '93 we got our entitlements, and I got serious about finding a partner. It took awhile but ultimately I contacted Bob Lurie who used to own the San Francisco Giants and was a family friend. Bob's father and my grandfather were great friends, and I knew Bob through golf, too. So I called him up and told him I had this new golf course project. He had just sold the San Francisco Giants, and I asked him if he was interested in going into the golf business. He said, "Absolutely not!" Then he paused and said to send him the information and he would take a look at it. So I sent him the information, and after a long due diligence, he and my family went into a 50-50 joint venture where we put the land in and he put the cash in and if there were any shortfalls, we would share them 50-50. We opened in 1995.

It was an extraordinary opportunity. The total property is 1,000 acres, including 150 acres of wetlands. We decided we wouldn't disturb any of the wetland areas, and in addition we would create another 100 acres of wetlands. We wanted pure golf. I knew it was an environmentally sensitive property, and I contacted Ron Dodson at Audubon International. At that time, 1992, it was the New York Audubon Society. I flew Ron out for several days. I was hoping I could just drop him off at the site for a couple days to walk the property with his binoculars and a note pad. We had already done our biological studies and didn't really think there was all that much going on out there on the property. When Ron came in from his first tour of the property, he said we had a veritable sanctuary. He told us it was unbelievable. He told us he thought there were 100 species of birds out there. There were Swainson Hawks and all kinds of other wildlife. He was just jumping out of his skin in excitement. At first I wondered if we would get our environmental approvals, but we did. Through that relationship, I joined the Audubon Cooperative Sanctuary Program, and we became the first Audubon International "Signature" golf course west of the Mississippi River and only the sixth in the world at that time. Subsequently, our company, Greenway Golf, is focused on environmental protection. That company is really another story, but we use old-world methods for maintaining turf. We use far less chemicals and fertilizers than any other golf course maintenance system. We have a very minimalistic approach to golf course design and maintenance.

In planning the course, I had wanted to find an emerging architect, someone nobody had ever really heard of. I had a bunch of the big-name architects come to the site. I brought out Tom Doak. At that time, Tom had done one project with Pete Dye, but few people had ever really heard of him. I picked him up at the Oakland Airport, drove him about an hour and a half to the site, and spent about five hours touring the site with him. During that day, I recognized his brilliance. I'm a student of golf course architecture, and with every architect I brought to the site, I took my role in selecting the right architect very seriously. I clearly knew that I might personally never have another chance to design a golf course. I wanted to be part of the design. Tom didn't want anything to do with that. He wanted to be the designer. It would have been interesting to see what he would have done with the property, and it would have provided him with his first West Coast design, but I wanted to be involved.

In looking for an architect, I stumbled onto John Harbottle. I wanted someone who was steeped in the traditions of classic golf course designs such as the old Scottish links courses. I hadn't spent all that much time in Scotland studying those courses, but Harbottle had. Not many people had ever really heard of John, and after we talked at length, I hired him and paid him a design fee of only $100,000. At that time, golf course construction was taking off, and some architects were already getting six figures and sometimes seven figures. John spent two days of every week on the site during construction. It was just fantastic. He brought a shaper with him named Tom Simpson. Tom had shaped all of the greens at the ocean course at Kiawah Island. While he worked for us, he stayed with my brother. We would be out on the site all day doing construction, and then at night we had these great dinners where we would talk about the course design. It was a fantastic time. I designed the routing of the holes as I had wanted, and John did all of the design features such as bunkers. John and Tom designed all of the green complexes. It is a sandy site, so they always carried a water bottle and would pour some water onto the sand so they could draw green complexes and bunkers in the wet sand. Then John would go off for a few hours on some other part of the project, then come back to meet with Tom and discuss the greens they had planned and that he had been thinking about. He'd tell Tom to plan details like fortifying back portions of greens, creating a 3-percent grade on this side of the green and then taper off in another direction. It just happened right in front of me. It was amazing watching them work. As a result, to this day I still think our greens are just great. They are so subtle and hard to read. They are really big. The average green is 6,500 square feet, but we also created extended collars around the greens, where we have bentgrass on native sand so the golfer can putt the ball or chip it. With the extended collars, the green complexes are about 10,000 square feet on average.

In 1995 we opened with great fanfare. *Golf Digest* rated the course "Best New Upscale Public Course in California" in 1996 and "Top 25" of all California courses in 1997. We hosted the U.S. Open Qualifying in 1996 and 1997. We were the first golf course in California to attain "Signature" status with Audubon International for our dedication to environmental excellence. Things were going fine in the early years. Then there was an onslaught of other courses being built, particularly in the Sacramento market. There had been no new golf courses built in 40 years in Sacramento, and then all of a sudden within a period of about 10 years they built 30 new golf courses. That was devastating to facilities like mine. We haven't really fully recovered. We were just breaking even or losing just a little money. In our best year, 2004, we made $300,000 profit, but with the collapse in the economy we've lost about $700,000 from where we were at our high point in 2004 to where we were in 2009. So, it's really a challenge. We have had to cut expenses accordingly. I'm always very mindful of not sacrificing quality. With our location, we are a destination facility and my feeling is that if we lower the bar, we would lose a big portion of our customer base.

I would have to say I'm kind of a maverick in terms of how I do things. I'm very, very open minded and inquisitive. I'm always looking for a way to build a better mouse trap. I've always wanted my golf course to play fast and firm, and I've always wanted it to be bentgrass. In 1999 I was involved in the development of a high-end private golf club in Sonoma County called Mayacama. It was working with Mayacama that I met my current partner, Marc Logan. Marc has a master's degree in Turf Sciences from Western Australia University. Marc is an Aussie, and he was hired to do construction management and grow-in at Mayacama. I had played on the Australian Tour and traveled with Aussies and I was so intrigued with and loved them. They are so hard working and such fun-loving people. Marc and I had long conversations about turf science and turfgrass. I told him that my greens were starting to get a lot of Poa Annua in them and get thatchy. I said my superintendent told me that it's inevitable in our region, but Marc said that was absolutely not the case. Royal Melbourne in Australia still had its original bentgrass greens. What he was telling me sounded too good to be true. So I ended up hiring Marc to consult with me at Stevinson Ranch, and I saw some unbelievable results in a very short period of time.

I started referring business to him for other courses. Then it dawned on me that I had the contacts and he had the technical expertise, so I called him up and asked if he wanted to go into business together. And so Marc and I started Greenway Consulting, LLC, in 2002. A few years later we brought on our other partner, Ken Campbell, and formed Greenway Golf, Inc. We have a very different, old-world methodology. We use a lot of ferrous sulfate on our greens. We have a more acid-based nutritional program, which is more akin to how courses are maintained in the U.K. and Australia. We are able to maintain bentgrass with our program. At Stevinson our greens are 15 years old now and there is virtually no Poa in our greens. They are beautiful. In *Golf World* magazine, we got recognized with the highest-rated golf course conditioning in the country for a public course. In Greenskeeper.org in California, we are always top-rated for course conditioning. Our company, Greenway Golf, is another whole sidebar.

The NGCOA (National Golf Course Owners Association) really advocates for golf course owners. At their conferences, like the one we are attending, they get the best speakers. This morning is a great example of the quality of speakers they bring. *(Chris Gardiner, author of* The Pursuit of Happyness*)*. About five years ago in Tampa, the NGCOA brought in Joe Calloway to speak. Joe owns a restaurant in Nashville, he's a motivational speaker, and he wrote several books. One of his books is *Becoming a Category of One*. I loved what he had to say about being distinctive. He gave a phenomenal talk about how you want to separate yourself from your competitors. If you don't, you become just another commodity. You want to be the default choice, and you do that through customer service and raising the bar, by making sure that everyone on your staff adopts a philosophy that we are going to do everything we can to make sure our customers' enjoyment of our facility is foremost. I bought his CD, took it home, and distributed it to all of our staff, and I brought them in for a motivational meeting. I told them we were going to move to the next level. I told everyone to take the CD home and listen to it, and then in two weeks we were going to get together again to talk about it.

In the following year, using Joe Calloway's philosophy, we improved our revenue. We went from losing $300,000 in the previous year to making $150,000 the following year. We made a $450,000 shift in our net turnaround. To this day, any new hire has to listen to the Calloway CD and then come back for a second interview. It's all about believing in the concept. Calloway talked about how in the early 1960s President Kennedy announced that by the end of the decade, we were going to send a person to the moon. Everybody in America was excited and rallying around the idea except for one group, NASA. Not only did many people within NASA think it was impossible, but they thought it was irresponsible for the president to make that proclamation. Over the years, Joe Calloway met many of the Apollo astronauts, and he asked them how they were able to accomplish that challenge. They said it was easy. They systematically got rid of the non-believers. That's my philosophy on customer service. We make sure that we hire people who are people-people. We want employees who enjoy people, who are engaging, like having fun, who are extroverts. It really makes a difference. We have the most amazing staff.

About two years later at the Golf Industry Show in Atlanta, NGCOA brought in Mike Veeck as a speaker. His topic was "Fun is Good." Mike Veeck blew me away! He talked about his dad's life and influence, and it reminded me about my dad. I was actually in tears listening to him. After the talk I went up to Ladd Brunner, my general manager at Stevinson who was seated somewhere else during the talk, and asked him what he thought about the talk. Ladd said he was in tears, too. Ladd is one of the most passionate people you could ever meet. We have people who are just so passionate about our business. We love what we do. So I got Veeck's book. I read it twice. The second time I read it I took handwritten notes and read it like a textbook. I put my notes into my computer and sent them to Veeck. Mike got back to me right away. He said, "Wow, George, this is amazing, man! Thank you for sending me your notes. You've just written my next speech!" I reminded him that it was his work. I just compiled it.

As a result of those speeches and philosophies, I see myself at the forefront of how we deliver golf to our customers. I believe that we have to make the game more fun. We have to have alternative ways to how we go out and enjoy the game. We have actually hired a Director of Fun. You'll see on our website we have a Constitution of Fun. I keep our constitution in my money clip at all times. All of our staff carry the constitution with them. It's become embedded in our culture. We do things differently than most golf courses. We hide colored balls out on the course. If you find one of our colored balls, you bring it to the pro shop, and you can get a free lunch or a free golf hat or a lesson. We dispense fashion police violations if we find players whose clothes don't match, we issue citations. The beverage cart girl might say, "Excuse me, Tom. Are you aware that your stripped shirt doesn't go with your plaid pants? Do you know that black socks don't go with brown shoes? I'm afraid I will have to issue you a citation." The citation looks official and scary, but if you get one, you get a free shirt off the sale rack, or you get 50 percent off any other garment in the shop. Things like that we love to do.

I'm the current president of the California Golf Course Owners Association, and we just had a "Grow the Game" conference. We talked about the fact published by the National Golf Foundation that more than one-half of core golfers, those who play at least eight times a season, never post a golf score, establish a handicap, or compete in a club event. It's a startling statistic to me. It got me thinking that everything we do to market golf as course owners or as equipment manufacturers or apparel retailers is marketed to fewer than half of our customers. Everything we are doing is about hitting the ball farther or straighter. There are over half of our customers who really don't care about hitting it farther or straighter or what their score is. So what I want to do is come up with four to six alternative games for golfers to play. We'll create the "rules" and laminate them. We'll create silly names for the games. We'll have games like you get one tee mulligan, one fairway mulligan and one bunker mulligan every nine holes. Or, you can throw your ball once per hole, and it won't count as a stroke. One of our ideas is that if you lip out a putt, where the ball hits the lip of the cup and changes direction without going in, then the putt is considered holed, and you get to take an additional point off your score. If you've ever tried on purpose to lip out a putt, it's really hard. We have a video that's on our website which shows me on our last hole trying to lip out a five-foot putt. Well, I made the putt 15 times in a row while trying to lip it out. Now I'm thinking I should try to lip out all of my putts.

I truly believe that in order for the game of golf to start growing again and get to a point where we owners can be successful again, we have to start delivering a completely different product from what we have been doing. We can still deliver the more traditional product, but we have to go beyond that. We must appeal to the half of our customers that just want to have fun. Whether they like the camaraderie, the fellowship, just being outdoors, or whatever, we should cater to them. Fitness is popular right now. We should have speed-golf events. For maybe 10 bucks, take a few clubs, and you have to play in less than one hour. Get a group of guys, hit and run to the next shot. If people like the idea, we can allocate the first hour of tee times to speed golfers. Tennis is branded around fitness. Tennis was dying. *Sports Illustrated* had a cover asking, "Is Tennis Dead?" In my estimation, we need to be asking that about golf these days. I wrote a piece titled, "Is Golf Dying?" One of the premises of the article was that what makes golf such a great game is its history and the traditions. Those qualities have tremendous appeal to many. However, those same aspects can hinder us from adapting to change. The United States Golf Association (USGA) is the governing body for rules of golf. Those rules are effectively no different today from what they were 40 years ago. Now, I have friends in the USGA, and I don't want to be disparaging, but in my estimation they are like dinosaurs. The Professional Golfers Association (PGA) isn't much better. With all of the crazy, zany things we are trying to do at Stevinson, one of my toughest jobs has been getting my PGA pro on board. He's an old-school, great guy. His attitude was, "This isn't what I was taught to do. This is stupid." He's on board with the Constitution of Fun now.

As an owner trying to make golf profitable again, I think some changes are needed. We need to involve families more. We need to get kids involved. We need to make golf fun. We need alternatives where nine holes are enough. We need to relax dress codes. My dress code is that I just don't want to see your armpit hairs. Other than that, you're fine.

If you look at what's happening in the golf industry right now, it's sad how many people are losing their golf businesses. But I think the contraction is necessary. One of our key leaders, Henry DeLozier, reported at this conference that only 7 percent of golf courses made a profit this past year. Supply and demand adjustments are needed. Creativity is needed to operate our businesses more successfully.

I'm generally an optimistic person. In my life I've always looked at the glass as half full, not half empty. But having said that, I am a little bit pessimistic about the future of golf. I think there needs to be some serious change, some serious introspection about what people really want. There are a lot of initiatives going on in the industry to grow golf. But why don't we engage in some conversations with people who don't play the game, or who are thinking about playing the game, or used to play the game and left the game, about what we can do for them? We are still going down the traditional lines. This new initiative, "We Are Golf[1]," is a good idea that should have been introduced 15 years ago. The lobbying in Washington, D.C. that is going on now is a good idea. We golf course owners are operating mostly small businesses. We have a significant impact on the economy as well as on the social culture of this country. There are lots of messages that need to be heard. If you look at young kids who play golf, they have better grades, they are less inclined to get in trouble, and they learn important life lessons playing the game. That's a great story. Kids who learn that in golf you call penalties on yourself can transfer that to their lives. Right now our country seems to be having lots of problems and going in some unfortunate directions. As an industry, I think we need to do an even better job communicating golf's values and benefits. Those benefits are real. We need more creative thinking to get this message communicated.

ℰ   ℂℛ

[1]*"We Are Golf" is a new coalition gearing up to tell the stories of golf's diverse businesses and their employees, the tax revenues it creates, the tourism it spawns, the charity it generates, and the environmental leadership it provides. Golf is a major industry with a profound impact on America's economic, environmental and social agendas.*

## Kelley's Lessons

- Nurture the network of friends and professional associates in your life for your own personal and professional development.
- Appreciating and protecting the environmental assets of your property can pay dividends. *(Stevinson Ranch became the first Audubon International "Signature" golf course west of the Mississippi River and only the sixth in the world at the time it was developed. Subsequently, George developed Greenway Golf, a golf course maintenance company focused on environmental protection.)*
- Even when competition and the economy can create difficulty for your business, the quality of your product and services must be preserved.
- Be open-minded and inquisitive. Don't accept what others tell you that you cannot do until you try it yourself. *(George took the risks to change from turfgrasses that were prevalent in his region to grasses and turf maintenance practices that he was told by some were impossible. The result of his risks were national and regional accolades for quality golf course conditions as well as the development of his company, Greenway Golf, Inc.)*
- Distinguish yourself from your competitors. Become a "Category of One." Make sure that everyone on your staff adopts a philosophy that they are going to do everything they can to make sure their customers' enjoyment of the facility is their foremost priority.
- Hire employees who enjoy people, who are engaging like having fun, who are extroverts.
- Fun is good! Make the game more fun. Create alternative ways to how we go out and enjoy the game. *(At Stevinson Ranch there is a Director of Fun and a Constitution of Fun that drive the philosophy.)*

- "I truly believe that in order for the game of golf to start growing again and get to a point where we owners can be successful again, we have to start delivering a completely different product from what we have been doing. We can still deliver the more traditional product, but we have to go beyond that. We must appeal to the half of our customers that just want to have fun. Whether they like the camaraderie, the fellowship, just being outdoors, or whatever, we should cater to them."

- "As an industry, I think we need to do an even better job communicating golf's values and benefits." Those economic, social, educational and recreational benefits are real. "We need more creative thinking to get this message communicated."

# Working Man

## Joseph H. Lightkep, Owner of Fairways Golf and Country Club in Warrington, Pennsylvania

ᛏ    03

*I interviewed Joseph Lightkep (Joe), single owner/operator of Fairways Golf and Country Club in Warrington, Pennsylvania, on February 2, 2009, at the Hotel Intercontinental in New Orleans during the Golf Industry Show. Fairways is a public 18-hole course just outside Philadelphia. The course was designed by William Gordon and built in 1965. The par-65 course has bentgrass greens, tee boxes and fairways. The course clubhouse is a converted farmhouse built in 1859. Somewhat unusually, no alcoholic beverages are sold or permitted at the course.*

### www.fairwaysgolfclub.com

ᛏ    03

I grew up in a middle class family. My mom was a nurse, and my dad was a salesman of lawn and garden equipment for Jacobson tractors. When I was a kid, Dad would drive the trailer home with tractors on it, and he would let me drive them. That's all I wanted to do was drive the tractors. During the summer I would go out with him during sales calls, and I got to meet lots of the Philadelphia golfers and superintendents. Also, as a kid I loved to trap muskrats. We trapped them on all of the golf courses in the area. So I got to know all of the golf courses by the creeks and lakes. I always wanted to be a farmer. As time went on, I wondered if I would ever get my farm, but I began to realize that I could enjoy this golf course work and still be outside.

My first real golf course work experience was out of second grade, at seven years old. I worked for my second grade teacher's husband at Fairways Golf Course, the same course I now own. A couple of times a week during the summers, I picked up sticks around the clubhouse, raked the lawns, and hand-raked sand traps. I didn't work for money, but for free golf. After my work Dad and I could play golf together. I loved it.

A little later, around 10 years old, I was on the school swim team, and the swim club had a chip-and-putt course on 14 acres. They were strapped for money, so my dad would bring home a tractor, I would cut their grass, and again my dad and I could play golf there. They decided they needed to change that chip-and-putt course, so my dad and I did the redesign, planted all zoysia greens, installed hundreds and hundreds of feet of drainage, and did all kinds of things for the swim club. We did this on nights and weekends. You should see it right now. Those zoysia greens are still there and they're beautiful.

When I was 12, I got my first full-time summer job at a golf course. They had two 18-hole courses. One was private and the other was public. I had a history with the owners of this golf course: My grandmother was their accountant for their hotels. Basically, my grandmother, or maybe it was my dad, got me the job. I worked 50 hours a week. By the time I was 14, I was in charge of all the herbicide spraying on both courses. They had no weeds and I just loved it. Then I got recruited to another course with a different owner. That course had lost its mechanic. Ever since I was a little kid, I took things apart and put them back together. So I worked on the mechanic's crew for that 27-hole course. I sharpened everything and did repairs on equipment. I worked there for two years, and then I worked for a cemetery for a year, in charge of their grass. That took me to the last year of high school.

I went to college to study chemistry, but I had a little too much hell in me and didn't do so well. In March of that year, I got a call from the owner of the first course I had worked for, Fairways. He also owned Hidden Springs, and he asked me if I would manage that course for him. I said I didn't think I was ready for college at the time, so I took the job. I was 19. Previously that course had been leased, and it was really run-down. The old farmhouse was gutted. Even the bathrooms were gutted. The course was overgrown. It was a mess, and I had a rough road ahead of me. We didn't even open the door the first year. If people wanted to go out and play the course as it was, we had a donations box for them. The owner wanted to bulldoze the old house down. He didn't want to spend any money in there. But I wanted a place to live. So I convinced the owner that I could bring the old place back to life. One of my friend's fathers was into air conditioning, and another friend's father was a plumber, so I told him my friends and I would fix the house up and not spend much money. The owner agreed, so two of my friends and I lived in the farmhouse, out in the middle of nowhere, and slowly fixed it up. We opened the course the next year. That's what eventually got me back to Fairways, where I started as a seven-year-old.

That first month of managing Hidden Springs, I only saw the owner three times. Then he moved to China for three years. He left me with enough money and a bank account so I could buy used equipment, and I ran that golf course on my own for years. He also owned a bank and probably could have afforded more than I spent, but I scraped by as cheaply as I could. The course improved steadily, and play picked up steadily. Before long, by 1985, we needed a tee book to reserve tee times. At first we only had one mower, and we mowed everything with the same equipment. We'd cut the whole course the same height and then a few days later go back to recut the fairways so they looked different from the rough. Eventually, in '88, we bought a triplex mower and started doing it right.

The course was designed by William Gordon in 1962. It was designed as a golfing community where the owners of houses on the property were to have ownership of the golf course. The course had its own sewage treatment plant, and the affluent water was pumped up to irrigate the course. That process is popular now to reduce water consumption, but we started doing it in '62. William Gordon designed a lot of courses in that area with his brother David. They designedd Saucon Valley Country Club where a U.S. Senior Open was held. For us they built the golf courses and some of the houses. But the operation went under, and an auction was held on the front lawn after three years of being open. About 80 percent of the houses were never finished. That's when I started managing Fairways.

In 1985 the owner returned from China. He was already an older man. That was when I really got to know him, and we started hanging out with each other. He wanted to sell the sewage operation, and the township wanted to buy it. It was pretty high-tech for the time, and the sewage system would help support other housing developments in the area. One summer he and I started rebuilding the cement structures that supported the manhole covers in the roads in the housing development. We did that work out of the back of his Rolls Royce. My dad wondered if the city would support the expensive equipment being used for the cementing work. After all, it was a Rolls Royce. But that was the type of man the owner was. He worked in a thousand-dollar suit, but he wasn't afraid of getting dirty. He just loved the work. So in '85, when I was about 23 or 24 years old, he and I did all the sewers, all the curbing, all the water mains, and helped build the roads. Then we were able to sell the improved housing sites to builders and they built the rest of the neighborhoods around the golf course. That's when I got my experience working with contractors. Up until then, I just did all the work myself. So I was running the golf course and working with contract builders who were dynamiting the streets so I could do curbing, water mains and the rest. That work lasted for two summers. It took eight years to get all the roads and work finally approved. I didn't have to pay for all of this, but I had to manage all of it, and it was amazing experience for me. It was the biggest learning experience I had up to that point.

I was doing the work, but I didn't have any formal training. So, I told the owner that I thought I ought to go back to school. He told me he thought that was a great idea, as long as I could keep the course running at the same time. So I went to Delaware Valley College of Science and Agriculture to study agronomy, because I figured I would be a golf course superintendent. The management side of the operation was coming easy to me, but I wanted to learn how to improve the quality of the course. I graduated in agronomy at the top of my class.

I was three years into that agronomy degree when the owner asked me what I was taking at college, anyway. I remember we were eating handmade German hotdogs in town one day. He loved those hotdogs. He asked me why I was studying agronomy and not business administration. I told him I loved the subject, the scientific management of soils. Then he asked, "Well, what are you going to do when I die?" I said I didn't know what he meant. He said, "Aren't you going to take over this place? You've been treating it all this time like it was your place. Don't you think it should be yours?" That was the first time it clicked for me that I could own and operate a golf course. We never, ever had another discussion about me owning the golf course.

He died four years later. His daughter and son took over the ownership of the course. His son was hard to work for, and I told his sister that if things didn't change, I was going to quit, so she took over and she was great. Two years later she came to me and told me that her brother wanted to sell the golf course. I just told her she had to do what she had to do. That's when she told me that her dad had said on his death bed that if she and her brother didn't want the golf course, they were to give me the first opportunity to buy it. She put me on the spot. She said, "Do you want to buy it?" Well, I had an agronomy degree and some business classes, and I really didn't know what I was doing, but something just told me to say, "Yes, I want to buy the golf course." Well, my parents didn't have any money, and I had a savings account, but nothing like the kind of resources needed to buy a golf course. My wife was operating a daycare center, and one of her clients was an accountant, so I asked this accountant if she would help look over the paperwork for the past five years. I just wanted to know if the course was worth it for me to buy. After she looked over the paperwork she contacted me and said it was absolutely worth buying the course. I can't remember the actual numbers, but I had been making the owner something like a 40 percent margin over his actual expenses. I didn't know this because I always just sent all the figures to the owner's office. They did all the payroll and finances for me. I had never even seen a financial statement. I was clueless. I didn't know if the course was making a profit. All I knew was that I wanted job security. I loved the place. Now when I look back, I think I was fortunate to not know about all of the finances. I just worked hard and didn't overspend.

So I took the accountant's figures, and I went to the local bank and told the banker I wanted to buy a golf course. The bank's branch manager asked me how much I wanted to borrow. When I told her how much I needed, she jokingly said that she didn't even know how many zeroes were in that number. She said someone would have to get back to me on the request. So corporate officers for the bank got back to me.

I sat down with them and told them my story about how I had started at Fairways and what I had been doing. They said, "Joe, just from your story, we're on! The cash flow is there and we'll lend you the money." My accountant set me up with a corporate lawyer, who drew up a 260-page agreement of sale. I had never even seen an agreement of sale before, much less a 260-page agreement. It seemed like it took me a month to read that thing and try to understand all that lawyer language. I did my due diligence, which I didn't know what it was at the time, had site one and site two environmental studies done. Every day I was learning and learning and learning. I loved college, but that year of buying the course was probably the best year of my life. All the steps that my accountant and lawyer made me go through made me a smarter person. I would have just signed the papers, but they made sure I did the job right. So in 1993 we went to settlement and I bought the golf course. I was 32 years old. I wasn't even afraid of what I was getting into. I was just excited. I hired a good accountant to do my payroll, pay my bills for me, and give me financial reports. She's still with me. I call her my assistant, but really she is my partner. She does a lot of my job for me. Some of the people working for me now have been with me for over 25 years.

I always wanted to be a superintendent, but after I bought the course I only lasted about five months doing the superintendent's job. One of my college friends had gotten a business administration degree and started selling mortgages, but he didn't like it very much. At night after his regular job, he would come to the golf course and water the course for me. So I asked him why he didn't come to Fairways as the head superintendent. He asked me what I was going to do. I just told him, "I'm a golf course owner now. I don't need the work of the superintendent too." He told me he didn't really have the knowledge to be a superintendent. So, I made him a deal. I told him I would pay for him to take the two-year turf maintenance program at Rutgers University and pay his salary if he would commit to work for me for a number of years. He asked his parents what they thought. They weren't at all happy about the arrangement, since they had paid for his business degree. Anyway, he accepted my offer and said he would work for me for 10 years. That was more than fair for me, and he has been my superintendent for more than 16 years now.

Since then I haven't changed a whole lot with the golf course. Obviously, the maintenance is quite different from when we started. With money coming in, we upgraded all of our equipment and upgraded the agronomics of the course. I had been doing everything on a shoestring budget, and I learned a lot. Once I knew there was money, I could invest it in the course. My operation is very simple. We have a snack bar, and we sell balls, gloves, tees, the things golfers need for the day. I'm surrounded by sports stores that sell golf products on sale cheaper than I can buy them, so my pro shop is pretty simple. My clientele is traditionally seniors. It's a shorter course at 5,006 yards. We have a tent for outings, and we also use a local Knights of Columbus hall where we can seat up to 200 people for an outing.

The farmhouse that the previous course owner had let me save was built in 1859. It has big windows, arched doorways, lots of wood inside. We stripped all the paint, re-plastered, rewired and re-plumbed the place. It was just a neat, old farmhouse, not a clubhouse. To make it into a clubhouse, we had to build in office spaces, lounges, and so forth, but we kept to the themes of the old house. We built cabinets like the original cupboards and spaces like the original butler pantry. Again, it was a great learning experience, and it was really gratifying to see my hard work really making a difference. I did the work without knowing I would someday own the course, or without knowing the previous owner's deathbed request to his children. I just worked and worked and worked. I just loved it.

I started coming to the National Golf Course Owners Association meeting that year that I bought the course, '93. I had been going to the Golf Course Superintendents national meetings before then, but I needed to learn about ownership and management. I didn't know anything about insurance for liability, worker's compensation, or any of that stuff. I had never negotiated cart leases or completed loan applications for new equipment. The only loan application I had ever made to that point was to buy a golf course. So my next step was to find out about all that stuff and the NGCOA annual conference was my resource. I really enjoy the classes, but it's the conversations with all the people you meet at these conferences that I enjoy. The next winter I went to Oglebay Resort and Conference Center in Wheeling, West Virginia. At the time, they hosted a two-year management program for golf courses and that helped me. I kept learning, and as problems arose, I just found the ways and means to solve them.

Right now I've got loyal customers. We have five weekly leagues, two for men, two for women, and one for juniors. The leagues all got started with the ladies who worked for me in the pro shop. They actually started their league before I owned the golf course. They started with 12 women and then word of mouth spread. When I bought the course, some of the men wanted to know why they didn't have a league. I just told them that I didn't start the women's league, they started it. If the men wanted a league for their own, then they should do it. So a couple of the guys started planning a league. I let them use the office space and make fliers and get started. After that I saw the financial benefit. Those are loyal customers. You know they will be there for their leagues. They feel a part of the course. At that time, we didn't even have memberships in the course. League became their membership to the golf club. Then they started bringing friends to play the course outside of leagues and began booking outings. It all just snowballed until I hired one of the women from a lady's league to run leagues and book outings. We have over one hundred league players now.

There are only four full-time employees at the course. That's me, my assistant Valerie, my superintendent Ronnie, and Malinda, the woman in charge of leagues. During the year we have as many as 47 employees. Except for the cart and grounds crews, the employees are all retired. They enjoy working two or three days a week, and they get their golf. In our area of Pennsylvania, it can be hard to find employees because it's seasonal work. But seniors really fit the bill. We actually have waiting lists to become a ranger or a starter. We have a waiting list to work in the pro shop.

Because we are in a neighborhood housing community, there are kids everywhere, and they get hired for the cart and grounds crews. I ask around to find the kids in the neighborhood who are the most trouble and then hire them. Once they feel a part of the golf course I don't worry about them and their friends screwing up the course that night. This process has worked, and it has worked very well. I actually try to find out which neighborhood kids are most likely headed for trouble and then try to hire them at about age 14. I give them the responsibility of cleaning and maintaining the golf carts. I think that's one of the hardest jobs at the course. That's one of the largest assets on the property, and I give that responsibility to one of the youngest kids working for me. They have a list of things to get done each night, but they don't even really have a boss or a supervisor standing over their shoulder. When the superintendent sees that guy make it through their first summer, then that kid has a job all the way through college. They learn how to cut grass and work on the grounds for a couple of years. Then I like to bring them into the pro shop, too, so they learn additional skills. Each year they want more and more hours. By the time they are home from college, they can make overtime. Some work over 60 hours a week. We never have a problem hiring grounds crew. The superintendent just watches who is doing cart maintenance, and we take them from there. I have never put an ad in the paper for an employee. The housing community has built-in employees. When I say I have some employees who have worked here for 25 years, I am talking about maybe 20 different people. All of these things fall into place to make my job easier. I take vacations, spend a lot of time in Florida in winters, go hunting in the fall, go fishing in Canada, and know the course is OK.

Right now we don't sell alcoholic beverages or permit them on the course. We used to sell alcohol, but on the weekends I had to referee between golfers who had too much to drink and homeowners with too much to drink. Basically, that's where that policy came from. It was easier for me to manage my golfers than it was to worry about what was going to happen with my neighbors. And there's a personal story behind the policy. Drinking was involved when I lost my best friend when I was 24. So I stopped drinking. That made it easier for me to say that if I'm not drinking, then nobody is. I do have insurance for alcohol for outings. I don't sell it or provide it, but the people in charge of their outing can provide it. Then I hire certified, professional bartenders from a friend of mine who owns a couple of bars. That helps keep things under control. Over the past four years, the outings have helped to generate some revenue. All the other courses in my area sell alcohol. I don't know if my alcohol policy attracts more people than it repels, but I do believe it attracts different people. Someone told me a long time ago that if your course can attract women on a consistent basis, then you are doing something right. I think we have more women and more families playing my golf course than any other course I know of. That's good for my business. You know, women get a bad rap from a lot of men for slow play. But I'll put my women's league players up against any men's league players for pace of play. The men won't keep up with them. The women might be shooting 30 over par, but they keep moving, much faster than the men. The bulk of my weekend play after 10 AM is men with their wives and families. Our junior program on Tuesdays is sold out for the season in two days. I think we have a mix of customers that a lot of courses would want.

We just started season memberships two years ago. I have about 40 members. The memberships aren't cheap. You have to play about three to four times a week to break even. It's for the people who want to play a lot of golf. That's the way I want it. I never had a membership in a course myself, and mostly I never played anywhere with memberships. In my eyes, that's the way I wanted it. I didn't want a hundred bosses. You know what I mean? I had heard from my superintendent friends that members can be a problem, with greens committees and all of that. Through the prosperity of the '90s I didn't need members anyway. Back then I didn't have extra room on my tee book anyway. After about 2001 there was a decline in golf and I had to make some changes. So we evolved. I started doing more outings and opened the course to members.

I play golf myself about three or four times a month. Even though I take time away from the course now, I used to work sunup to sundown seven days a week. I was always at the course working. Now when I play, it's usually at someone else's course. I enjoy playing my course, but when I am out there, I always see all the work that needs to be done. My back gets sore from fixing 20 ball marks on greens and filling divots. Or I'll be out there making to-do lists. That's not play, that's more work. My superintendent has other superintendent friends at some of the best courses around Philadelphia. When he takes me with him to those courses, he knows we won't be coming home with a new list of the things he needs to do.

This summer we had our best accolade ever. We hosted an outing for the Philadelphia Association of Golf Course Superintendents. Their letters to me and the press we got in their superintendents' newsletter stated that anyone who didn't play Fairways this summer really missed a gem. They said it was the most fun and maybe the best-conditioned course they ever played. That's with us being an 18-hole course with an annual maintenance budget under $250,000, including labor costs. Those other superintendents work at courses with over one-million-dollar maintenance budgets. That's something I'm really proud of.

September of last year I made my last payment on the course. I paid it off in 15 years. It's just a small 5,000 yard course, with no restaurant, no liquor, but with people. I've never put an ad in the paper. People are always asking when they get their turn to work at the course. And I'm living every superintendent's dream. What superintendent wouldn't want to make all the decisions at the course they are managing? The whole story is so exciting to me.

It's hard to make business decisions based on revenue you may or may not have. But I've surrounded myself with really good people. The accountant who got me into this thing is still my accountant. I have two good attorneys. One is my corporate attorney, and the other is my risk management attorney. I always enjoyed those risk management and liability classes in school. I can honestly tell you that I have never had a worker's compensation claim and that I have never needed to use my liability insurance. That history keeps my insurance costs down. Not having alcohol on the course cuts my liability insurance costs maybe in half. You have to make the place safe for the people who pay to play, but you have to make it twice as safe for the people who work there. I pride myself on that. We have a revolving capital budget where the equipment is continuously updated. There's no broken-down equipment where the kids or other employees can get hurt. I lease the golf carts with their warranties, so we don't have to work on those to keep them running.

*(I asked Joe if all of his greens keeping equipment is Jacobson.)*

**Joe** *(laughing)***:** Even though my dad did sell Jacobson tractors, yes, our equipment is all orange *(Jacobson)*, with the exception of one Toro Sand Pro. When I was a kid, all I ever wanted for Christmas was my own greens mower. My dad had a huge Jacobson estate mower that we cut our front lawn with. We used that mower to cut the greens at the swim club, and he would let me use it to cut neighbors' lawns for money in the summers. It was a big, walk-behind reel mower. I always wanted one of those for myself. I love that stuff.

*(I asked Joe to comment about the golf industry as a whole.)*

**Joe:** People have been playing golf for a long, long time. Some parts of the industry may be recession-proof. Lots of courses still have retired people who have enough discretionary income playing during the week. They have worked all of their lives to then live their lives. They are going to play golf. For me, that's a blessing, because I'm surrounded by communities with 55-plus people. But golf is cyclical. It has its ups and downs. When Bobby Jones played golf, the whole industry thrived. Now there's nothing bigger than Tiger Woods. The national economy wasn't all that great when Tiger came out, but with Tiger, golf boomed. As long as we can position ourselves to stay in business during downtimes like this, then that's the key. I don't have lots of the problems that some other owners have. I've grown up with this golf course. I know what I can and can't do.

Some of those who built courses in the '90s at the height of the golf boom are having trouble paying down their debt now, with fewer golfers for revenue. Sometimes the property is worth more money as housing developments. Some of the mom-and-pop courses aren't going to their children because inheritance taxes are so high or because the children see that the course is never going to make as much as they can get for housing developments. Golf courses were overbuilt, and now that market is adjusting. In my area for the past two years, not to mention the last six months, those who are feeling the effects of the economy the worst are the higher-end private clubs. I know one exclusive private club in my area that had 310 members and lost 130 of them this year alone. The bulk of their membership is people between 45 and 55 years old. These are the people who might have lost their jobs, been downsized, or suffered in the economy. Those very high-end private clubs with members age 55 to 75 aren't losing their members. Those people have their money. It's all about who plays your course that influences how owners are going to get through this economy. I'm going to be OK.

## Lightkep's Lessons

- Hard work is its own reward. This is a philosophy that builds experience and resourcefulness for benefits that will follow, both planned and unforeseen at the time.

- Learning is its own reward. Again, planned and unforeseen benefits will follow.

- A community golf course is an integral component of the community. The course is a source of fun, recreation, social interaction and employment for the community. The community is the source of revenue for the course.

- Hiring older, retired employees is cost effective and creates loyal golf customers.

- Hiring neighborhood kids for the grounds crew keeps them busy, benefits their development, and creates job security. *(Joe has had some youth work for him from childhood through college. He has never had to advertise to fill work positions.)*

- Alcohol is not a requirement for golf. While the sale of food and beverages, particularly alcoholic beverages, is the lifeblood of most golf courses, not having alcohol can reduce costs for risk insurance and create a profitable customer mix of women and families with children.

# Old School

Jeff Hoag, Owner of Scott Lake Country Club in Comstock Park, Michigan

ಉಂ    ಆಟ

*I interviewed Jeff Hoag, who owns and operates Scott Lake Country Club in partnership with his brother Paul, on February 6, 2009, at the Morial Convention Center in New Orleans during the Golf Industry Show. Scott Lake is a public 27-hole course in Comstock Park, Michigan. Scott Lake's motto is "Where Golf is Fun!"*

*Scott Lake opened its first nine holes of the current 27 holes in 1961. The NGCOA named Scott Lake the 2012 Course of the Year.*

www.scottlake.com

ಉಂ    ಆಟ

My introduction to golf began with my parents, who were members at a private club. We grew up swimming on the club's swim team and taking golf lessons at the club. Then my dad decided he needed to build a golf course. Dad started building the first nine holes in 1960, opened in 1962, and opened the second nine holes in 1965.

Dad *(Oliver F. Hoag)* had been a member at Green Ridge Country Club for over 20 years. He had played competitive golf as a young man, playing in the National Tournament for Left-Handed Golfers and in local citywide tournaments. His decision to build a golf course was based on three ideas. First, he knew that people wanted to play golf but either couldn't afford to belong to a private club or didn't want to belong to a private club. The second reason was that his industry, furniture manufacturing *(Cherrymasters, Inc.)*, was on a down-hill path, so he sold his business with the idea of replacing one business with another. At that time Dad also owned the Grand Rapids Dinette. The third reason was that the combined family had six sons, and building a golf course would keep them busy. I was 10 years old, my brother Paul was nine, my brother Joe was 11, John was 17, Jack was 21 and Jim was 21. The youngest three brothers (Joe, Paul and I) grew up on the golf course.

As we were growing up, we would be home at Sunday dinner sitting by a picture window overlooking the golf course, we would see a car coming up the dusty gravel road, and either Mom or Dad would go down and check in the golfer. Then they would come back home to finish dinner and get back to the course again to serve a hotdog or a pop. That's where I learned what you need to do. When people come in, you get up, and you do what you need to do to serve them. In all these years, those principles have not changed.

At age 10 I was out there doing whatever I could do at the golf course. In the beginning, it was picking rocks, hauling brush, raking, hoeing, and watering. We helped install the irrigation system, planted the greens, transplanted trees, and filled in washes. Later we did maintenance activities, mowing, watering, and fertilizing. Back in the old days, we took a 20-inch rotary mower out to mow around the trees, and, man, there were a lot of them. When we were in high school, it was normal to get up on the weekend and beat the golfers out to mow the greens. After school during the week, we would come home to rake leaves. Except for one summer in 1967 when I was an exchange student to Uruguay and Argentina, I worked at the golf course.

Then I went to college at Michigan State and graduated from their turfgrass program planning to be a superintendent. I was 20 years old, and I thought I knew everything. I tried to get a job, but I couldn't find the right one. I didn't want to be working at just any golf course. I wanted to work somewhere with some challenges and a chance to use some of the skills I had developed. I couldn't find what I wanted, so I went to work in the retail business at a Zayre's chain department store. I worked for them in Chicago for a while. Then, one day I was standing at the front door at a picture window, looking outside at the sun shining, and I realized that I had been in the store for the past 27 days without being outside. And I said to myself, "Is this it?" I came to the conclusion that "No, this is not going to be it!" I decided that I was going to quit my job and get back into the golf business.

In 1973 I went back to the Grand Rapids area to work at the golf course my parents owned. I bartended and helped around the shop the first year and then actively helped with the day-to-day operations until 1975. In 1976 my parents decided to retire. An older brother (Joe), a friend of ours, and I bought my parents' course. My parents made us a good offer and helped us with a buying structure that we were able to do. None of us had any money at the time. My brother and I needed the friend to help because we didn't have enough money to put the deal together. Lots of golf courses were bought or built in the late 1970s on land contracts. That was during President Carter's years and interest rates were over 20 percent. Actually, having lived with the recession of the 80s helps us make our business decisions during the recession we are in today. As time went on, my older brother got out of the business, and my youngest brother Paul bought in. Our friend in the partnership got out, too. So now it's just Paul and me in the partnership. I was 25 and Paul was 23 when we became golf course owners. That's where I am today.

When my brother and I took over the golf course, it wasn't where it needed to be. I'm still surprised my parents were able to make a go of it, and I'm surprised today that we were able to survive. In the ensuing years, we were able to build up the business, and we built another nine holes in 1998, 36 years after the original course was built. There was a property across the street owned by an older lady I had known all my life. She was an old farm gal. I told her we would really like to buy her property, but she said no, that would never happen, she had plans for her property. She wanted to give it to her nephew. She said, "My nephew is going to build a house, and then he's going to take care of me." The nephew took over the property, built a house, and they lived there for a few years. One day he sat down on his chair and he passed away. Now her plans had all changed, and she called us and asked if we still wanted to buy the land. We told her that we probably would be interested in buying, and she told us to make her an offer. We made her an offer, and she handed it back to me and she said, "You know, I have to be able to eat." It was a fair offer, but we came back with an offer for a few more thousand dollars that she accepted. Now that we had the property, we had to decide what we were going to do with it. We couldn't afford to have the debt service and not do something with it, so we built a third nine holes. We then renovated some holes on the existing

18-holes, and we built a driving range, and that's where we are today. We have 27 nice holes of golf that players can play in three 18-hole combinations, and we have a wonderful teaching facility. It's been an interesting business to be in. We have grown our business from a relatively small operation into something where we have a lot of golfers and lots of people who really appreciate what we do.

At first, when we bought the course we thought we could just do one or two things to the course and we would be on easy street. The next thing you know, you have to buy carts, you have to buy equipment. So for the last 35 years, we've been on this capital expenditure train that there is no relief from. Equipment and carts wear out, you need to make technology upgrades. We never thought about technology in 1975, but now it's a big issue. The interesting thing is to learn how to build your business by building your relationships with people. That's been key.

Our children have worked at the golf course, but we have always encouraged them to do what they want to do. We have one son who went to the PGM program at Ferris State in Michigan *(PGA Golf Management University Program for aspiring PGA professionals offered at 20 PGA accredited universities)*. With his degree and some excellent internships in that program, he came back to work for us, and he did a great job. But he got married and had a child and decided he didn't really want to work nights and weekends. Besides that, he was ready to take over the course, and I wasn't ready to go. So he started another career and he's doing very well; probably better than he ever could have done in the golf business. It's ironic, though. He's working in the medical field and he's on call nights and weekends. I tease him, though. I ask him, "How's that plan for nights and weekends going?" He just laughs. He's very happy. The other kids are happy, too, but they're just not interested in the golf business. My brother and I both have personalities where we are drivers, not followers, so I think it makes it hard for the kids to follow in those footsteps. The kids have made the right decisions for their lives.

We don't expect to pass the course on to our children. Right now it's not important to us. We did have an offer from someone to buy our course a few years ago. At the time, we weren't interested in selling. We had our own plans for growing our business, and we just wanted to complete our vision. Now, looking back and with the current economy, we wonder if we made the right decision to not sell. But our business is performing well, the way we thought it could, and that's very fulfilling.

Before college I worked for my parents doing the work of a superintendent. Then I went to Michigan State and got the turf degree, but at about that time I decided I didn't really want to be the "dirt" guy. In my experience in retail business, I got additional training. Since owning the course, I have gone to lots of seminars to continue my education and build new skill sets. I would tell anyone starting in their careers that continuing education is the key to their long-term success. It's not just about financial success, it's about how you feel about what you do. Do you like your job? Do you like the direction you are going? Can you change the direction you are going? Too many people today are stuck with the direction they are going because they don't have the skill sets to change. We see that now with the industrial demise in the Midwest. Auto workers at the same jobs for 25 years may not have the skills they need to make changes. My advice is to keep learning.

We are hard on our staff to deliver what we want our customers to experience. Our course motto is "Where Golf is Fun!" We are always trying to define that. We consider ourselves to be in the recreational business, not the golf business. We are in the repeat-business business. When we write our employee manuals, we always start off with who we are and who we are trying to be. We are really just a place that popped up one day. We aren't trying to be upscale. We cater to the blue-collar customer. My dad was a member in a private club, but he thought the costs were too high for most people. He wanted a golf opportunity for people where they could feel like they were members of a private club for a day, if that was all they could afford. That was his vision, but he never really got it to a reality. It was just too difficult. My brother and I have a different vision. We are a public, daily-fee golf course. Our customers aren't looking for the private club experience. They just want to play golf, have some beers with their buddies, and go home.

During the season we have 64 employees. There are five of us who work year around, and the rest of the staff are seasonal employees. Many of them have worked for us year after year. Some start at age 16, but we do have a job for a younger person. We have a job for a kid to recycle cans and bottles. We call him "Can Boy." When they get ready to transition to another position, we call him "Can Man" because it's like a promotion. It's a fun thing for us. We love the ability to work with young people, to see the kinds of attitudes they bring, and to help them develop to succeed.

My brother is the superintendent at Scott Lake, and he does a wonderful job. He's driven to do much with nothing, because that's where we came from. We learn how to be plumbers, electricians and janitors. We learn how to patch roofs when it's needed.

Our assistant superintendent has been with us 14 years. Our food and beverage Manager, my wife Nancy, has been with us for 33 years. My assistant, our director of golf, started with us as a cart boy. He worked for us through high school and college. He graduated from the University of Michigan as a chemical engineer. When he graduated, he took a position as a chemical engineer (*telephony*) consultant for a big company and traveled all over the world in that job. After five years, he decided he wanted to get back into the golf business. He was making six figures for a salary, but what was important to him wasn't being met. He didn't have a family, didn't have many friends, and he was never home. So he and I had a conversation about him coming to work for us at Scott Lake. I told him what we could pay him to start and what his position would be, and he was fine with it. He's been back with us for three years now. He has an incredible skill set. It's kind of funny, but I was at lunch lately with the owner and the golf pro of another course in our area. I asked the golf pro where he went to college, and he also went to the University of Michigan and graduated with a degree in chemical engineering. That's two chemical engineers who chose to work in the golf business!

The competition in our market is fierce. We have about 40 daily fee courses within a 30-mile radius of my facility. At one point it was the number-two market in terms of number of courses with the fewest number of golfers. Our area and

Michigan in general is overbuilt with golf courses. There are nearly 900 courses in Michigan. So we have had to find our edge. We've found in the golf business that you are not going to be 100 percent great every day. We've had long times of flooding rains, we've had times with 90-degree days where we've lost grass. How you overcome some of those obstacles has to be with the strength of your personality. Are you truly glad to see your guests? We have to work so hard during the season. We say to ourselves that we are so glad to see our customers come in the spring, but we are so glad to see them go in the late fall. We work so hard seven days a week, we're so intense, and we try so hard to not take anyone for granted.

You know, our motto is "Where Golf is Fun." When a guest first shows up, it's important that we recognize them with a greeting and ask who they are, who they are playing with, if they know where the range is, and that sort of thing. After that, it's pretty easy to make their golf fun. The golf course is fun to play. It's not overly long, and it has lots of topography changes. The course has lots of par-3 holes and we emphasize that because mathematically it increases their chances for a hole-in-one. Besides that, we have three 9-hole combinations that the guests can play. We have lots of special events such as the Great Golf Giveaway, where guests can participate as a first-time golfer at our course. We put a card in their cart, with prizes like a free round of golf or a bottle of water. The golfer fills out the card to give us information about themselves that we can use to promote the course and to get to know them better. In return, we give them gifts. We give away 140 gifts a month in that program. Our staff is particularly friendly and helpful. We continually ask our guests if there is anything we can help them with.

We take a keen interest in being hospitable. During the last big growth period for golf, I believe the industry made a change from being about hospitality to being about numbers. How many rounds a course generated in a year became the main goal, it seemed. It was all about numbers. How much are the greens fees, how many carts got rented, how many balls got sold? For me, the success of our business isn't about the pluses and minuses of the financial ledger; it's about having a customer tell us how much fun they had and that they can hardly wait to come back. That's how we should measure our success. That philosophy is how our motto, "Where Golf is Fun," started.

Throughout the season we have Friday scramble tournaments open to all golfers, another event we call the Scott Lake Tour, and a series of events for women called The Women's Charity Challenge. In these events, players of all skill or ability levels are encouraged to play, and we give prizes for not only winners but for random places in each event so that everyone has a chance to win.

We have gotten involved with so many different things in our community, and we try to be helpful where we can be. I've been on the board of the Michigan Golf Course Owners Association, and I was president of the association. I was president of the National Golf Course Owners Association from 1990-1991. I've been on our local Education Foundation board since 1987. We think it's important to be involved, not only with the golf community, but with our local community, as well. This isn't about business or building customer loyalty or new customers. For me, it's about adding depth to my character. At events like the Golf Industry Show, I try to come home with some good ideas, but I spend more of my time trying to help other owners. Just today I spent lots of time on the NGCOA listserv answering questions from other owners. I have enough experience in the business that I can help them. I want to project the point of view that we are in the hospitality business.

People come to us to get away from their problems, to get away from their families if they need to, or to be with their families if they need to. We have programs that are family-based. Families can play golf for next to nothing at Scott Lake. We really believe that golf is a family game, and we want to create the opportunities to back up that philosophy. Actually, we take some ideas from minor league baseball, which has had resurgence. They understand that it's about creating family entertainment for a few hours at an inexpensive price. We've seen the price of golf expand at a faster rate than the cost of living. I don't think that's been good for the game of golf. At

Scott Lake, kids under age 17 can play free golf after 4 p.m. on Saturdays, Sundays and holidays with a paid adult green fee. No carts are required and we encourage kids to walk the course.

Our "Afternoon Approach Family Golf Plan" developed because of our awareness of the time and money constraints on families and golf. One of our guests loved to play golf but couldn't find the time. He got home from work and there was always a list of chores. The wife had to take the kids to T-ball and handle all of her responsibilities. At one point, they all went to the driving range and had a great time. Then they went out to the course to play, and they all had a great time again. But they had trouble finding the time and the money to regularly play more golf. We decided that we could solve the money issue. We could provide families the opportunity to play golf for one dollar a day. In our season there are 66 Saturdays, Sundays and holidays, so we only charge $60 each for the year to play. So the father, mother and a child can play for the year for $180. Families can play all the golf they want on weekends and holidays. So the money issue should not be a big burden. Now the family just has the challenge of scheduling the time. We've had a very good response to this program. The program helps develop tomorrow's golfers, and it addresses one of the biggest challenges the golf industry faces: finding the time to play golf. It doesn't take any longer to play a round of golf today than it took 10 years ago. The problem is finding the time in your schedule to go to play. We think our program helps people create that schedule, just like they schedule a soccer game, T-ball, or other family activities.

In recent years, one of the most interesting things we have done is provide an adaptive golf cart for guests with physical disabilities. We aren't aware of another course in our area that has an adaptive cart. If we are going to have open golf, grow the number of players, and be hospitable, then how can we exclude that whole group of our citizens? We've seen people with physical limitations do things like hook wheelchairs behind golf carts, just so they can play. They just hang on with the strength of their arms, just for a chance to play golf. Because we are in an area with lots of medical facilities and rehabilitation centers, there are lots of city programs for people with disabilities. So we got connected with those programs, and now we help conduct clinics to help disabled people learn to play golf. We run a golf league for the disabled through one of the recreational centers. It's really cool! You can't help but have tears come to your eyes some days when you see not the struggle about the game but their smiles when they make a putt or hit a good shot.

This last year we had a young man come out, and he wanted to use our cart. John can't use his legs, and he's paralyzed on one side of his body. He comes out, gets on the cart, and we see he doesn't have any golf clubs. We asked him what he was going to do for clubs, and he tells us he has a "gizmo." Working with an inventor, they created a golf gun. It's like a potato gun. Put your ball in the gun, pump the air in, pull the trigger, and there's your shot. I thought this was a great idea. This would be fun if you didn't need it because of a disability. He's got a little portable compressor with him that's battery operated, he gets on the cart, and off he goes. The first time he played about five holes and then had to go. You learn that many disabled people have time constraints, places they have to go, or rides they have to catch. He came back a couple more times and we really started to get to know the young man. He let us try his gun. One time he said something to me that illustrates his love for the game. He said, "You know what? I can hardly wait to play golf with somebody who can really play. The people I've been playing with are just hacks!" I told John that he sounds just like most golfers I know. Most think their games are good enough to play with better golfers. I told him, "John, you're a golfer now." John drives 60 miles one way to play our course. It's just so fulfilling to be a part of that. All it took was providing a cart.

We had another guy come to the course last year who had lost the use of his legs. He came with his wife and his daughter, who was about 35 years old. They used the adaptive cart and played, but I didn't have a chance to talk with them that day. About a week later, I saw his daughter and asked how the golf had gone. She told me that I just didn't have any idea how good it had been. Her dad had been struggling with his leg problems for a couple of years, and she and her mother were very worried about his depression. She said, "Since playing golf, his whole life has changed and all he talks about is the next time we can go to play golf again. Now we know my dad is back with us." He plays at our course regularly now with his family and with business associates. His drive to the course is 22 miles one way. Golf is a big part of his life now. Having that cart has made it possible.

Honestly, I'm ashamed of our industry when we say we want everyone to play, but then very few spend the money to purchase an adaptive cart to make golf accessible to the disabled. I try to stay off that soapbox, but sometimes I just have to speak up about it.

I love to remember all the characters who have played at Scott Lake. You think you can categorize some of the guests, but then you get to know them and their unique life stories. That is really the beauty of our industry. You don't get to know customers by their golf game, you get to know them for who they are as people.

*(I asked Jeff about the most noteworthy successes he and his brother Paul have experienced.)*

I don't know if I would focus on any earth-shattering successes. We provide organized recreation that leads to small personal successes such as opening golf to our disabled guests, teaching women to play golf, or seeing a league operate well. We don't want to just take our golfers' money and send them off to the course and forget about them. We want to make sure they feel welcomed. We direct them to the starter on the first tee and tell them we'll see them at the turn *(after their first nine holes)*. We make a point of learning our guests' names. If you play our course three times, then we not only learn your name but the names of the people you typically play with.

Of course, there are milestones. When we upgraded our irrigation system, when we put in cart paths, when we made those kinds of step-by-step improvements, then we can look back with pride. The best part of all those improvements, though, is that we were always able to bring our customers with us. We have customers who have been playing with us for 35 years. Every improvement we make to our facility creates a sense of renewal for those customers. It's like we keep creating a new place for the guests.

*(Are there any noteworthy challenges that come to mind?)*

We had an underground fuel storage tank that we removed. It took about a quarter of a million dollars and three years for that process. Fortunately, the state of Michigan had an underground storage tank fund that was really beneficial in helping us pay for the removal. Even with that financial help, we were under the gun the whole time because it had to be cleaned up. Having that underground tank tied us up. We couldn't sell the golf course or mortgage the golf course with that problem unless we went to a nonprimary market. Because of the environmental threat, we were a subprime loan for our capital improvements that were needed. It cost us a little over $25,000 to do the cleanup, but all the while we had to pay subprime rates for loans. That was a challenge.

There was a time in 1984 or '85 where it rained from the 28th of August to the 15th of October. It was about 47 days of rain, and we were only open about 15 of those days. It was terrible, terrible weather. There were floods, and even the days we were open weren't good days. Sometimes we could only open nine holes. Because it was regional flooding, FEMA was there to provide some disaster loans and we could have borrowed some money, but we didn't. We just didn't know how we would survive as a business, but somehow we did. The fact that we could overcome those challenges made the experiences into successes. In business you always have to be prepared for things you know are coming, but you also have to be prepared for things you don't see coming. In business, there are no excuses anymore.

Now we believe there is another transition coming. I think we'll see shrinkage in the number of golf courses. I'm hoping we'll be able to weather this economic storm. I hope we have enough money set aside to stumble through, if that's what's going to happen. We need to upgrade some of our buildings to continue that sense of renewal that we have a reputation for . People who come to Scott Lake comment that there is always something new going on. That's what we have been doing for 35 years. It's normal for us. Some of our competition hasn't done a thing for their golf courses for the past 15 years, so we started to wonder if we were the exception with the changes we made. But my brother, our superintendent, doesn't want to just mow grass every day. Where's the satisfaction in that? When he's able to build a new tee box, renovate some golf holes, or change the way things look a bit, then that's exciting. There's fulfillment in change.

For us, we also need to consider what the secession plan is going to be. I'm 59 and my brother is 57. How long are we going to work? With the current economic situation, we wonder if we'll see a recovery in our lifetimes. Personally, I don't believe we will ever see an economic situation as good as what we have already seen. We used to see an alternative use for golf property as real estate for housing developments. Now we know where that option has gone, so we have to make the property profitable as a golf course. Part of the succession plan has to be how I can retire off the current business. These are important questions and they may not be answered by me. They may be answered by the marketplace. In my father's generation, I watched his friends work until they were 75 years old, or they worked until they died. I'm prepared to do that if I need to, because I'm in a great industry where people are having fun.

People always ask me what I do in the winter. They assume we must always go to Florida during winters. We spend almost the whole winter cleaning, planning, or doing whatever is necessary to get ready for the next season. It's surprising how much time that planning takes. We have to get budgets set, and that is always changing. Last year I thought our budget was on the money, except for a couple of issues I couldn't control. For example, with the cost of fuel I had estimated about a 25 percent increase, but it ended up costing us about 50 percent more. It was a huge impact on our budget. And then we had to deal with a Michigan minimum wage bill that was in excess of the federal government minimum wage. For the first year or so, we were able to make adjustments, but this last year, that minimum wage bill had a huge impact on us. In Michigan we are in our eighth year of the recession already. I blame five of those years on our current governor and legislative houses because they have not keyed on jobs. Jobs didn't seem like a big issue a year ago, but now all of a sudden it's the main issue. How are we going to get people back to work? Now Michigan is planning a new ergonomic standard for workers that will add an additional layer of costs for employers and an additional layer of bureaucracy to administer and enforce the program. How are we going to pay for that? If we are not ergonomically correct, then an employee can sue us. We'll see if that bill passes. Small businesses like ours are worried. But this gets us into some political issues that we can't solve.

For the industry as a whole, there are a number of golf course owners and operators that are not qualified in today's economy to successfully operate their golf courses. They just don't have the necessary skill sets to succeed. Many owners got into the business when business was really good. Now, when they are faced with dwindling players and dwindling revenues, they don't know what to do. The typical comment by someone saying they are not very busy is that they looked into their parking lot, and there aren't as many cars as they used to see. Their next conclusion is they need to lower their price. Now their parking lot might be busier, but they don't always consider what their pricing has done to their financials. Being busier doesn't always translate into higher income. Being busier with no additional revenue means those owners have incurred extra costs that may not show today. There will be extra wear and tear on the course, carts and equipment, and there may be additional costs for personnel to process more golfers, clean and maintain carts. These are all cost-creepers that have the wrong impact on financial statements. Too many owners and operators make quick decisions to impact customer traffic instead of considering their bottom line and what is needed to make the golf course profitable.

Besides this economic issue, reducing costs to the customer for golf encourages the customer to believe that previous costs were too high and they had been getting ripped off all along. Now the customer starts to think to themselves that they will never pay full price again. These customer perceptions are really important and need to be considered in making any pricing changes. I think it's better to convince the customer that they are getting quality and added value. The minute we start to charge less for the same services, we risk not only our financial status but also customer perceptions. I would bet that if you asked most golf course owners what their average cost is per golfer, what it costs them to put a golfer on the course, you would get lots of blank stares. Golf business has to be intelligent. On the other hand, when some of these less-skilled owners get out of the business, it will bring a new set of owners who I believe will be higher skilled. In the long term, it may be beneficial to the industry.

The business decisions are important, but for me, golf will always be fun. The real bottom line is that it's all about the people.

## Hoag's Lessons

- "Build your business by building your relationships with people."
- You work seven days a week, and there are always obstacles to your success. Still, you have to work hard to not take anyone for granted.
- Take your time to complete your vision. Hoag's 27-hole complex was built over a 40-year span.
- "I would tell anyone starting in their careers that continuing education is the key to their long-term success. It's not just about financial success, it's about how you feel about what you do. Too many people today are stuck with the direction they are going because they don't have the skill sets to change. My advice is to keep learning."
- "For me, the success of our business isn't about the pluses and minuses of the financial ledger; it's about having a customer tell us how much fun they had and that they can hardly wait to come back. That's how we should measure our success."
- "We think it's important to be involved, not only with the golf community, but with our local community, as well. This isn't about business or building customer loyalty or new customers. For me, it's about adding depth to my character."
- Golf is a family game. Create opportunities to back up that philosophy.
- If you are going to have open golf, grow the number of players and be hospitable, then don't exclude people with disabilities. Hoag provides an adaptive cart for people with disabilities and finds the rewards gratifying.
- "Every improvement we make to our facility creates a sense of renewal for customers. It's like we keep creating a new place for the guests."

- "In business, you always have to be prepared for things you know are coming, but you also have to be prepared for things you don't see coming. In business, there are no excuses anymore."

- "The minute we start to charge less for the same services, we risk not only our financial status but also customer perceptions."

- "Being busier doesn't always translate into higher income. Being busier with no additional revenue means those owners have incurred extra costs that may not show today. Too many owners and operators make quick decisions to impact customer traffic instead of considering their bottom line and what is needed to make the golf course profitable."

# North to Alaska

## Melinda and Roger Evans, Owners of North Star Golf Club in Fairbanks, Alaska

ᔕ ᘓ

*I met with Melinda and Roger Evans while attending the 2010 Golf Industry Show in San Diego. I interviewed Roger on February 10, 2010, at the Omni Hotel while Melinda visited exhibits. Roger is a civil engineer and Melinda is a physician.*

*North Star Golf Club is the northernmost USGA golf course in North America. The 18-hole links course is underlain by permafrost, creating an ever-changing pattern of dips and mounds reminiscent of the links courses of Scotland. North Star may be the only golf course that includes an animal checklist on the scorecard. The open grassy meadows attract hawks, owls, eagles, red fox, Sandhill cranes, lynx and moose. A local rule is that when a raven or fox steals a golf ball, a replacement may be dropped without penalty at the scene of the crime.*

www.northstargolf.com

ᔕ ᘓ

**Roger:** My father was a golfer. He grew up in Coronado, California, and planned to become a professional golfer. He tried to model Sam Snead, but then came Pearl Harbor, and he was at an age, like others at that time, where he got the call to serve in the war. He was asked if he would rather walk or fly, so he became a pilot in the Marines. After the war, he flew a new airplane for a flying service to Fairbanks. Once he got to Fairbanks he found there were lots of needs for pilots, so he stayed there. After a while he became a Cessna dealer. I was born and raised in Fairbanks and grew up around airplanes, but I also learned golf from my dad. Fairbanks had a nine-hole course built before I was born. Dwight Eisenhower played the course when he visited in the '50s. It was a bit crude and had sand greens, but we could go play. Dad was a really good golfer. He won the Alaska State Championship a couple of times in his 50s and 60s.

Even though I enjoyed golf, I was more involved with skiing, living in a place with ice and snow. After I got over being a traveling ski bum, I moved back to Fairbanks, got married, finished my degree in civil engineering, started raising kids, and I actually built a ski area. I found land that was owned by the local borough government. In the mid-'80s things in Alaska were not good. Oil was $10 a barrel, people were leaving, and the economy was poor. Since I was a guy who wanted to build something, the borough gave me a good deal and I bought the land for the ski area. At that time I was about 40 years old.

My parents divorced and later remarried in the late '60s. In the early '90s, my stepfather, another golfer, went to the same borough government that had repossessed some cleared land from a guy who couldn't afford to pay his taxes. Initially, he leased the land from the borough. My stepfather scratched out nine holes for a golf course on that leased land. To help get things going, he got some donated equipment and buildings. He was in his mid 70s, and the 14-hour days at the golf course were hard on him. I had been spending my summers helping him at the golf course, and I realized right away that this was pretty easy land to work with. There were no rocks, and there were long slopes that easily drained. The only problem with the land was that there was a lot of permafrost and every year the land would settle differently. When an area settles so much that it starts holding water, you have to either drain it or fill it. I developed a saying, "You know you have casual water problems when shore birds start moving into your fairways."

In the mid-'90s, my wife and I and two of my sisters, bought out my mother and her husband, and we kept going from there. When we decided to take over the land from my stepfather, I went to the borough government and told them that no one would loan money to improve the land while it's being leased. I told the borough that they should sell us the land. I talked them into selling us the land at the appraised price before my stepfather had made improvements. The economy wasn't so good at the time, and the borough sold us the 160 acres for $60,000. Then I was able to get financing for improvements if I needed to, and I knew we could always sell the land for residential development if we needed to.

We were committed to golf, and I built nine more holes and rebuilt most of the original greens. It's just dirt. You can shape it any way you want it. I didn't know a lot about golf course construction, but being a civil engineer, I did know a lot about earthwork. I joined the golf course superintendent's association and started taking all of their courses. I learned about the modern green from Dr. Michael Hurdzan. I learned about routing holes. I read every golf course architect who had ever written a book. Then I figured out which strategies would work best on our land. Some architects like lots of trees. I don't like trees that much. They're trouble for the golfer and for the grass. There were architects like Alister McKenzie and Tom Doak who were pretty minimalist, and that seemed right for me as I designed the course. I know how to run bulldozers and excavators and lots of heavy equipment, so I designed and built the course. I did all the green shaping and everything. In fact, *Golf Digest* came to the course, and one of their guys said that whoever drove the dozer on those back holes should be working for Jack Nicklaus. I told them I had just made it smooth, and then the permafrost did the rest. Most of the mounding and undulation was created by freezing and thawing in the permafrost.

If you were to classify our course, it would be "meadow/wetland." I have to say, it looks great. It looks like some famous landscape architect designed the vegetation. There are cattail clumps, fireweed, and lots of decorative vegetation. Of course, we keep the playing areas mowed, but we leave as much of the property as possible in its natural state. That's the short story.

On our scorecard, we have an animal-sighting checklist for the moose, bears, muskrats, eagles and all kinds of other wildlife. It's really rare to see lynx, but we have had guests see lynx. I've lived in Fairbanks for 60 years, and I've only seen lynx three times. The only animal that is rarer to see is the wolverine. I've seen two of them and one was while flying, which is cheating. Seeing animals from the air is much different from walking around and running into one. There's no reward for checking animals off the checklist. It's just for fun for the tourists, mostly. Luckily not too many bears have been seen. Moose are common and seen almost every day. In Alaska they are almost like wild cattle. If you walk toward them, they will get alarmed and go into the woods, but if you ignore them, they just hang around. If a golfer stays in a golf cart, the moose don't seem to get alarmed at all unless you drive toward them.

We have something else that you'll never see anywhere else that I know of. With climate change and global warming, one of the things that people worry about is the permafrost melting and releasing methane gas. That happens on our course. During really wet periods when the turf gets worked and muddy, it gets sealed and gases can't get through. Then a bubble will come up under the roots of the grass. You get a big hollow bubble of soggy grass. It took me a while to figure out what was going on, but one day I poked one of the bubbles with a tee and lit it with my Bic lighter, and it released a big flame. I started showing that little trick to our golfers, and now it's one of their favorite things. Anybody who finds a bubble will poke it and light it. I've never had one blow up. What clued me in was an old-timer who showed me something when I was a kid. Before the snow comes, you can walk out on the ice on the frozen ponds and see cone-shaped bubbles under the ice. You can poke the ice with a nail and light the gas, and it will just blow-torch as the water comes up the cone and finally spurts out of the ice, ending the flame. The methane gas trapped under the turf is the same thing. As the gas escapes, the turf bubble settles back down until it's over and the flame goes out.

The clubhouse was built from a recycled building. Back in the days when the pipeline was being built, a lot of modular buildings were brought to Alaska. There were a couple of those buildings near our airport, and my stepfather made a deal with the pipeline company to buy one of them. He was a master at getting people to help him, and he got some guys to take the building apart and then reassemble it at the golf course. We're still paying off some of those "lifetime passes." It was a building, but it was a real eyesore. It took me six or seven years of remodeling to make it look good and be functional. We put in plumbing, but we have to drain everything for the winter. Right now, in February, it's probably 20 degrees below zero inside the building. There is no point in heating it.

Our golf season is mid-May through the end of September. The snow melts away in April, but the ground is still frozen hard. It has to thaw down several feet because all of the water in the ground can't drain down because it's frozen so hard. The ground is just too spongy on top to work with it. Members can go out on the course before we open our regular greens in May and play to some temporary sand greens with flagsticks. They have to park outside the gate if we haven't opened yet, and they have to walk. Sometimes there will be 20 cars outside the gate in the spring. The golfers can't wait to get out there, and if it means rubber shoes and a flag out on the fairway, so be it.

The season may seem short, but it doesn't get dark from mid-May until the end of July. It doesn't get dark at all. During that season, we are open from six in the morning until two in the morning the next day. Then we close so people can go get some sleep and the grounds crew can get out on the course at 2 a.m. to do their work. When tourists come to Fairbanks they will typically ride on the sternwheeler riverboat, they'll pan for gold, go see the pipeline, go back to their hotel and have dinner. But then what? The sun is up and not making a move downward, just sideways. It might be 7 or 8 p.m. and they look for something else to do. Well, there's golf. They find us on the web. They'll take a taxi out to the course. Many of them want to tee off at midnight, just to say they have. We encourage them to try to get out around 10 PM so they can finish by 2 a.m. Most of the tourists are really unprepared, so we have a "visitor's special" that includes golf with a golf cart, some golf balls, rental clubs, a bottle of water, a logo ball, and a certificate that they played America's northernmost golf course. For 69 bucks, they usually think that's a pretty good deal.

I don't show up as early as the grounds crew, but I stay a lot later. I'm kind of the special projects guy. I need to rebuild at least one green every year. What happens is there are a lot of subterranean ice lenses. That ice thaws out because you've cleared, thereby removing the natural insulation from the land. Then the water drains away, and it leaves a void and the soil sinks. On the greens, that can create some dramatic contours. When it gets totally out of hand, we can hardly mow the green anymore. I don't want to just tear up the green in the middle of the summer, so I build a new green next to the existing one. Then it takes about a year to get the new green up and running. When the new green is in play, the original green just becomes part of the fairway.

Nobody in Alaska has been able to use bentgrass very successfully. Our choices for grass have been developed by trial and error. We have both pink and gray snow mold. It leaves a spider web of gray fungus on the grass after the snow melts. The mold thrives on wet and cold, and bentgrass is killed by it. Where the grass is killed by the mold, it doesn't come back, so you have to replant. Replanting takes weeks and weeks to grow in, and those parts of the course wouldn't be playable. Poa grass is considered a weed on a lot of greens. They do like it in California because it's quite playable, and after it's been growing for a long time, it turns from an annual into a perennial and stops creating so much seed. Basically it morphs into a very playable grass. There is actually a company that sells a poa annua product that is created from the best genetic examples of poa they can find. That's what we buy. It does OK in our climate. We have Kentucky bluegrass on the fairways, and it can get all blighted and white in the spring from the snow mold, but bluegrass comes back. After a couple of weeks, the bare spots in our fairways and on our greens caused by mold are green and growing again.

Also, in the winter we cover our greens with waterproof tarps. We do have to poke a hole in the tarps about every yard or so to let the methane escape. If we don't, the methane will kill the grass under the tarps. The first year we used the tarps, we didn't poke holes in them. When we pulled them off in the spring it smelled like a landfill, and there were dark, dark green areas. The next day all of those green areas were dead. With the holes, the gases can escape, and we don't have snow touching the grass and helping the snow mold. There is a lot of trial and error.

We're competing with a $10 million military golf course. They've started covering their greens in the winter, too, but I haven't been very good at sharing my secrets with them, nor have they ever asked. They haven't shared their 10 million with me, so I don't feel too guilty. Their course allows civilian players, but it's quite a bit easier to get onto our course. To play the military course, you have to get a security pass to get on the base, so we do have some advantages. To get a season pass to play the military course, you have to buy a three-way pass through the Fairbanks Golf Association that includes the old nine-hole course and our course. So we do get included in that way. Most military bases are built around airfields and have flat land. Their golf course is flat, too. Ours is much more unique because we are built on a slope and we have much more undulation. They have some advantages we don't have, though. They can start serving liquor at eight in the morning. We are in a borough that doesn't allow it until 10. As a result, they get a lot of outings that we don't. Lots of guys want to start drinking as soon as they start golfing. On the other hand, when they have an outing, their course is closed to others, including military personnel, and those golfers will come to play our course. Overall, we do quite well competing with the military course.

Only about 10-20 percent of our guests are actual tourists. Most of our players are local residents. Our weekday business is mostly after work hours because of the daylight. About half of our play is for nine-hole rounds. We have people who come out and play every day after work, even if it's only nine holes. The Fairbanks Golf Association set up the handicap system so that people can play the front nine on one day and the back nine another day and create an 18-hole handicap. We have Eskimos, Indians, miners, trappers, construction workers, businessmen, all kinds of people play the course. Some of our most avid customers are Koreans. They are nuts over golf. Just look at the percentage of Korean golfers on the LPGA.

My wife, Melinda is our businessperson. She set up our webpage and our Internet system for tee times. She does all of our buying for merchandise like shirts and balls. Also, we have a clubhouse manager. Actually, I wouldn't want to be the clubhouse manager. We have three shifts of employees each day during the summer because of the long hours we are open. The scheduling of employees is really complicated to allow staff some time off. We have about seven or eight people working as the grounds crew, compared to about 30 on the military base. In the clubhouse there are at least two people working at all times. So including part-time workers, we have about 20 employees for the three shifts.

The ski area is much simpler. That's only open three days a week. It takes two people to run the lodge, and some people to run the lifts. They aren't conventional lifts. They are transit buses. I built a road around the mountain all the way to the top. So I have skiing in the winter and golf in the summer. There is a brief season between skiing and golf, but that is really spent getting the golf course and clubhouse going for the summer, or vice versa.

Thinking back on my challenges, we just never had much money. I spent many years going to auctions down in Seattle looking for turf equipment. A lot of our equipment is surplus from the city of Seattle. For a while we were mowing our roughs on the course with a 42-inch mower. We'd mow for days and days and then start over. Getting the right equipment has really helped with our labor costs, and it gives you the time needed to make improvements. Getting geared up without a lot of money took us awhile. Getting that clubhouse renovated took lots of time. I've done a lot of carpentry, and one step at a time I did the roof, the kitchen, bathrooms, whatever was needed. Now it's a pretty nice clubhouse. When you're competing against a $10 million facility, you are never sure you'll be able to attract people away from it. So I've tried to pay as I've gone with construction projects and improvements. It's come around very well. The original nine-hole course was lucky to gross $50,000 a year, and now we do 10 times that. People really like the course. People who come out to play are amazed at how beautiful the property is. I just tell them that it's Mother Nature. They love the vegetation and the wildlife. We get a lot of predators because we have red-backed voles living in the deep grass between fairways. They attract the foxes, the eagles and the cranes. Lots of wildlife are after the voles. In Alaska, dry grassland is rare, unless it's high altitude and then it's tundra. Usually if it's dry land then trees take over. Grassy fields attract moose and other wildlife, and it's good for us.

We used to lose thousands of golf balls on our driving range, so I designed a driving range net. In Alaska you can't just plant a pole and expect it to say there. It will either tip over or jack out with the frost-heave every year. The oil companies use lots of heavy-duty drilling pipes to drill 10,000 feet deep looking for oil. When they're done with the pipes, they surplus them. I found a company in Fairbanks that will drive those pipes down into the permafrost so that they are permanently frozen. They won't jack out or tip over. I bought some of the poles and had them planted for the driving-range netting. Most of the poles are driven 20 feet, but a few had to go 30 feet to get the necessary resistance. They were left a foot above grade. Then I surveyed and calculated the necessary heights of the welded-on poles to create a perfectly straight grade across the tops of the poles. Remember, I am a civil engineer. It looks great. Now we don't lose too many golf balls. I love those kinds of challenges.

I went to college at the University of Alaska in Fairbanks. They have an excellent engineering school. Living in a place that has a 150 degree range in temperature, the engineering degree is really pertinent. Very few materials remain unchanged in this climate. Growing up in Alaska is like growing up on a ranch or a farm. You learn to do a little bit of everything. I may not be an expert at many things, but I'm good enough at most things. If I don't know how to do something, luckily I can read and I can figure it out. In my 20s I really wasn't aware of how valuable my education was. People with a sound education may not even pursue the field they studied, but the foundations enable them to go in so many different directions. That seems particularly true in science and math. Our older daughter is a veterinarian who is in Norway on a Fulbright Scholarship. Now she's helping Norway with their wolf studies. She can do anything she puts her mind to. Our younger daughter is just graduating from college this year. She wants to pursue medicine. My wife, Melinda, is a physician.

I love coming to these trade shows to see all the new equipment. I used to go to the classes on turf science, but now I mostly like to see the new equipment for groundskeeping. I can't afford it, but sometimes I will copy what I see at the shows. I just go home and make what I've seen at the shows for a lot less money. In fact, I've always been a designer and an inventor. I invented the snorkel stove (www.snorkel.com)

for my wilderness cabin north of Talkeetna, because I had lots of wood and water and wanted a hot tub out there. It's the only thing I've invented that I ever patented. Most of my inventions I just use. The snorkel stove is a wood-burning hot tub heater, made out of aluminum, that's actually submerged in the hot tub. I sold that company in about 1984, and there are about 50,000 in use now. I like to think that if 20 people have used each hot tub, then I've made a million people happy.

In Fairbanks, the biggest growth in golf is with women golfers. To respond to that growth, for the last three years our pro has been a woman in the LPGA. There hasn't been much of a golf culture for women. They may have had a dad who taught them, but otherwise most women are really beginners. They can be intimidated by golf. Playing with guys who can smash the ball over 200 yards when they are just trying to hit the ball isn't that much fun for them. The LPGA pro and a ladies' league create an environment where they can struggle to play well but still enjoy it.

People don't come to Alaska for the golf. Our economy is pretty good, and people come because they can make some money, or they come to see what Alaska is all about. Once they are here, we can offer them golf. Over time I was able to buy some parcels of land around our golf course. That's enabled us to keep houses away from the course and keep it as natural as possible for the golfers and the wildlife. It's really nice. I feel lucky to be able to spend my summers working in such a beautiful environment.

## Evans' Lessons

- "You know you have casual water problems when shore birds start moving into your fairways."
- Building a golf course usually means shaping or moving dirt. It's just dirt. Allowing nature to take its course in parts of the course that are not in play creates beauty.
- If you have the skills and the ambition, do it yourself.
- There are many ways people can have fun on a golf course. At North Star the golfers can tee off at midnight during the summer, keep track of the wildlife on a score card, poke holes in the methane bubbles under the turf, and light the escaping gas to create a torch.
- Getting the right equipment for golf course maintenance really helps with labor costs, and it gives you time needed to make improvements.
- Embrace the challenges of innovation.
- People with a sound education may not even pursue the field they studied, but the foundations enable them to go in so many different directions.
- "I love coming to trade shows to see all the new equipment. I can't afford it, but sometimes I will copy what I see at the shows. I just go home and make what I've seen at the shows for a lot less money."
- North Star has an LPGA pro and a ladies' league to create an environment where women might struggle to play well but still enjoy it.
- Count your blessings. On a golf course, you get to work in a beautiful environment.

# Italian Stallion

Frank Romano, Owner of Scenic View Country Club in Slinger, Wisconsin, Blackstone Creek Golf Club in Germantown, Wisconsin, and Fire Ridge Golf Club in Grafton, Wisconsin

ᘓ  ᘔ

*I interviewed Frank Romano at the 2010 Golf Industry Show in San Diego on February 10, 2010. I had met Frank on several previous occasions.*

*Scenic View Country Club has been owned and operated by the Romano family since 1978. The first nine holes were built in 1959, and the second nine added in 1961. The public course includes banquet and meeting rooms, three bars, a sandwich grill, golf shop, driving range and full-service locker rooms.*

www.scenicviewcc.com

*Fire Ridge Golf Club, built in 1994, formerly the Country Club of Wisconsin, was purchased by Frank Romano in 2003. The course has hosted many amateur and professional events and has received numerous awards, including being nominated "Best New Public Course" in 1995 by* Golf Digest. *The course was awarded a four-star rating from* Golf Digest *"Places to Play" in 2000-2007. Fire Ridge is an International Audubon Sanctuary golf course. Since 2002 it has been the Monday qualifying site for the PGA Tour's U.S. Bank Championship.*

www.fireridgegc.com

*Blackstone Creek Golf Club, built in 1974, is an 18-hole public facility. It is a traditional parkland course with mature trees lining most fairways. The Menomonee River runs diagonally through the course. An additional nine-hole course at Blackstone Creek was sold for conversion into condominium and commercial space after purchase by Frank Romano in 2006.*

www.blackstonecreekgc.com

ᘓ  ᘔ

When I was a kid, my dad was superintendent of schools in Germantown, Wisconsin. He was in his 40s and had been superintendent for about 10 years. Ironically, he had supported a referendum to add some elementary schools that got voted down pretty hard. He was sulking about the outcome because he had put so much time and effort into it. One Sunday morning in 1978, he picked up a newspaper with a classified ad that said, "Golf Course for Sale." At that time I think he felt his next career move would be as a school superintendent to a major urban district, which would have a lot of political headaches. He thought the golf business might be better than what he had been doing, so he cashed in his retirement and bought Scenic View Country Club in Slinger, Wisconsin. I was about 12 years old at the time.

Dad was undercapitalized and overchallenged. Not knowing much about it, he overpaid for the property. When I was 12, I started working to help him in any way I could. Originally I worked on the maintenance crew during the summers and washed dishes in the restaurant in the winters. I did that all through high school, and by my senior year my title was superintendent of the grounds. My parents had both worked on their Ph.D.s and education was important for them. As I was growing up, they made it clear that I couldn't work for them without an education. It took me a couple years to figure out where I wanted to go and what I wanted to study. In the meantime, I traveled when I was 18 and 19. I lived in California for a couple years and worked at the golf course during summers. Eventually I settled on the University of Oklahoma. I was interested in marketing and journalism. I got an aviation minor, so I was doing some flying, but I always worked for them during summers.

The year I graduated from the University of Oklahoma, the school's golf team had just won a national championship. The university owned a golf course, but, believe it or not, their golf course didn't have any irrigation. Can you imagine a golf course with 100-degree summers that didn't have any irrigation other than for the greens? The people who ran the course wanted somebody to come in and sign a 20-year lease to make the improvements they wanted. I worked really hard at getting that lease. I had kind of an inside track, being a recent graduate and having a golf course background. I put the whole proposal together and went to many meetings and presentations of my proposal. It was to be a one-dollar-a-year lease for 20 years, with the condition that all of their improvements had to be made. The improvements included a clubhouse addition, rebuilding holes, and installing irrigation. Back at Scenic View in Wisconsin, we had been doing the same kinds of improvements, so I had the numbers for irrigation systems and other costs. I had real-world bids for Scenic View, and the university had academia bids. Their irrigation bids were three times what we were paying at Scenic View in the private market. So when I put the proposal together for the university, it looked like a very attractive deal to them. We could get everything they wanted done for a lot less money than what they thought it would cost. The deal-breaker was that they had given lifetime free memberships to the golf course for all retired faculty (*imagine the irony for me, a recently retired faculty member always hoping for some subsidy for my golf addiction*). When we put our organizational plan and fee structure together to present our proposal, the retired faculty turned out in droves, carrying signs saying, "Don't take our golf course away!" Eventually the university regrouped and got 18 sponsors to underwrite each hole, and they rebuilt their golf facility without me.

Of course I was disappointed, and I went home licking my wounds. My parents' course was really getting busy by that time, in the peak of golf in the '90s. What we saw was that the World War II generation was playing a lot of golf at our property, and the baby-boomers were starting to play a lot. Bill Clinton was making it fashionable to play golf and smoke cigars on the course. He was playing golf with Greg Norman, and golf was getting lots of attention. A little bit later Tiger Woods came along, and all of a sudden, everybody was playing golf. My parents were getting a little older and Dad didn't want to continue to deal with all the headaches, so I got involved at Scenic View as general manager and did the marketing for the course. My older brother was our golf professional. He had played at Pepperdine University and for a while on the professional mini-tours. He and I got together and worked hard on building up the business during the summers.

In the mid-'90s I also got involved drilling oil wells and putting drilling projects together during the winters. I had an office in Dallas through some family connections. So I was putting together oil deals in the winters and working the golf course during summers. My job was as a promoter putting together wildcat deals with 20 or 30 investors to go drill wells in Nevada and Texas. It was kind of funny because golf was really booming, and I was putting together oil deals when oil was only $23 or $24 a barrel. I remember meeting with investors and telling them that if we could get to $25 a barrel, then we were going to have a pretty good deal. Since golf was booming, I chose to dive into golf instead of oil. By 2007 oil was up to $140 a barrel, and there weren't enough golfers on the golf course. You never really know how those things will work out.

At Scenic View we had one of the more inferior layouts in Washington County *(just outside Milwaukee)*. We knew we couldn't change the property overnight, so we decided to make it the best-conditioned property we could and raise our customer service to be better than anybody else. We tried to outdo our competitors by being as attentive as possible to our guests. We had a full-time restaurant at the time. Now we have an all-out banquet facility that can seat 300 guests. Our strategies worked out really well for us, and as business grew, my brother started up another company of ATM machines and financial services. At the golf course, we had a good market share and good retention of our loyal golfers.

In 2002 I decided to take a bit of a break from full-time management at the course. I hired a golf pro away from a nearby club with 45 holes. That year I was in Dallas for the Christmas holidays, and I was reading the December 23rd *Milwaukee Journal Sentinel* online and I saw an article about the Country Club of Wisconsin going through foreclosure. The foreclosure auction was December 23rd, and no one had bid on the course, so the lender bought it back. I remember wondering why they would hold the auction on December 23rd when no one would be prepared; people would be off on holiday. It seemed to me that they were trying to close a deal by the end of the year. The capital company that bought back the course was a Japanese firm that just happened to have their office in Dallas. So I went down and banged on their door on December 24th. Of course, everybody was gone for the holidays, so I went back to their office on the 26th. I talked with one of their people, who didn't even know what property I was talking about in Wisconsin. Then I had the NGCOA (National Golf Course Owners Association) fax them a letter of introduction for me to the president of their U.S. office. He called me back the next day and invited me in to talk about their property. He told me the gross revenues at Country Club of Wisconsin had dropped by 50% from 1994 or 1995 to 2002. That was in less than a 10-year period. I told him that I thought one reason might be because of competition from a new Arnold Palmer course, The Bog, which had recently opened around the corner from Country Club of Wisconsin. I knew that was part of the case, but not likely all of it.

At that time, the Japanese finance company had just taken back a group of courses from Pennsylvania and the upper East Coast. There had been a couple hedge-fund guys from Harvard who had the idea that they would buy golf courses when they were declining in value. They kept buying more and more courses with their hedge-fund money, and the Japanese company had underwritten all of those courses. So, at the time I was there to discuss the Country Club of Wisconsin, the whole portfolio of the East Coast companies had just come back to the underwriter. I was talking about buying the Wisconsin course, and they tried to make a deal for me to take over all of those other courses, too. They were willing to finance all of them for me. I would put in the sweat equity, and they would put in the money. Their terms were way above market rate; they wanted a 12 percent return on their money. It wasn't a good deal for me, so I declined. However, we ended up putting a quick theoretical deal together for the Country Club of Wisconsin before the end of the year. We tried to fast-track a closing, but we ended up closing the deal for the Country Club of Wisconsin in May 2003.

As I was closing on the Country Club of Wisconsin, I held some events at Scenic View, and I asked some of our regulars and members what their impressions were of CCW. The consensus that I got on the west side of Milwaukee was that in order to play CCW, you had to be a member of the Milwaukee

Athletic Club or CCW. They thought the course was private and the only way to play there was as a guest. Even though I liked the power name, Country Club of Wisconsin, I knew there would be problems marketing the course because of the private club misperception. We had to rename the course. I wanted an aggressive name, so we named the course Fire Ridge Golf Club after witnessing a beautiful winter sunset from the patio at the course. Changing the name helped us get off to a good start. People in the general Milwaukee market now knew it was a public course they could play.

The other thing we did to get off to a good start was open a good restaurant. Fire Ridge is 17 miles north of downtown, and I thought a good restaurant would help to tap into the white-collar market. I was worried about doing food and beverage on my own at that time. There was low unemployment, and I knew it would be hard to hire good people. Also, just for my sanity, I wanted to bring in somebody else to help. We convinced some friends of ours who had three restaurants in the city to open a restaurant at Fire Ridge. One of their well-branded restaurants was Flannery's, an upscale Irish pub. They fed a lot of the white-collar lunch clientele in the city. I thought that if I could connect with that lunch crowd at Fire Ridge through the quality of food and invitations to the course for outings, it could work well for me. In order to make a committed arrangement with the restaurant owners, we put together an equity deal to create a partnership between Fire Ridge and the restaurant. So we opened a Flannery's Restaurant at the course. The restaurant is open year around. It works really well for us because we tap into their very large clientele from Christmas parties and other events they do for people downtown. That helps us sell events at the course, as well. We were very successful capturing the downtown market we were after.

At Fire Ridge, not exactly by design, we ended up at a successful golf price point in a location that doesn't have a lot of competitors north of Milwaukee. We see our competitors as the more expensive Brown Deer Golf Course and The Bog. We had wanted to price ourselves in the $50-$60 market, and we don't really have any competitors in that price range in the huge population base on the north shore. If you go west of

Milwaukee, there are a lot of golf courses in our price range, but not where we are. Really, from Kohler south to Milwaukee, we have a very good market. When the Kohler property at Whistling Straits hosted the 2004 PGA Championship, we got a lot of traffic on our course, and that has helped us a lot, too.

I quickly brought the gentleman, Troy Schmidt, I had previously hired to be general manager at Scenic View to be the head pro at Fire Ridge. After a while he was having some frustrations, so I invited him to go play golf with me at another location. I was going to be his sounding board, just to let him express some of his frustrations. So we went to the course where I had learned how to play golf in Germantown, where my dad had been superintendent of schools and my pro was a resident. It's a bedroom community for the city of Milwaukee. It was a 27-hole course, right in the middle of town. While we were there, we talked quite a bit with the owner of the course, whom I have known since I was a little kid. When Troy and I left the course, I asked him if that owner had been trying to sell me his golf course, or trying to paint a picture of why I should buy the course. Troy said that was exactly his impression. The other owner had been talking about selling the course, without saying it exactly. At that time, we were in the top of the real estate bubble. He had 27 holes on 275 acres in the middle of a highly developed area. A lot of his course acreage was buildable. The owner didn't know what his exit strategy was going to be, even though he knew he had a desirable, valuable property. It was going to be complicated for him. He would need a rezoning process to turn golf into real estate. That was the end of the golf season in 2004, and the owner soon packed up to go to Miami where he spent his winters.

One of Troy's goals was to own his own property. It made sense to me to put Troy on the ground there, and give him some sweat-equity, so that he could be one of the best golf course operators and partners I know. So Troy and I jumped on a plane, flew down to Florida, pounded on the owner's door and said, "Let's make a deal." It was crazy. The owner said he wanted $10 million for his property. I asked him to give us an option, to give a year to look at the deal and kick the tires. The golf course had been extremely neglected. They were maintaining 27 holes with a maintenance crew of about five or six people. They hadn't recapitalized on a lot of their equipment. Lots of issues needed attention. The owner's interests were going elsewhere.

Troy and I got a sense of what we needed to do to bring the property up to speed. I had signed that option for 10 million when I was thinking that it was worth only one million on a good day. Troy and I talked about what parts of the property were buildable and what parts were best for golf. The original 18 holes had been one of the first championship designs in the Milwaukee area. In the '70s and '80s, it was a go-to place for experienced golfers. They had hosted lots of tournaments and outings and had been very popular. Another nine holes had been added in the early '90s, and we thought that had kind of chopped up the original course. We came to the conclusion that those last nine holes were buildable for real estate. We decided to separate those 60 acres.

The other component in our plan had to do with the clubhouse that sat on Mequon Road. It's a busy main street in town with strip malls. Ten thousand cars a day were on that road. The 275-acre golf course had this huge frontage on Mequon Road. As we did our due diligence to buy the property, we realized that land on Mequon Road was selling for about $300,000 an acre. So we decided to split off 10 acres where the clubhouse was located for real estate. It's right at a major intersection and was a desirable piece of property. Those 10 acres and the additional 60 acres divided off for development would still leave us with the original 18-hole golf course. As we were making these plans, we realized the owner knew the real value of his property during that boom in real estate.

For the 60 acres, we worked up that we could get four condo units per acre approved. The plan was for 60 or 70 condo units on that land. It was going to be oriented to empty nesters, right on the golf course. The 10 acres looked like it would hold about seven different retail buildings with a couple hundred thousand square feet of space and parking. Then we were going to build a new clubhouse as an anchor to the retail space. The first hurdle was to get the property rezoned. It was zoned for mixed-use recreational and some residential. We put the plan together to present to the village board. In the meantime, we hadn't yet closed on the property. We still had the option but hadn't closed, so we knew it would be a leap of faith by the board to let us go public with 180 acres of golf, 60 acres of housing and 10 acres of commercial retail. However, their incentive was that the village tax base would go from about $60,000 a year up to a couple million dollars a year. There was a lot of economic incentive to do it, but there was also a lot of political push back the other way. Some people didn't want to see the land redeveloped. They didn't want to see roof tops and that sort of thing. We worked hard at getting the proposal through the local planning commission. At the public hearing we were fortunate that a lot of my customers from my other two golf clubs turned out. We must have had several hundred people show up. Usually you might get 10 people for a hearing like that. In fact, there were so many people who showed up that the board didn't want to start the meeting. They stayed in the back room trying to get a sense of why so many had shown up. When they finally opened the meeting to speakers, one guy spoke in favor of redevelopment and the next guy spoke against it. When the third speaker spoke in favor of the proposal, my brother, who was in the audience, started to clap. The next thing we knew, about a hundred people started to clap in support. Then the board members realized that the huge crowd was there to support us and our approval became a rubber stamp. We had walked into the meeting without enough votes to make it happen, and before we knew it we had a nine-to-nothing vote of support.

In August 2006 we closed on the course. Then we sold those two development portions to a real estate developer at a negotiated price of about $2 million less than we originally wanted. However, we sold those two pieces for about the price we had paid for the entire 275-acre property. We knew we had to reestablish the reputation of the course. Our plan was to have at least one worker for every hole so that they would be highly visible and build confidence in our customers about changes we were making. We had about 22 employees out on the course in light-colored shirts, trimming trees, cleaning up the riverbed for the river that runs through the course, placing rocks and that sort of thing. So we made a splash in 2007 with the golf community. They were impressed with our effort, and we have had a steady incline in golf participation and revenue. It's become a really good performer for us. Even with the economic decline in 2008, we had an uptick in revenue into 2009. Even people who had been laid off at their work were buying memberships.

I have come to realize that in the golf business, what you are doing is competing for people's time and entertainment dollars. Once you realize that, it helps you develop programs to meet those needs. I see our biggest competitor is people's time, not the golf course down the street. In the Milwaukee market, the Milwaukee Brewers baseball team has been playing really well for the last couple years. They've been doing three million in attendance. I see them as a competitor of ours because they get people's time and entertainment dollars instead of golf. In a down economy, people travel less, have less destination golf, and play more golf locally. We've seen a big uptick in customers in the building trades. Four or five years ago they didn't have enough time to play because they were so busy. Now they have the time to golf. If we keep a reasonable price-point and they feel they get value for their money, then it works out for us.

The terrorist's attack on 9/11 was a gamechanger for the economy and for golf. In the late '90s, Wall Street made money easy to attain for golf operations or any business growth. At that time, when I walked around a show like the Golf Industry Show, I had financial people grabbing me by the arm to ask if I wanted some extra money for golf operations or new acquisitions. I remember one conference in Monterey, California, when Mercedes Credit was there, and they were giving away a new Mercedes sedan if you borrowed money from them for golf operations. "Sign up today, and you can drive this new Mercedes home." What happened was that a lot of golf properties got built. Then as we moved into the 2000s, we lost the World War II generation because physically most of them couldn't play anymore. Then we hit that 2001 recession, and the baby boomers were getting downsized at their work. Their home entertainment budgets got trimmed, and their expense accounts disappeared. There was a surplus of golf properties and fewer and fewer golfers. From 2001 through our current recession we have had a reshuffling because of too many courses and too few golfers. The supply-and-demand curve got turned on its head. I think many operators are beginning to get that sorted out. They are figuring out what their business model needs to be to survive, what their market share should really be, and who they really are. We had done that with our original property at Scenic View when we knew we had a large blue collar clientele and we focused on golf outings and events for company employees. At Fire Ridge we focused on golf outings for people's clients, who were mostly white collar. We targeted marketing efforts differently for the two courses.

For Scenic View, if we thought the employer wasn't going to pay for outings and the company employees might just throw their money into a hat to share expenses, then we would go to their human resources departments to recruit outings. We'd tell them that we would set up an outing for them at a good price, create online registrations for golfers at their events, and do everything we could to make it convenient for the company. We didn't want to wait for them to call us; we called on them to invite them to the kind of entertainment we provide. We wanted to help them make the decision to come to our course and that's worked for us.

At Fire Ridge, we started to see a real drying up of corporate dollars. Originally we had big companies like pharmaceutical companies bring doctors out to play and drop a lot of dollars for their entertainment. But we have lost a lot of that market share. Company credit cards aren't available. So we retooled our approach from the corporate business and went back to focus on the walk-in, daily fee customers. We got a lot of the private golf club customers who didn't want to spend their money to maintain relatively expensive private club memberships, but who still wanted a quality golf experience. We softened the price-point just a little bit to increase volume of business. The approaches have been working.

At Germantown, we're still working on the right strategy. We're thinking that because the course is in town, we want to create in-town loyalty and encourage walk-in play, become a place to host weddings and group events. When we make these kinds of plans, I obviously get to make the decisions, but to do it right you need to take input from all levels. For instance, the starter on the first tee box has more information than anybody. I need for him to pass on all the input he gets from players. Same thing goes for the guy behind the desk who checks people in. Are the guests telling him that $75 is pushing the market, or are they tossing their credit card down without any concerns? His input is important. I like to get on the phone and talk to my customers myself, particularly the big event customers. I like to carve out a little time every week to make those calls to find out what they liked and didn't like. Just the other day, I had a regional training meeting that we hosted at Scenic View. Afterward I called the guy that presented at the meeting, and he told me our easel is a piece of junk. That costs too little to not make the improvement immediately. Those phone calls give me lots of information for my decisions.

We use a marketing company that surveys golfers in our area. Scenic View is always rated the highest of our three courses, and it has the weakest layout of the three. This past year, out of several hundred golf courses in Wisconsin, we ranked number one in having our guests recommend the course to somebody else. I think that's because we delivered up to their expectations. It may not be the greatest golf course in the world, but the combination of the right price-point for greens fees, the culture that we have established with our employees in providing good customer service, and the product we deliver have hit the right notes with our customers. We haven't gotten it quite so right at the other two courses yet. When you walk into a higher-end course, your expectations tend to be that much higher. Meeting expectations is important. I'm proud that building our businesses around the principle of exceeding guests' expectations at a price they think is fair is successful for us. If customers leave feeling satisfied, they will tell somebody else.

Even though my education was in journalism, I love business. Thankfully, my degree program was very interdepartmental. It allowed me to go into other schools at the university and take courses. I took courses in political science, creative writing, art, including video and broadcast technologies. I got exposure to a lot of disciplines. I had somebody tell me recently that I have "shiny object syndrome." I belong to a group of CEOs who get together monthly to talk about their businesses, what problems they have, what solutions are working. It's designed to be a peer group, so you can discuss your issues with somebody in a similar position. The only reason I got into the group is because I host them at one of my clubs, and probably because I talk a lot. Most of these guys are running $100 million companies, so I'm just a little teeny guy in there. It feels like I'm getting an MBA being with these guys.

One of my advisors in the group told me he thinks I fail my way to success and I have "shiny object syndrome." I had been telling him about a guy I met on a skiing trip who is a global representative for a precast concrete company. That company had created precast concrete houses that can be erected in one week for a cost of $60,000. The houses are hurricane proof, somewhat earthquake proof, and even flood proof when located at an elevation. They had been building these houses in Barbados, and when Hurricane Katrina hit New Orleans, he got involved with trying to get contracts to build his homes in the Gulf states. There was actually about $40,000 in recovery money to replace each house that had been lost in the hurricane. For political reasons he didn't get the contract, and the houses are mostly rebuilt from wood. But then he told me that China had just added a new building specification that is ideal for precast concrete houses. This national building code created a huge new market for this guy's concrete houses. Anyway, I got all excited about the precast concrete business and how to put together a capital group to fund construction. When I told this story to my monthly business group advisor he told me I have this "shiny object syndrome." He said, "If somebody puts something in front of you, you get so distracted. Focus on golf." I guess he's right. I jumped all over in college, did the oil thing, and so on.

I think it's easy in golf. Imagine yourself at a golf course all day. We have the three courses doing about 100,000 rounds a year. That's 100,000 people passing through the door who have interesting stories and have 100,000 different things to say. If you're inquisitive and you like to talk, not only do you end up getting a great seat at a restaurant because you know so many people, but you get new business ideas. I listen to our guests talking about what they are trying to accomplish, and I then consider how I can use my golf property to help them. If the guest is trying to get their sales managers more motivated, then I want to arrange a solution on the golf course. Bring those sales managers to play nine holes of golf. It won't take that much time, and then they can have space in the clubhouse afterward to do some cheerleading and get them fired up again. One of the best examples of this was with Club Car, who went around their plant to find out how many employees were playing golf. The answer was very, very few. They are making golf carts and not playing golf. It didn't make sense. So they integrated themselves with a local golf property, got some golf lessons arranged for employees, put up some putting greens around their plant, and got more integrated with golf.

Our course in Germantown is right next to an industrial park, and there are plants all over. So I went into these plants to explain how golf could help them with employee relations. At first they didn't really see the value of what I was talking about, so I started taking a DVD that Club Car had done to show how recreational golf helped their employee relations. Just 10 minutes with the DVD started making my point. The light bulbs went on, and they saw how they could use golf to improve morale or whatever.

When there are problems with employees, it's not usually about wages. It's more likely to have something to do with work conditions, their work environment and culture. Some time at the golf course can help. I call it my "golden handcuffs." Get those guys away from work for some fun with each other. Almost all local golf courses can create these kinds of opportunities. Of course, the people operating a golf course have to be aggressive enough and figure out how their golf product can be of benefit to other businesses. Just simple things like moving the tee boxes forward in the evening can create a par-3 tournament. Or even a putting contest can create a fun getaway. These kinds of things don't take much time but can help reshape a work culture. And guess what? We sell food and drinks during and after the golf. Sometimes we'll get a band and have a bit of entertainment, too. Now, all of a sudden, we've created a night out for your employees. Friday nights can be slow on a golf course, so that's when I try to arrange the business outings. Now I fill those tee times.

For all three courses, I employ about 150 people during the summers. Each course has a head superintendent, a general manager, a director of golf, a mechanic and a banquet manager on annual contracts. I am passionate that the golf clubs are built on their personnel. Every customer's experience at the course is based on their interaction with somebody who works at the course. I would like nothing more than to have good people with me for years and years. We pay 100 percent of the insurance, including dental. We have a 401K program that we fund to the maximum that we can. When I get to budget crunches, I look everywhere I can to save money without hurting employee benefits. Those benefits create employees who have pride in what they do and they promote our businesses. I try to be as honest as possible with my staff. I let them know just how much the company is making and just how much I am making and it adds to their trust and commitment. I want them to know how much revenue their area took in and how much their expenses have been. When they understand that, it enhances their sense of purpose, and they respond in their roles. They know I'm not some magic man that works miracles. They know that their performance really matters, and they learn to enjoy the challenges. I've even had staff volunteer to take temporary layoffs during downtimes to help with the bottom line. I don't like to do it, but it shows their sense of responsibility and awareness.

Take, for example, the hot-button issue of healthcare. We have a fairly youthful group and they're not hugely expensive, but I've never asked the employees to make any contribution to their health insurance. That act alone has built so much loyalty and respect from them. If I look at the whole balance sheet for the businesses and I need to cut somewhere, I might cut a bit off the advertising budget or cut back on the number of cell phones to save on costs, but I won't touch benefits to employees. I think the employee benefits pay longer-term dividends.

My day-to-day involvement at the three courses is always changing. If I start running around from course to course, I miss what I like to do, like pulling a pro shop shift and getting deeper into what goes on at a specific course. I do visit with the managers to encourage them and help solve problems they might have. Sometimes it feels scary. Originally I was doing everything. I was the superintendent or the general manager and running around working crazy 100-hour weeks. Now it's at the point where on some days I have trouble finding something important to do at one of the clubs. It doesn't feel right to me yet to be going home early on a Saturday, because there must be something I should be doing. I guess it's a testament to my staff. And, like I said before, the more honest I am with my staff, the more I feel like they have my back.

Looking ahead, I think one of my futures in the daily-fee market is to build a regional group that can share expenses and outperform the competitors. In the golf industry, a lot of consolidators, such as American Golf Corporation *(operates more than 110 courses in 30 states)* and Club Corp *(operates over 100 courses around the world),* have looked at the country or the world as a whole. I've seen them try to compete across markets and make some miscues on their big scales. I think the local market is a little different. I looked at a property in Oshkosh where the original owner is a friend of mine. He sold the property to a New York City-based firm. He thought the new owner didn't have a good understanding of what they were doing. They brought in a general manager from Texas, and the first thing he said was he didn't understand all the nine-hole rounds that were being played, that golf is an 18-hole sport. So he cut off all their golf leagues. It was a small community course that thrived on local bowlers and the local golf leagues. With the new owner and operator, their revenue dropped 50 percent in the first year or two. The original owner thought I should buy that course from the New York owner and then return it to what it had been, because I understand that market. I've seen this kind of problem with some of the larger multicourse owners who specialize in member-only Sunbelt private clubs. I don't think you can roll into the Midwest and use that profile. Price-point and location are important, and one general strategy just won't work everywhere.

What I want to do is look at the market that I know, Milwaukee and Wisconsin, and focus on that market by building the best team that I can. In putting the numbers together, it looks like if you go over five courses in a given market I see savings and ways to outperform the competition. For example, if I've got that much inventory to sell in a given market, rather than having somebody contracting golf outings at individual courses, maybe only on a part-time basis while they are managing the course and involved in day-to-day responsibilities, I would rather go get a "rock star" who really understands sales and have them sell all my events across courses. Then that sales specialist, who is expert at selling, up-selling and recruiting, can hand off the execution of the events to the people at the individual property level. For me, I can take the expense of staffing that specialist and really divide it five ways or more across courses, and it starts to make sense. At Scenic View, we do 2,500 to 5,000 outing rounds a year, with about 100 players per outing. Theoretically, one person could manage selling and recruiting those larger groups. We could make decisions about multicourse memberships at our courses, make them part of our VIP club, bring those customers together, develop better long-term retention, even make arrangements for them to get together for events like Milwaukee Bucks games off the golf courses.

I think these kinds of plans will make us even more competitive. Frankly, in the long term I'd like to add a ski component to the plans, as well. Four years ago the Little Switzerland ski area near Scenic View closed up. They had been in business since 1941. I always thought it was a perfect match for golf, because our same people who operate the golf course during the summer could operate a ski business during winter. That would be true for food and beverage, maintenance, operations employees and others. That creates year-round jobs that would be appealing to my staff. My vision is to buy some existing ski properties, and then long-term, I hope to be a ski and golf company based in Wisconsin.

For the industry in general, I am very optimistic, mostly because of the baby boomers. If you circle back to my comment about our biggest competitor being people's time, I see this huge segment of our population over the next 10 years having the time for golf. They are an active group of people who may slow down physically a bit as they age, but golf perfectly fits their profile. Right now is a great time to buy properties, because a lot of the current owners are scared and banks are concerned about financing courses. At these Golf Industry Shows, there was much more vibrancy five to eight years ago. Now that vibrancy is just not there. The industry is going through doldrums. But there is a market. You just have to be in the right place at the right price-point to supply that market. I would be nervous on the resort or the real high-end property part of the industry during this economy. I'm getting players at my $30 clubs, Scenic View and Blackstone, who used to be private club members. Now they are playing my courses three and four times a week. They might play once a month at a high-end property, but for $30 with a cart during the week they are choosing us. The volume is at the lower price-point.

Also, I think that people in the golf industry have gotten better at looking at how they spend their capital dollars. At this Golf Industry Show, you can look at all the new maintenance equipment and be impressed. But how many $55,000 lawn mowers can you really buy? Maybe a lease of equipment or buying used equipment makes more sense. I've seen this with golf carts, too. That's probably a quarter of a million dollars investment at a golf property that needs to be spent every five years or so. As the technology has gotten so much better, there's no reason those fleets shouldn't last 10 years or more. We used to lease them and then roll them every three years. They used to break down too often, and we always wanted guests to see we had newer equipment. If the customer can see it, feel it, touch it, then we should provide the best we can. Rather than spend $55,000 for a mower that the customer won't likely see, I would rather get a used one for $15,000 and buy six brand new golf carts that the customer will touch and use. As we go forward in the industry, I can see how some of those capital expenses will change, mostly because the products are better made than ever before.

I also think that the golf industry is going to pay more attention to the quality of employees. Looking at the amount of employee turnover that has occurred in the last five or seven years, the numbers have been huge. I think the standards for hiring employees are going to improve. Some got into the industry because they were good players or pros, but they didn't have the needed management skills to succeed. I think the industry is going to look for personnel who have a better, broader knowledge with better business and management skills. Once the better-prepared staff starts to generate performance in their positions, then lots of owners are going to see the benefits and want those performers on their teams. If you look at private clubs, they are starting to get it, too. Typically, they have committees with guys who own a bunch of car dealerships, a guy who owns an air conditioning business, insurance salesmen, and what have you. The presidents of the clubs turn over every two years. As they study their clubs' balance sheets, they may begin to see how dedicated golf business talent is needed. Performance is needed, and I think talent is going to be rewarded. We just saw this in my area, where the new owner of Erin Hills Country Club hired a new general manager whom they recruited at an enormous salary from Ozaukee Country Club. The salary is way out of industry norms, but the new ownership understands the importance of hiring a person who really gets it, who can perform.

It always amazes me when I go to the new multiplex movie theaters. They must spend $25 million for those buildings, but then they hire young people at very low salaries to run them. The places are often messy, the food is not very good, and the customer service is poor. Their investment is huge, but they don't spend anything on their local management. That just doesn't make any sense to me in any business, including the golf business.

I was president of the First Tee program for the Wisconsin Golf Foundation for a year. I got on the GCOW board *(Golf Course Owners of Wisconsin)* in 1994 and I got on the NGCOA board *(National Golf Course Owners Association)* in 1997. Those experiences, and particularly the NGCOA board, have been terrific eye-openers for me. I've been able to meet so many owners and suppliers in the industry and to see how people function within the industry. These bigger perspectives on the industry have been an education for me.

## Romano's Lessons

- "Every customer's experience at the course is based on their interaction with somebody who works at the course." Build employee trust, commitment, loyalty and pride. They respond in their roles when they understand their purpose.
- To get the information you need to make the best informed decisions, talk to your customers and employees on the first tee box, at check in, in the clubhouse, at every opportunity.
- Exceed customer expectations with the right price-point for your market, an employee culture of providing quality customer service, and a good golf course product.
- Show local businesses how they can use your golf property to advance their own employee relations and work culture.
- Know your market competition and customer demographics to target marketing efforts.
- The course opening sets the tone to establish your course's reputation.

# Partnership

## Dick and Nancy Schulz, Owners of The Oaks Course in Covington, Georgia

        ℬ    ℘

*I interviewed Dick and Nancy Schulz at the Golf Industry Show in Orlando, Florida, on February 9, 2011. The Oaks Course is an 18-hole public course one half-hour east of downtown Atlanta. The original nine holes were conceptualized by the legendary Bobby Jones in 1938, and the additional nine holes were designed by Dick Schulz in 1989. Dick and Nancy first entered into a partnership ownership of the course in 1989 and assumed majority partnership ownership of The Oaks Course in 1992. Southern hospitality and the natural beauty of Georgia are features of The Oaks Course.*

http://www.golfoaks.com

        ℬ    ℘

**Nancy:** The Oaks Course is owned by a limited partnership in which Dick and I have the majority shares. Dick is the general partner, and I am the majority limited partner. We own 75 percent of the course, and there are 10 other limited partners. In the last 20 years, there are some partners we have not seen. There are two partners we see about once a year. We think of the course as ours.

**Dick:** I became a golf course superintendent straight out of the University of Tennessee in 1979. I had played sports through college, but I got injured and had to make decisions about how I could stay involved in sports. Coaching sports wasn't really an interest, but the turf side of the golf industry gave me a chance to work outside, which I love.

After graduation, Nancy and I moved to Pennsylvania. I was an assistant golf course superintendent at Lord's Valley Country Club. We moved there so I could get experience in northern turfgrasses (bluegrass and bentgrass). Then we moved back south to Tennessee, first to Fairfield Glade Resort to gain construction experience and then to Gatlinburg Country Club to formulate a 10-year program to renovate the city golf facilities. We moved to Atlanta in 1984 when I took the position of superintendent at the Atlanta Country Club.

I was at the Atlanta Country Club in 1985, and a gentleman came over to see me with a picture, an aerial photograph, of a golf course that was built in 1938. He told me that Bobby Jones *(legendary golfer and founder of Augusta National Golf Club, where the Masters Golf Tournament is played each year)* had laid out the original nine holes of the golf course in the picture, that he and his partners wanted to restore the course and wanted me to do the work. We were having children at the time and I was already working at a very, very nice golf course that was taking good care of us, so we said, "No." Our conversations about the course continued, and in 1988 I created a design for the second nine holes at that course. I got paid for the work but still wasn't interested in building the golf course. Then in 1988 that gentleman came back to see me again and made a much more substantial offer for me to be a junior partner in that golf course. I accepted the offer at about 30 percent of the ownership shares, I began working at The Oaks Course as superintendent, and I got to design and help build the second nine-hole layout.

During the construction phase of the course, from 1989 to 1990, things didn't go as planned. My dad and Nancy are both very good with finances, and we began to figure out that something was wrong. We went to our attorney to see what our options might be. To make a long story short, we filed for bankruptcy and in 1992 after 10 months of hearings a judge redistributed the ownership shares. Nancy and I ended up with the majority of the shares because we convinced the judge that the golf course had the potential to be successful as a business. Because of the court ruling, there are still parts of the experience we cannot discuss.

**Nancy:** We actually took the course through a chapter 11 bankruptcy. At the end of the chapter 11, the judge awarded us the majority of shares. One of our ethical dilemmas was that when you enter a bankruptcy, most people don't pay back all of the creditors. That was not an option for us, and thus we paid our debts in full.

**Dick:** Everybody who worked with me on this project had worked with me for years on other projects. They were friends or business acquaintances that we felt we needed to take care of. It was not an option for us to ignore their investments during the bankruptcy.

**Nancy:** So we agreed to pay the creditors back 100 cents on the dollar. I think the judge perceived that our ethical standards should be rewarded, and he awarded us the majority of shares.

**Dick:** We were up against American Golf Corporation and Club Corp, some big businesses. It was the two of us against the corporate world and there didn't seem to be much of a chance for us at all. We did have a great legal team. We spent more on that legal team than we have ever spent on anything else in our lives, but it was the smartest decision we ever made to hire them. It was the best legal team in Atlanta, maybe the state of Georgia, maybe in the United States. In the end, not only did we pay back the creditors 100 cents on the dollar, but we told the judge we would keep the original limited partners. In preparing to render his judgment, the judge looked down at us from the bench and asked me, "How old are you, son? Nobody has ever done this. Have you lost your mind?" We were in our early 30s at the time and looking at $4 million of debt. Obviously we had a very big challenge getting started as golf course owners.

**Nancy:** When we took on that mortgage, we started at a very high interest rate. The financial institution was part of a big corporation, but it was struggling at the time. Their chairman of the board had been involved with the Reagan administration and had written some books on finance. I read some of his books to see how he and that financial institution thought. I think the insights helped. We started negotiating with them, and they gave us a pretty deep discount on the interest for the mortgage.

**Dick:** That saved us. It was another of many acts of God that helped us.

**Nancy:** At that time, we had really small children. Our oldest child was five years old and our youngest was three. I remember the day we had to go to our first bankruptcy hearing, and both kids came down with the chickenpox *(laughing at the memory)*. It was a time in our lives when I figured we could take the risks now, and whether the risks either paid off, or if they didn't, we would have time to recover. When we were awarded majority ownership, we just jumped in and we did it!

The next year, 1993, we made the decision to come to our first NGCOA conference. We thought that if we were going to do this, we needed to get all the help we could get. The help we have gotten is one of the biggest reasons we've made it. The meetings on running a golf business have really helped us to climb out of a big hole.

**Dick:** We started out with a loan that had a 13.5 percent interest rate. Our mortgage payment was almost $50,000 a month. Every time I think that it's bad now with the recession, I look back at how hard it was when we started. Our 6 percent interest now isn't all that bad.

We still have more debt than I wish we had. We have heavily reinvested in the golf course. It's important that the condition of the course is great, that the paint looks fresh on the clubhouse. We invested in a new irrigation system and redesigned some holes. We have really tried to take care of our customers, when sometimes I wish we had stored that money away.

Golf is a capital intensive business that is driven by weather and the economy. If the economy is good, golf business is good. If the economy is bad, golf business is bad. Running a golf course is a puzzle. If you don't like solving puzzles, don't get in the golf business.

**Nancy:** All of our decisions about investing in course improvements were prudent at the time. Our operating budget is very efficient, and repairs and maintenance have to be addressed. Any entrepreneur makes good decisions and makes a few mistakes. That's the nature of the beast. If you are not prepared to make some mistakes and then learn from them and move on, then you have no business being an entrepreneur. Look at Walt Disney. He was in bankruptcy five times before he created Disney World. People don't remember those five times that looked like failure. We remember his eventual success.

Our children are in their early 20s now, and they worry about our business. Even some of our staff is like, "Oh, what are we going to do? The sky is falling! The sky is falling!" Dick and I just tell them to get over it. Just put one foot in front of the other one and keep going. You have to keep your focus on the silver lining, especially in working with your staff. Staffs seem to get beat down very easily, and you have to keep their spirits up.

We are very competitive, too. That's essential in running your own business. You have to be willing to get up every morning and say, "OK, the chips are down, but that's the way I like it!"

**Nancy:** The property was originally owned by a mill in Covington. It was part of the recreational facility for the mill workers. One of the owners of the mill, Jack Porter, had a relationship with Bobby Jones. He had money and knew the movers and shakers in Atlanta. Mr. Porter brought Bobby Jones to the property. Bobby went around the course and laid out the original nine holes. Then over time the mill closed, as many do. That mill had made twine as well as uniforms for Confederate soldiers during the Civil War. It was a very substantial mill, but over time it went out of business and the golf property was sold.

**Dick:** Jack Porter, Bobby Jones and Charlie Elliot, who wrote for years and years for *Field and Stream* magazine, were fishing buddies. That was their connection. That was how the nine-hole course got started.

In the 1970s a group of guys bought a neighboring property next to the mill and tried to add nine more holes to the original layout. They created a terrible golf experience. There were odd yardages for holes and fictitious yardages. They would post that a hole was 396 yards long, when in reality it was 312 yards long.

When we were first approached about involvement in the property, the plan was to restore the golf course and use Bobby Jones' name to help market it. Having the chance to help create the course and then own it, all of it together, the ego part of it to own my own golf course, the freedom to bring in the children, was so exciting. For me there was something about creating jobs and being able to help other people make a living that was so attractive. Going from a superintendent to being a superintendent who owns a course was a dream for me. For a long time I had thought how much fun it would be to own a course. Then when that first general partner came along with the offer of ownership, I thought it was like an act of God.

**Nancy:** I think there is another piece involved in our desire to own our own business. In the late 1980s, both of our fathers had been in businesses for many, many years, giving their loyalty, and then were let go because of their ages. They were given severance packages that were not consistent with the loyalty they had shown. That really rubbed us the wrong way. We wanted to be more determinant of our long-term financial destiny, rather than be completely dependent on someone else.

**Dick:** In the superintendent's profession, your position is as stable as the weather, and that worried me. We were planning a family, and having some control over the future was important. Nancy's family is from Europe, and at the time her grandmother still lived in Europe. We thought that owning a golf course might give us time to visit her family in Europe. If you are a golf course superintendent, you can't get away. We considered a lot of factors in deciding to own a course. We knew it was high risk, high reward. At the time, golf was at the beginning of its growth cycle and really exploding. It was the right time to do it.

The course is in the Atlanta metro region, and there is a lot of competition. It's about supply and demand, and we are in the classic oversupplied market. There are 128 public access courses in Atlanta. It's really ridiculous. Banks own some of these courses. If they would close some of them or bring in someone who really knew how to run a golf course, it would help. The banks want every penny they can possibly get out of those properties before they will do anything with them. There are just too many right now, and it's wrecking the industry. Government competition through municipal golf courses and banking practices are really hurting golf ownership. The municipal courses don't really have to make profits and they don't. Municipal courses are managed to lose money. This may be my next career, to walk into a municipality and present a plan that will guarantee it some set number of dollars in profit without ever asking for more money. With our golf course, if we didn't have to pay taxes like municipal courses don't, if we didn't have to pay the mortgage like government places don't, then we would be making some good profits.

**Nancy:** I'm a Type A personality and I'm very left-brain, logically oriented. My role with the course is as controller for our finances, the bookwork and accounting. I manage all of our policies and procedures or anything having to do with the organizational side of the business. We have a chef, but I oversee the food and beverage side. Dick is our creative force, but I keep us on target with rules and regulations we need to follow. My training is as a nurse. I am a nurse practitioner, and I practice one day a week. That's a good dovetail for me because I emphasize health maintenance as a nurse. Golf is a healthy activity. Sometimes I get a little frustrated because some of the food we serve is unhealthy, but it's what customers want. Also, I was recently elected to a local position as county commissioner.

**Dick:** Any form of exposure as a team gives you business opportunities. Nancy is so oriented to the letter of the law and doing everything ethically that she would never take improper advantage in any way, shape or form. That's her reputation. Because she is so active in the community, people ask her, "Where is The Oaks?" Her work off the course gives us repeated exposure and that's been enormous help.

*(At this time in the interview, Nancy had to leave for another obligation. She was meeting with a group of female owners and told me, "You know, men bond by playing golf. Women bond while shopping, so I am going shopping and bonding.")*

**Dick:** Nancy's family is an affluent family from pre-war Germany. They barely survived because of their political position. Her grandfather was an engineer, and that's the thing that saved their lives. Our son is planning to write a movie about the family's experiences during the war. As I said before, superintendents don't get away from the course very much, and I knew we had to find another way to be in the industry. The good Lord just threw the golf course in my face. Although it did blow up in our face, too, that experience actually made us stronger. We just had to figure out how to get through it.

Our first child died. When that happened, we were told that 96 percent of the couples who lose their first child end up divorced. That experience was what hardened the steel for us. With all the things that happened to us before getting into the business and then initially in the business, we feel that our ownership is destiny.

The east side of Atlanta, where we are located now, was the new frontier when we started there. There just wasn't much development on the east side then. The first time I went to our location, I couldn't believe how far out of the city it was. It seemed like the other side of the earth. The second time I went out, it seemed like half that distance. We thought the area would grow. When we got there, there were 38,000 people living in Newton County in 1990. Now there are 100,000 people in the county. The area exploded with growth, mostly during the mid-'90s. That growth has helped our business.

A lot of the people who come to The Oaks do so because of the course's condition. My reputation as a superintendent helps to market the course. In the club where I worked before The Oaks, we held a PGA Tour event every year. It was known as one of the premiere courses in Atlanta. I got a lot of good exposure at that course and I worked with John Deere and with the Atlanta Braves baseball team, so I had a very good reputation. I'm on the USGA Green Section *(branch of the USGA responsible for turfgrass research)*, and we have held a USGA Qualifier Tournament each year for the last 15 years at The Oaks Course and that has gotten us special attention.

I'm considered a big risk taker within the business by people who know me. There have been lots of magazine articles in the USGA and other publications about some of the programs we've used for turfgrass management and for building membership at The Oaks. I'm part of a group presenting at the Golf Industry Show on Friday *(in February 2011)* about a revolution we started in Atlanta with a new type of Bermudagrass that we used to replace bentgrass. We brought in the new Bermudagrass in '05. We had to close the course to make the changes. We invested $400,000 with this controversial change. When I brought, it in there was an enormous backlash from a golf course superintendent who said the new grass would hurt the superintendent's profession. They just didn't really understand what we were trying to achieve. Once we were able to explain our process, it's become the hottest, greatest advance. With our process turfgrass maintenance expenses can be reduced by up to 30 percent and that usually means the customer will benefit. Everybody is starting to make the changes we did in '05. When we started that program, I mean I got chewed up and spit out by a bunch of my old colleagues. They thought it would hurt the value of the superintendent, because you could put a monkey in charge of this grass. The value of the grass is survivability. If you don't work this grass on a daily basis, it can become a nightmare, but it will survive no matter how hot or cold it gets. The only thing the grass doesn't like is the shade. It needs eight to 10 hours of sunlight a day. The golf course superintendent at East Lake, where they have the Tour Championship every year, was having trouble keeping the greens really nice at the end of the golf season, so they went with our grass program. The PGA Championship in August this year will be held at the Athletic Club in Atlanta, and they will have the same greens we have.

Once us little guys can get the big guys to understand that it's OK and they start doing it, then eventually those big guys start taking credit for it. That doesn't bother me all that much. I've had some really nice articles written that give me the credit. Our golf course superintendent is a young man who is really good and has worked really hard on our grass program. One of these days we'll lose him to a big club. I'll hate to see him go, but I'll be tickled to death to see him succeed.

The golf course is open 364 days a year, every day but Christmas. We have not had to lay anybody off, but we've had two full-time people leave during the economic crash. Their managers have elected not to refill their positions until things turn around. Those managers have just rearranged hours with the rest of their staff. I serve as general manager, but we have a superintendent, a PGA golf professional, and a food and beverage manager who serves as chef. Nancy handles the food and beverage side, and I handle the golf operations side. All of my managers have the autonomy to set their own schedules and their staff schedules. If we want to make any changes to the course, that's my expertise and part of my value to the partnership. If we want to make presentations to the community, I do the formal presentations, but with Nancy serving as county commissioner for two years, she can help communicate what we do to the community. Of course, when decisions are made that have any relationship to our business, she has to recuse herself from any vote that could be a conflict of interest. I spend most of my day trying to shake as many hands as I can, patting people on the back and wishing people a good day. I suppose that right now I'm most annoying for always saying, "We're one day closer to good weather." The staff is starting to hate that statement, but you have to keep a good attitude or you'll go nuts. Some of the staff are starting to preempt me by telling *me* we're one day closer to good weather.

Keeping everybody employed is one of our secrets for keeping the course open and making the mortgage payment. Our pro has been with us for 16 years out of our 20 years. Our superintendent has been with us for just over eight years. Our head mechanical technician who keeps the turf maintenance equipment going has been with us for 15 years. Two years ago he came to us and told us his kidneys are failing, that he may not be able to do all he used to do, but he really needs his job for the insurance. I got emotional and he had to talk with Nancy. He's a cantankerous fellow, but he does a phenomenal job. He's on dialysis three times a day now. We've told him, "Until the day you have to walk out, you have a job here." The food and beverage manager is the newest, and he's been with us for three years now. Of course, we have had some people who worked for us move on to other positions and become very successful. That's a very good feeling for us. I've seen some of those people here at the conference.

We went through a process with the University of Georgia to evaluate our facility, set a mission statement, and define our core values. Honesty is our first core value, and the way things filtered out loyalty ranks number five, even though it's one of the most important values to me. That value of loyalty is part of my commitment to keep our full-time employees employed. Right now, with the down economy, we have a total of 24 employees: 13 full-time and 11 part-time. I sat down and talked with them and told them that we had been working really hard and it seemed we got at least as much done now as we did with more staff. Their conclusion was that we used to be overstaffed. I'm an efficiency nut, so this conclusion makes me happy. I want my employees to feel like they are treated well. Even our university interns are paid minimum wage. Sometimes their schools don't like it, because they don't think it's a precedent they can support. If the schools don't want us to pay the interns, then we don't, but we give them a scholarship when they have finished working with us. When I had interns at the Atlanta Country Club, the interns didn't get paid, but the club provided a dormitory for them and fed them. Having the Atlanta Country Club or Augusta National on your résumé can make it valuable to the student even if they don't get paid. I like our scholarship program the best of all the options, though.

For me, the opportunity to complete the construction of the golf course was maybe the biggest thrill. I had been construction superintendent for other golf courses, but The Oaks was my own. That first day of construction was exciting, but at the same time about as scary as anything I had attempted. Then when we opened the course, there was a lot of community excitement. We had planned a playground facility at the elementary school our kids were getting ready to attend. The school had no playground. We connected with the community and with General Mills to ask for their help. All the Cheerios east of the Mississippi are made in Covington. General Mills liked our idea and pledged to match any money The Oaks could raise for the project. They didn't know at the time that Nancy and I had lots of fund-raising experience. Pretty quickly we got together a plan with the county for the playground, and we raised about $50,000. General Mills was not prepared for that. Probably our best friend on this earth is a vice president with General Mills to this day. We built the playground; it's called an outdoor learning center. There is an outdoor track, trees, a berm around the property for security and for helping teachers control the children. As you walk up to the playground, there is a granite plaque in the ground that says, "Thank you to Dick and Nancy Schulz and General Mills for their dedication...." All of the kids who read the plaque assumed Nancy and I had died. That was kind of funny, but doing the project really helped us build community relationships right from the beginning.

We got heavily involved with the schools, and we are one of the largest sponsors for schools in the area. Right now I'm chair for a 501(c)3 coalition that is raising money for a miracle field for disabled people to play athletic events. It's a tartan field that can be used by people in wheelchairs or people who have a hard time with motor skills. We're building a complex so that those with disabilities won't be isolated, but they can do their activities next to those who are not disabled and are doing the same activities, whether it's baseball, softball, golf, or having a movie. It's about a $2.6 million project. Nancy is working with the county, and we're getting ready to hire a grant writer who will be contacting the NFL and MLB to get their support. They have foundations that we think will want to be involved. One major league baseball player, Tim Hudson, has donated a jersey, bat, ball and glove that we will be raffling to get us going. In the last eight months, we've already raised about $125,000 in a very bad economy. Now with the 501(c)3 nonprofit designation, we will have a better chance of getting some of the grants we need. These kinds of things make us feel good, and at the same time they make our business more visible in the community.

By owning the golf course, we got to spend a lot of time with our kids, going to ballet practice, football games, baseball games, recitals, and that sort of thing. Both kids are in their 20s now. As a golf course owner I had opportunities to be with my kids while they were growing up that I never would have had as a superintendent at Atlanta Country Club. Our daughter plays very little golf. Our son loves to play golf, but he has no interest in going into the golf business. The kids were around the course a lot when somebody would come into the clubhouse after a bad round and look for anything negative to say. The kids never liked hearing people talking to their dad like that.

That angry guest has caused some problems in the golf industry. It's common for somebody to come into the pro shop and just lose it, for no other reason than they just played a bad round of golf. Nobody likes to be around that kind of negativity, and it's bad public relations for the industry. We've had members and regular customers at the course ask us to bar some customers from ever coming back. They tell us that our facility is so nice and our staff is so nice that we never need to have the angry, disruptive players come back. In the 20 years we've been open, there are eight to 10 people who are not allowed back to our facility. I've taken those angry customers aside to an isolated place and said, "You have to cool out your attitude. If you don't think you can, then please don't come back to The Oaks." In a couple of cases I have actually pulled them aside and told them, "If you ever step foot on this property again, I will have you arrested." Those are instances where the customers have abused our staff. You cannot justify humiliating another human being in a public arena. You can have an argument with me in my office, and there have been some knock-down, drag-out arguments in my office, but we will not do it in a public arena. We will not shame anybody.

If Nancy and I had not had an upbringing in a belief that there is a higher power and that there are certain commandments that should guide us, we would not have the success we have now. I would rather be penniless and have 1,000 friends than have a million dollars to spend every day. Relationships with people are extremely important to us. We were both raised by parents who were very involved with their churches. I was raised with nine brothers and sisters, and our Catholic school was attached to our church. That upbringing and belief that each person is a little piece of the universe to be respected is key to who were are. I've had to fire three people in the last 20 years, and those were some of the worst days of my life.

From the beginning, Nancy and I were thinking about and planning for the kind of retirement we want. To do that, you have to be ahead of the curve. Nancy and I decided that at the end of this year, we need to put a secession plan together. Our children are not interested in running the course, but if we have a relative or employee who would like to take over, then we have to come up with a doable plan. The number one thing for us to do is reduce our debt so we can be in a place to do some owner financing. We have to take care of the partners, who are a lot older than we are. I imagine that fairly soon they are going to want out, so we have to figure how to let them out and still have the capital to reduce our debt. Then we can find a relative or someone we trust to take it over, and then we can tutor them through what it takes to be successful. It's a demanding business and you will not get wealthy, but you can make a good living and you can enjoy every day. If you want to do it, it's a great way to meet a lot of people and have fun. For our secession plan, we've done a lot of research, and we've been to a lot of seminars on how to approach it. Nancy is very good with financing. She is very strong with gathering and organizing information. I give her my opinions based on what I read. I have a big imagination, but I need her to listen to my ideas and be sure that I really understand what I read. In the bankruptcy hearing, we had what I believe were the best attorneys in the country. When we need help, we don't fool ourselves into thinking we can handle things by ourselves, so we will probably look for help. I've talked with some financial people here at the conference about how to proceed. Their advice is to not even try to get out right now. Get through another year or two and then get serious about secession.

With our big families I have some ideas about what we could do next. I have an idea file on what I would like to do. Recently one of our employees brought me a patent that he applied for and got. He gave me a demonstration with his new product and as soon as I get home we are going to figure out what he needs to do next. One of the things I want to be involved with is making the sport of golf more universally accepted and accessible. I'd like to help golf course ownership be more efficient and based on better business models. In this industry, we have associations on top of associations, foundations on top of foundations, and it's terribly inefficient. We are paying thousands of people hundreds of thousands of dollars and duplicating services. It's one of the reasons the game of golf is so expensive to play. A greens mower costs $32,000 because you have the executive director of this group and the executive director of some other group who all get paid. The pyramid has gotten so tall that we can't support it anymore. The industry needs a survival plan. We could lose a huge percentage of the big players in the industry the way things are going; the financial people, the corporations, the technical people. The industry is such a limited field. If we lose these kinds of big players in the industry, then the game of golf will suffer. Golf is such a great game. It teaches kids physical activity, mental toughness, honesty and self-rule, stem to stern. The business of golf has to be more efficient to preserve the great game of golf.

I would like to be involved with an NFL owner who wants to build a new stadium complex, and I would like it to be the first totally environmentally friendly, green football stadium. I've already talked to some important people about this idea, and there is some encouragement. Taking care of the environment and cleaning up the environment are important to me. Golf is so good for the environment, that it's unbelievable and that is something too few people understand. Golf courses are a filter for all the things that are bad for the earth. We have 50 species of animals wandering around our golf course every day. We even had a fox squirrel on the course this year. It was the first one ever seen in Newton County.

I'd love to build one more golf course in my career that was developed based on all that I've learned in the last 20 years. The game was supposed to be entertaining and fun. We've turned it into competition, which is fine. I'd like to build a course that can be flexible enough to be both competitive for those who want that challenge, but fun and entertaining for others. I'd even like to build a course where if your ball goes into the pond, it's caught in a net and you can get your ball back, take your penalty stroke and go on from there. The ball manufacturers might not like that idea, but give the golfer his ball back, and he will be happier.

I'd like grandkids one of these days. I may have to be patient on that one. I want to travel more with Nancy. I'd love to teach the United States government how to be more efficient. It really shouldn't be all that hard. We both have lots and lots of future plans. For the immediate future, we will continue to offer a highly conditioned, beautiful golf course that is for our guests and our community to enjoy.

## Schulz's Lessons

- Due diligence does not end with investigating risks prior to acquisition decisions. Ongoing due diligence is necessary to evaluate business finances and to help assure business health and stability.
- Ethical integrity is good business.
- "If you don't like solving puzzles, don't get in the golf business." (Dick)
- "If you are not prepared to make some mistakes and then learn from them and move on, then you have no business being an entrepreneur." (Nancy) *A similar philosophy was stated by Bob Swezy representing Myrtle Beach golf businesses at the same conference. "If you aren't making mistakes, then you just aren't trying hard enough."*
- Leadership must maintain a positive organizational culture. Sometimes your staff must be reminded to "Just put one foot in front of the other one and keep going."
- Treat employees with honesty and respect to create employee commitment and loyalty.
- Take every opportunity to build community relationships.
- The angry guest should not be tolerated. Have a plan for how to handle the disruptive and abusive guest. Be clear that other guests and your staff are not to be abused by the angry customer.
- For the independent business person, retirement or secession planning takes time and professional guidance to be thorough and successful.
- The phrase "mom and pop" is popular in the golf industry to describe independent family golf course ownership and operation. Dick and Nancy Schulz exemplify the importance of partnership for collaboration and breadth of skills in working toward a common goal. Additionally, they remind us that mom-and-pop operations are about companionship, as well.

# The Firefighter

Richard J. Hampton, Jr., CEO of the New Orleans Fire Fighters Pension and Relief Fund that owns Lakewood Golf Club in New Orleans, Louisiana

℘   ℭ

*I interviewed Richard Hampton (Richie), CEO/secretary-treasurer of the New Orleans Fire Fighters Pension and Relief Fund, at Lakewood Golf Club in New Orleans on March 13, 2011. We were joined in the interview by William "Bud" Carrouché, president of the New Orleans Fire Fighters Pension and Relief Fund, and Cynthia M. Rico, vice president of operations for Lakewood Golf Club. Richie, Bud and Cynthia are natives of New Orleans.*

*Lakewood hosted the PGA Tour for 26 New Orleans opens, and the course is currently in its 50th year. The New Orleans Fire Fighters Pension and Relief Fund, with nearly 700 active members, purchased Lakewood Country Club in 2003. A multimillion dollar renovation of the course by the noted architect Ron Garl preserved its original character while making improvements in irrigation, drainage, course contours and bunkering, as well as adding numerous fire fighting themes. After repairing the extensive damage caused by Hurricane Katrina, the course reopened in 2009 as Lakewood Golf Club, a public 18-hole facility with options for traditional memberships with initiation deposits and membership dues.*

*The Lakewood golf course is the first phase of a multimillion dollar resort plan for the property that includes a hotel, four-story clubhouse, conference center, golf villas, condominiums, retirement center, office suites, restaurants and specialty retail businesses. The Lakewood story, like the New Orleans story, is truly inspirational.*

www.lakewoodgolf.com

℘   ℭ

**Richie:** I'm born and raised in New Orleans and I love this city. While I've traveled to many places, I cannot imagine living anyplace else. All three of us were born and raised in New Orleans.

I am a retired district chief of the New Orleans Fire Department following 33 years of service. I've had a very enjoyable and rewarding fire department career. I'm very proud of what I've been able to accomplish on the fire side of the business. Alongside of my fire department career, I've always been engaged in the fire service through the local union, Local 632. Well over 20 years ago Bud Carrouché, the president of the New Orleans Fire Fighters Pension and Relief Fund, convinced me to get involved with the board of trustees for the Fire Fighters Pension Fund. For the last 16 years I've been the CEO/secretary-treasurer of the pension fund. While my firefighting career goes back a good ways, Bud was instrumental in getting me involved in the pension side of the business.

I will have to say that the most rewarding and the most challenging moment in my career was during Hurricane Katrina in 2005. I served as the incident commander for the New Orleans Fire Department during Hurricane Katrina. The city was devastated by flooding and wind damage. Our firefighters were involved in fighting fires, evacuations and search and rescue. Communications were broken, transportation was broken, electrical power was out, gas lines were leaking and buildings were collapsing. The terror among our citizens and the chaos of criminal looting of the city was such that firefighters had to be armed for protection. I was in charge of the operation when the entire fire department relocated to Algiers on the West Bank of New Orleans, because there was no clean water supply on the East Bank. I had the very distinct honor of being in charge of that entire operation as it expanded to mutual aide with fire departments from New York, Illinois and Maryland, who came in to work side by side with us with hundreds of firefighters and equipment. Logistically, the coordination of the mutual aide firefighters, our own firefighters, who were suffering personal losses caused by the storm and who were not able to communicate with their own families, and the other agencies engaged in responses to the storm, was an experience unlike anything I could have imagined. Every fire officer always looks at the opportunity to be in charge of a significant fire emergency and do a good job. As a fire chief I had been in charge of a number of large fires in the city, but never in my lifetime could I have imagined anything that went to the extent of Katrina, and how an entire city, really the entire Gulf Coast, was devastated by a storm. To survive we had to be very innovative and creative with respect to moving forward with all of the challenges that were placed in front of us. I'm quite proud of the work all of our firefighters did. I couldn't speak more highly of the officers who worked with me to keep the fire department running and responding in a highly dignified and honorable manner, performing an incredibly great service to our city.

I don't remember the exact date that we got involved with the golf side of the business. We were attending a police and fire conference on the West Coast, and we were introduced through a friend of ours to a group that owned and managed a golf course in Monterey, California. We thought it was a bit of an odd thing for a pension fund to be involved in, so we did homework and due diligence for well over a year. We found out about the Alabama Golf Trail, which is owned and operated by some Alabama pension funds, and we began to realize that it wasn't so out-of-the-box that a pension fund would be involved in something like a golf business. As we began to look at the business side and what the investment return might be with a golf business, we started to get excited. At that time, golf was just steaming down the tracks, doing really, really well. So we began to look at the opportunity to get double-digit returns from a golf course investment, and we have to look at every investment we make for commensurate returns on every risk we take. One of the things the golf course business offered us was that we could mitigate the risk by basically having a mortgage against the golf course, so that we would have ownership of the land if anything went wrong. We would have a mortgage underneath so that at least we owned the property. It wasn't just a business that we were investing in. If you lost your business because it didn't do well, then you could lose everything. We knew we would have very valuable real estate. We also had two of the very best investment partners we could have had in the golf industry as we got involved with golf course investments. Even though we looked at golf courses in Monterey first, we actually ended up investing in a golf course outside of Houston, Texas. That was the first golf course we invested in. Without getting into too many details, we ended up selling that course a few years later and I think we made about 13 percent rate of return over the course of the investment, which was a decent return. For us, our actuarial assumption is 7.5 percent, so anything over that 7.5 percent is what we call in New Orleans "lagniappe." It's something a little extra from what you thought you would get.

**Bud:** The history of lagniappe is something like a baker's dozen that you may have heard of in other parts of the country. It's a French word for something that's a little extra. It's like when people go to the store to buy some beans, and they get a little rice, too, as lagniappe.

**Richie:** Getting an investment return over and above a desired level is a little more than lagniappe. It's actually something that we strive to get at all times. When we first decided to invest in a golf course, it was because we expected double-digit returns. In fact, with the contract we signed we were more or less guaranteed to make those kinds of returns. Not many people are willing to put their signature on the line and say that no matter what happens, you are guaranteed a double-digit return. We mitigated the risk by having the property mortgage underneath the golf course, and we had the ownership guarantee that we would get double-digit returns. That's exactly what happened when we sold the golf course in Houston.

Then we invested in two golf courses out in Monterey, or actually Seaside on the old Fort Ord property. They were beautiful courses and they did really, really well. We invested money to help upgrade the quality of those courses. Ultimately we were going to make that property into a golf resort destination. The city of Seaside had control over the permitting for those courses and the construction. We struggled for a long time to get that permitting, and many times we thought we were close to the finish line in getting the upgrades done. Then something else would occur on the governmental level that slowed us down or even stopped some of the plans. Eventually our partners came to us and told us that as hard as we were working, it was going to take us longer than we originally thought to reach our goals. Since we had an opportunity to sell those courses with a double-digit return, the partners recommended that we sell while we could make that kind of profit. We thought that eventually, when the resort was completed, we might make even more money, but given the time it would take, it was to our advantage to take our money and reinvest it someplace else. That's what we did.

We had some options on a couple of golf courses in Austin, Texas. With one of those courses, we flipped it in less than two months and made a bunch of money in the transaction. We were ready to take over the course, and somebody else made us an offer we couldn't refuse. We are in the pension fund business, the investment business, to make money. No matter how much you love a particular property or golf course, at the end of the day you have to be able to walk away if you are confident that it's the best decision to make a good return on the investment for the pension fund and its members. As a result, we sold that course.

The other course in Austin is called Falconhead Golf Club. It was the first TPC-series course ever built. We were minor co-investors in that course. The partners we had were either not doing a very good job of running the property, or the golf industry got into such a state that they were not able to make sufficient money on the course to pay debt service. They ended up filing for bankruptcy. We were at a crossroad in our golf businesses at that time, but we thought we had the opportunity to buy it out of bankruptcy and create value where there was none. That's exactly what we did. We have turned that course around to the point that it's finally making a profit. The partners we were in it with were supposed to be smarter and better, but they could never do anything with it. As you well know, the golf business is a tough business. We could have cut our losses and walked away, but we felt like we had enough invested, and we felt strongly enough about that golf course's potential that we believed we could make money. Right now we are doing over 47,000 annual rounds of golf at that course. In an industry that is struggling right now, that's not too shabby! We still own Falconhead.

For a while we thought we might get out of the golf course business. Then the PGA came to us with respect to the TPC course that they wanted to build out in Marrero, Louisiana. They couldn't arrange the financing they needed to build the course. Because of our golf course experience, they asked if we were interested in partnering with them. We negotiated with them a good while. They were pretty tough negotiators, but I think we ended up getting exactly what we needed to get in order to get that property done. Our money was the last money in, so the golf course had to be good to go before we put our money in place. Right before they were ready to ask us to write the check for that golf course, they were able to get cheaper financing. They asked if we would allow them to replace our financing with the cheaper financing but still enable us to maintain our equity position. So without putting in a dollar we were able to take part ownership in the TPC course. Having no money at risk at all and still have some part of ownership was probably the best investment strategy you could ever have. That's what we did to get involved with the TPC Louisiana Golf Course, the home of the PGA Tour Zurich Classic of New Orleans.

We didn't get into this business blindly at all. Our board of trustees is the hardest-working board of trustees I have ever had the pleasure of working with. They do their due diligence. They get their arms around the risks and understand the potentials in what they invest in before they put up their first dollar. Nobody can control the stock market. It does what it does, but we are consistently thorough in all of our investments, and we have worked with good partners. Partnerships can make or break just about any business.

That brings us to Lakewood. Lakewood Country Club was suffering through hard economic times and hard golf economic times. It was in a position where it couldn't meet its debt service. The shareholders were frustrated because they were asked again and again to put up more money without seeing any opportunity to ever get it back. Originally they tried to sell the golf course with covenants on it that required it to remain a golf course. Because there is so much risk in the golf business, they didn't get any takers on the sale. Lots of people had other ideas about what this property was worth as real estate, outside the golf arena. When they finally relented and released the covenant restriction on the sale of the property, we got very interested. We knew this was a valuable piece of real estate. No matter what we did with the property, we would have the opportunity to make money.

The property is situated between Park Timbers and Tall Timbers, two of the very nicest subdivisions in the area. Nearby Lakewood South is a high-end community. This is some valuable real estate. So initially we purchased the golf course in 2003 knowing in the back of our minds that we could develop a high-end subdivision and make money just out of building homes. The pension fund has successfully developed residential neighborhoods before. We felt comfortable that we had the background and experience to go in any direction we needed to go with the property. Also, we knew it was being sold at an extremely low price. It was a very good investment opportunity. It was not our first dance in owning real estate or golf courses, so we were comfortable. And, around here we believe in eating your own cooking. The taxpayers put up money for the fire service and the police department. They put up money to pay salaries and pensions. Our thoughts were to reinvest in the same communities that support us. We wanted to show the public that we could in turn, support them by reinvesting in the city. We feel very strongly about that. As a business investment and as another way to support our city and its people, we saw nothing but good things with this property.

When we first started at Lakewood, we knew how tough the golf course business was, and we knew that the golf course was in a bad state of disrepair. At first we started to run the business as a golf course as it was when we bought it. We had done two simultaneous due diligence studies. One study was based on use of the property solely for real estate development. The other study was based on keeping the property as a golf course, and maybe doing some real estate development as well to get some more bang for the buck. We went with the golf course plan and made commitments with all of the homeowner associations on this side of the river. Cynthia (Rico), our general manager, has worked closely with these associations, and she can tell you that they represent very tight-knit societies. The neighborhood associations are active, they communicate with each other, and they work together. They have regular meetings and when they meet they always have a quorum. They have a very strong say about what goes on in their neighborhoods. If they don't like what you are doing, you will hear about it.

We made a commitment to them up front that whatever we did was going to be transparent, that there wouldn't be any surprises about what we were doing. We met with every one of the 14 homeowners' associations to let them know the firefighters' intent with the property. We told them we were doing the double-tiered study and that the pension fund would make the best investment decision, whether it would be for a real estate subdivision or for a golf course. Of course, they all wanted the green space. They never wanted to see the golf course go away.

Lakewood is a very historical golf course. It's 50 years old, and it has hosted 26 New Orleans opens for the PGA Tour. Hall of fame golfers, names like Nicklaus, Player, Trevino, Casper, Watson, Ballesteros and Crenshaw, have won the New Orleans Open on this course, and it's somewhat hallowed ground. We wanted to preserve that history as best we could.

As we considered our options, we were able to buy some parcels of land around the golf course. The golf course itself had a very tight footprint. As we acquired those extra properties, our real estate options grew, and we began to see the golf course as a very high amenity for other real estate developments on the property. Little by little, we bought every adjacent piece of property that touched the golf course.

Then Hurricane Katrina hit in August 2005. It certainly set things back for the whole city and for us. Like the city, we had to reconsider what we might be able to accomplish. Not only had the economic landscape changed, but the physical landscape had changed to the point that it was going to be a real challenge. Cynthia can tell you better than anybody about the number of trees we lost and had to haul off, and the costs we had to incur just to clean up. Insurance doesn't really come close to covering that type of devastation.

**Cynthia:** It was 2,600 tandem-truck loads of debris that we had to have hauled off the golf course. We didn't have any flooding here, but we had siding off houses, satellite dishes, all kinds of things from the wind damage.

**Bud:** We don't really know the number of trees we lost. We had to cut the trees into pieces and haul the pieces to the curb for FEMA to haul off. Thankfully FEMA would take them away from the curbs, but it cost us $600,000 just to get the downed trees to the curbs. That's how many trees we lost. We still have a lot of trees left on the course, but they are just a very small fraction of what was originally on this property. We salvaged some of the trees, but we lost so many big, beautiful cypress trees, that it's really sad.

**Richie:** The cleanup was a challenge in itself, with the cost of the cleanup and the cost of being out of business for that time. We had to develop a new plan for how we went forward, especially in an economy in the city of New Orleans that was so devastated. The city lost a large portion of its population, and there was no way to know when or if they would return. The last dollar the people had was the luxury dollar to spend to play golf. We had to seriously think about what we were going to do. We had made a commitment to this development, and we didn't want to just walk away from it, but at the same time, before we invested any additional dollars, we had to figure out what we were going to do going forward. It took some real soul searching and some heart-wrenching decisions on our part. I have to give the board and the investment committee credit for a lot of courage in believing that we could turn this golf course around and ultimately develop it into the real estate development we've always wanted it to be. We wanted to help our neighborhood in Algiers, but we also wanted to help bring New Orleans back from the storm. We not only wanted to bring the city back, but take it forward from where we had ever been, even prior to Katrina. That's really what our long-term goal is to accomplish over here.

For the golf course, we knew we could make cosmetic changes to make the course even more playable than it was before, but ultimately we decided on a more long-term plan. We knew we had to do right by the golf course for our long-term plans. Patchwork repairs would be just cosmetic touches that wouldn't make it the golf course we wanted it to be, especially if we wanted the course to be the premier amenity or centerpiece for our complete development plans for real estate on the property. Our plan from the start was to have a very high-quality golf course and a very high-quality real estate development. They have to go hand in hand. There was no way we could just piecemeal a repair with an inexpensive do-over, so we made a commitment to do the golf course right.

We've taken our knowledge and experience and coupled it with the expertise of the golf course developer out of Florida, Ron Garl. Ron is one of the leading golf course developers in Florida. I think he's done over 200 courses around the world. Right now he is doing golf course development in Asia. We interviewed Tom Fazio and other name-brand, high-end golf course developers, as well as some of the golf professionals who develop golf courses, like Hal Sutton who did a course in Louisiana. We talked with Jack Nicklaus' people who did English Turn, a local course in New Orleans. We didn't really consider going back into partnership with the PGA. Our experiences with partnering with them at the TPC course in Louisiana and at Falconhead told us to look elsewhere. Obviously the PGA is very successful. We aren't smarter than them. We just think differently from them. We interviewed many people, and we visited some of the courses that Ron Garl had designed and built in Florida. We liked Ron and his work from the start.

One of the things that tipped the scale from the start, other than the kind of quality person that he is, was he had already rebuilt one golf course in this area, called Money Hill. If you know about Money Hill, it's an award-winning course. It's been number one in Louisiana for several years. I'm not much of a golfer myself—I call myself a hacker. I just don't have the time to play much golf, but I've been on a number of very good golf courses. You can see quality in a golf course and you can talk to the people who take care of a golf course, to learn about quality. We liked Ron, and we knew he had local experience. One of our biggest concerns was the Louisiana mud and muck. We knew that somebody who had never worked in this area would be in over their heads, because they wouldn't know what they were fooling with. With Ron, he had created an award-winning course in our area. We liked his work, and his price was the fairest price out of everybody we talked with. He was so down to earth in talking with us. He told us he would tell us just what he would do and what it would cost. When we had questions or had to consider possible directions to go, we just sat down at a table and talked it out until everyone was comfortable with the decisions. I think that with some of the other developers we considered, it was usually their way or the highway.

**Cynthia:** Our course maintenance plan with Ron was on a three-year plan. We had a little over a one-year grow-in plan and then $875,000 to finish the reconstruction. With Tom Fazio, for example, the expense would have been $2 million after grow-in. It was a good budget for us to work with, and it kept us focused on long-term maintenance for the course.

**Richie:** We did two things early on with drainage and irrigation that improved our long-term course maintenance. We sand-capped the entire golf course. It was very expensive, but we knew that in this city with the rain we get and the quality of the soil here, we might be the only golf course in the city that would be open after a hard rain. When we first bought Lakewood, it was like most of the local courses. After a hard rain, we had puddles everywhere and some days just had to shut the course down. Even in sunny weather, it sometimes took two days for the rain water to drain. So we invested in the infrastructure of the golf course for the longterm. Once again, I give kudos to the board for making those courageous decisions to spend a little more money up front than most people would want to spend, but knowing that if you didn't do things right at the beginning, then it would cost you much more money down the road. We did a lot of things right at the beginning to mitigate long-term maintenance expenses.

I don't get out to Lakewood all that much. Cynthia and her staff run the course. I have 40 other pension fund investments that I oversee, but Lakewood is near and dear to us. It's important that the course looks good and plays good and that we are successful as a business. The folks we have in place at the course are doing an outstanding job. I'm very proud that the firefighters can call Lakewood their course. I hear people bragging about our course; unsolicited people I don't even know. That makes you feel really good to know that people appreciate what we are doing.

For our management structure, we have worked very, very hard to get quality people to work alongside us. Our mindset is that we want our staff to want what the firefighters want, which is to be the best, to work toward quality, and to have pride in what they do every day. When our staff goes home, I want them to know they had a good day's work and they made people happy. They helped to create a quality experience. If our staff doesn't have that mindset, then eventually they won't be working out here. That's the attitude we want not just from the golf pro, but even from the guy who cuts the grass or weed-eats around the trees. If we maintain that thought process, we can't help but be successful. Cynthia, as our general manager, oversees our course and our staff. She does a wonderful job and ensures that our staff has the attitude we want and takes pride and a sense of ownership in their work. With the quality of people we have in management now, the quality of our golf course is going up by leaps and bounds.

**Budd:** I've been a fire chief in New Orleans for 36 years. I've been working with Richie for most of that time. Even though I don't play golf, this project has been my baby. I'm here four or five days a week. I have to say that in all that time, the smartest thing I did was to spot Cynthia. She was in charge of food and beverage and worked at Lakewood before we bought it. I realized that she was the go-to girl. Even though she had many managers over her, when people had any kinds of problems, it was Cynthia people went to. Right now Cynthia is running Lakewood and Falconhead in Austin. I don't know how she does it. She does everything from the smallest detail to the biggest. She speaks fluent Spanish and that helps a lot. Plus, she's almost the "Mayor of Algiers," because she knows so many people and has so many key relationships with people here.

**Richie:** Jimmy Headrick is our director of public relations and golf development. He has received numerous awards for developing young golfers. He was inducted into the Gulf States PGA Hall of Fame, he has received the PGA's national Junior Golf Leader of the Year Award, the inaugural Gulf States PGA Junior Golf Leader Award and was named to the prestigious list of Top 50 Kids Golf Teachers by U.S. Kids Golf Foundation. The ranking is reserved for an elite group of golf instructors nationally and around the world who focus much of their time and energy on developing young golfers in their communities.

We are committed to developing junior golfers. We have weekly junior golf instruction, and we host a variety of competitive junior golf tournaments. This year we will host the Gulf States PGA Junior Championship. This spring Lakewood will be opening a six-hole course designed by Jimmy solely for youth golfers. We want a fun, family atmosphere, and we want the kids to not only learn to play golf but also learn the values associated with golf.

Our golf course experience tells us that it takes about five years to break even on finances. While Lakewood is an old golf course, we basically made it a new golf course by rebuilding it from the ground up. After Katrina, we were building a new business. It was a new business plan, a new economic environment, a new world. Even though we are sitting on an old golf course property, we created a new golf course here. We don't think it will take us five years to break even. In the first couple of years, we are ahead of that expectation. With the economy and all that has happened to New Orleans, things have been slow to come back. Most golf courses can make money Friday, Saturday and Sunday. It's Monday through Thursday where most golf courses struggle. We now have a business model and a manager, Jay Maumus, who is our director of tournaments and corporate events, bringing in tournaments and outings during the week, and that is putting us far ahead of what we imagined. There is hardly a week that goes by when we don't have some kind of tournament, charity event or corporate outing. We have so many great people working at Lakewood.

Our price per round is not compromised. If you give golf away, anybody will want to play your course. We made a commitment early on that we would not get into a price war with our surrounding courses. We have to be cognizant of what other courses are charging, but if you get into a price war, then you reach a point where you can't make any money, and you can price-war yourself right out of business. Our commitment was to have quality and to charge for that quality. Reducing fees would bring a lot of hackers to the course who would tear up the course, and then the regular golfers would look elsewhere to play where the course isn't chopped up.

It has been a struggle the first couple of years, but I think our price and quality are beginning to pay big dividends. We have developed a lot of respect in our golf community. I believe we are one of the very best golf courses in our region, and there are some very good golf courses here. I also think we are going to be one of the most profitable golf courses in this area. We can't be concerned about how badly the other courses are doing right now. We have to be concerned about what we have to do to be successful here. I really look forward to this year, because we've put all the right things in place on the course maintenance side and on the management side. Cynthia is so in touch with the community and with the people who make things successful around here. She brings so much to the table with knowing people and developing relationships that we keep raising the bar, climbing that ladder of success. I couldn't be happier with where we are today, and I look forward as we get started on our plans for real estate development around the golf course this year. We have several commitments already to begin some of the real estate development. The Fire Fighters Pension Fund, the Fire Fighters Union and the Fire Fighters Credit Union have already committed to being on this property, as well. The firefighters not only have their name in ownership, but they will also have a physical presence, as our offices will be located on this property.

I've been focusing on the big story of our ownership of Lakewood. Of course, there are a lot of little stories along the way that are every bit as fascinating as the global story. After Katrina, what happened to our trees was devastating to us. Our fairways were lined with mature cypress trees and oak trees and we lost so many, over 1,000. We had a number of pieces of trees that didn't get uprooted. Cynthia came across a guy from Indiana who was doing tree sculptures with trees that were snapped off or broken. She got the idea of bringing him over to Lakewood to see what he could do here. Once he came and got started, we realized what a unique idea it was. Building sculptured monuments on the golf course became a tribute to the trees we lost. You won't see anything like these tree sculptures on any other golf course. Some of the sculptures are of Louisiana wildlife, and others pay tribute to our firefighters.

When we started working with Ron Garl to rebuild the course, we knew we wanted the firefighter's signature on the course. He was very receptive to our ideas. One of his Florida courses that we visited had a long stretch of waste area that was in red sand. So we built a flame bunker at Lakewood out of cucina red sand from Florida. It's totally unique. That firefighting tribute is really our signature hole. We developed a process to make the sand even more red to make it obvious that the bunker represents flames. The sun bleaches it, so we keep trying new paints and dyes to keep it as red as we can. On one of our par-3 holes, the bunker is designed to be a Maltese Cross badge, and on the first hole a bunker is designed as a fleur-de-lis. The firefighter's Maltese Cross is known around the world and represents honor and courage among firefighters. The fleur-de-lis is an official symbol for Louisiana and has become a symbol representing support for the recovery of New Orleans following Katrina. We painted the fleur-de-lis black and gold during the Super Bowl that our Saints won in 2010. Also, we built a very unique series of ornate, paved cart paths through our waste areas. Those paths are functional, but they also complement the designs of the waste areas. Unique ideas like these give a real identity of the fire side of our ownership but also distinguish the brand for our golf course.

I think one of the biggest strengths we have brought to this business is our innovative thinking, our ability to think outside the box. We do things differently from others, and that's the mindset of our pension board. If we have a problem, we don't just want to solve it. We want to turn it into a positive. I'd like to tell you that we are the wildest and greatest outside-the-box thinkers in the world, but we're not. But we do pretty good!

Our Fire Fighters Pension Fund is somewhat unique in that we're independent. Most of the firefighters in the state of Louisiana belong to the state Fire Fighters Fund. All of the city employees in New Orleans belong to the city fund. The New Orleans Police Department used to be independent like us, but they merged with the statewide system. We are one of the few pension funds that don't belong to either state or citywide systems. We are totally independent, and believe me, we like it that way. Being independent thinkers and investors like we are we would feel very restricted if we had to dance to somebody else's tune about how to do things. We think it has been a real advantage to have control over our own destiny, and we have made many good decisions to make that destiny come to fruition. Independence has been good for our city, for our citizens and for the members of our pension fund.

Ultimately, we are at the very beginning phase of what we believe is going to be one incredible real estate development. We want to see this become a $400 to $500 million real estate and resort destination. Our long-term thinking is what a great trophy property this would be for the city and for the firefighters. Our planning includes a hotel, four-story clubhouse, conference center, golf villas, condominiums, retirement center, office suites, restaurants and specialty retail businesses, with the golf course as the centerpiece. We want to make money for the pension fund, but we want the city to prosper from our work.

## Hampton's Lessons

- The risks of investing in a golf course are mitigated by ownership of the real estate. Even if the golf business doesn't thrive, the land itself can be valuable real estate.
- "No matter how much you love a particular property or golf course, at the end of the day you have to be able to walk away if you are confident that it's the best decision to make a good return on the investment."
- "Partnerships can make or break just about any business." Good partnerships can produce good investments with thorough understanding of business risks and potentials.
- A golf course investment that mutually benefits a city or locale and its people is a good investment.
- Transparent communications with surrounding communities when planning for a golf business produces valuable feedback and trusting community relationships.
- When things get tough, the tough get going. Hurricane Katrina was the costliest, and one of the deadliest, natural disasters in the history of the United States. Among the costs of the disaster were at least 1,836 lives, over $81 billion in property damage, and a relocation of over one million people from the Gulf states. Responses to the disaster showed the worst in human nature and the best in human nature. The New Orleans Firefighters and the people at Lakewood are among those showing the best.
- "If you don't do things right at the beginning, then it will cost you much more money down the road." Initial costs for reconstruction or construction should be weighed against long-term benefits for maintenance and quality.

- Management must assure that each and every employee takes pride and has a sense of ownership in their work and understands that creating a quality golf experience makes people happy.

- Problems and crises can create opportunities. Lakewood Golf Club in its recovery from Hurricane Katrina created on-course tributes to firefighters and hurricane recovery that branded the golf course as distinctive, generated pride among employees, and became an icon for pride in the city.

- Golf course businesses are supposed to make money. They also have the value-added qualities of serving their communities with economic benefits, green spaces for quality of life and environmental assets, recreational and social centers.

# A Change of Pace

Rick and Gina Budinger, Owners of Chippewa Valley Golf
Club in Menomonie, Wisconsin

ᘓ   ᘔ

*On the evening of October 13, 2008, I interviewed Rick and Gina Budinger
at their home, less than a mile from the Chippewa Valley Golf Club that they
have owned since 1995. Throughout the interview Rick did most of the
talking. He is a people-person, quick with the names of all his business
associates and friends. Gina was quick with any lapses in Rick's memory and
was continuously given the credit for taking care of the details of many of
their business transactions.*

*Chippewa Valley Golf Club is a public 18-hole facility on the outskirts of a
small college town in west central Wisconsin. Chippewa Valley is a
prototypical example of what the golf industry calls a "mom-and-pop"
operation. This is my "home" golf course.*

ww.cvgolf.com

ᘓ   ᘔ

**Rick:** I started TCR Graphics in the Chicago area after being
a salesman and running a printing press for another company.
After about two years in sales, the company I was working for
got into financial troubles. I told my partner we had no future
there. I told him we had all the connections to put our own
place together, that I knew sales and he knew the inside of the
business operations. That was in July 1972. In September we
started our new company, TCR Graphics. We then picked up
a third person. We thought we needed another partner. There
was a new bank in Woodfield Mall, the world's largest mall at
the time. The president of Woodfield Bank was a young guy,
and he was a client of one of my partners. We talked to the
bank president, and he thought our proposal sounded
promising, but because we were just starting, he wanted us to
downscale our business plan. The third person we contacted
as a partner had just tried to buy his own printing company,
but that deal fell through. He had money, though, so he joined
with us, and we went back to the bank. We sat down with the

bank president and he listened to us. Even though the bank president didn't think we'd make money the first year, he went along with us and granted us a loan. That was a time where you could never do it again.

We bought all used equipment and we leased our building. Our third partner was in sales, because he had all the connections in Chicago. In 1972 we started, and by 1974 we bought out the third partner. He got all his money back plus a profit. The business grew, and we moved into our new facility in 1976. A little while later, my first partner's wife committed suicide and he began to sort of drift away to other interests. I was working sales in the Chicago suburbs all day and then into the city at night. I was busy. He and I were having real difficulties in our relationship with each other. When it got real bad, he suggested that I just buy him out. Gina was a part of all this turmoil, discussion and planning. We tried to work it out but just couldn't, so we had a board of directors meeting and we just fired him. He took us to court when we fired him. He still had all of his stock in the company, but he was fired as an employee. Well, he took us to court. (*At this time Rick asked Gina for half a glass of wine. The experience with his partner brought up a lot of emotions.*) We had only two-color equipment in those days, and it was getting to the point that you needed a four-color press in order to get business. We had already ordered the four-color printing equipment when the judge held a hearing and told me to refrain from our ordinary course of business until our disagreements were resolved. After a year and a half and a lot of struggle, we did buy out the second partner. We actually bought him out with money he had helped us make. It took us like three to five years to pay him off, and then we started making some money and growing.

Soon we bought a six-color press. Thanks to Gina, who was doing a lot of PR for the company, we began to develop a national reputation. We even promoted ourselves as the "number one" printing company in the Chicago area. At this time we actually weren't as big as everyone thought we were. I wanted to grow TCR to a $50 million company, but I couldn't acquire all the business I wanted. I thought that if I couldn't grow it bigger, I didn't know if I wanted to continue. We were profitable, but not as big as I wanted. I sat down with my general manager, and we decided we just didn't have the loyalty in our customers that we used to have. At one time I could walk in a door and people would just hand me jobs. Then I had to bid for jobs, and I didn't respect the people I was dealing with. Gina and I started to think about selling the business. Gina had her own marketing business and I was a client. But Gina was a big part of TCR. She was our director of marketing. I had a manager for everything. I had a general manager, a plant manager, a color separation manager. We had managers in all aspects of the business. There were 125 employees working three shifts a day, six days a week.

We gave our employees profit-sharing and pension programs, but then we decided we were having trouble paying them with all the benefits we were providing. So I hired a new general manager. He was an older guy, kind of an expert in the field. He knew everything about running that business. He showed us how to make money, and we made money every month that older general manager was with us. So we had made some money, and I was frugal with the money I had. Now we had a company that I could sell for money.

My accountant sent out inquiries to companies all over the world. We were asking them if they might have interest in buying our business, and at first we didn't have anybody that showed interest. Finally we got a local company that was very interested. Now, they were a bigger company than me, but we were way ahead of our time with our quality and our marketing. We were winning important awards in the industry and making the magazine covers of national publications in the industry. The company that was interested in buying our company did labels for some major national contracts. They had been around for a real long time, and they were making more money than me. Gina convinced them of our size and our impact in the industry, and the deal was made. They bought the business in 1990. At that time, we had national recognition. Our aggressive technology advances, marketing and creativity got lots of press in the printing and advertising industry. I was selling $3 million a year in contracts myself.

This business was like a golf business. If you don't treat people nice, you won't succeed. The new owners didn't pay attention to our former clients, and they lost a lot of the business we had with TCR. At the same time, I had a smaller express printing business facility doing smaller jobs. It was like you have a 36-hole golf course, but somebody wants to play nine holes. Well, of course you can play just nine. The express company served us well. But the new owners closed it down. They just wanted the big jobs. The bottom line is that they bought my company but didn't treat customers or employees very well. We continued to lease them our building on a 10-year lease, but after a while, with different legal representation, we forced them to a position where they just bought our buildings. Those people who bought my company were like a soap opera. One guy got divorced, and the other guy's wife had an affair. Both of those guys are dead now. Their business just went downhill fast, and eventually they sold my business that I had made successful.

I sold in 1990, but in 1989 I started looking at golf courses while I was still in the printing business. I knew I wanted to get out. Gina and I had lived together for a few years, and in 1987 we bought a house together. Gina was with me through all of the decision-making turmoil to get out of the printing business. I'm not a big golfer. All of my life I typically had three jobs before I owned TCR. When I was starting, I had four kids, a new home, and a new car. I started out selling for $150 bucks a week plus a small 5 percent commission. I was always working so I never had a chance to play golf. Every now and then I would take a couple clients out to play golf or to an outing as part of the Printer's Guild. At these golf outings with the Printer's Guild, just ask Gina, I'd fill my pockets up with money to take clients out. I'd buy drinks, dinner, whatever. These were pretty rowdy events with the drinking and the entertainment. We got to thinking, why not just do this instead of corporate? This is kind of fun. So we started looking to buy a golf course. Most of the courses we looked at didn't have good finances. They were struggling; they didn't seem to have good business people running their facilities. We looked in Florida, Georgia, South Carolina, North Carolina, Michigan, Indiana, Illinois, Wisconsin and Minnesota. When we looked for golf courses, we had a list of different things we wanted to accomplish.

**Gina:** It wasn't so much based on size or price, we were looking for a quieter lifestyle and a smaller demographic than we were accustomed to in Chicago. We were looking for beauty in the course, our ability to grow the course. We really had a lot of different points that we used to evaluate the courses we considered.

**Rick:** At one point we started asking the owners and managers to tell us how much they were actually working because we'd been working so hard with the printing business. I was 47 years old when I sold TCR Graphics. I was too young to retire, but I didn't want to work at the same level I had. One owner told me he'd come out at 10 o'clock in the morning if they had an event, or he might come over after league and have a couple of drinks. Well, that sounded pretty good. I didn't really want to work-work, but I wanted to be able to say I owned a golf course and then enjoy the beauty of the land. Hey, Gina, that's what we were looking for, huh? But I should have known. This guy I was talking to had an adult son working for him, he had employees, older employees who had been with him for 10 years, and so he really had a functioning organization that enabled him to be more leisurely in the way he approached his business. Just about everybody we looked at had old-time employees, or they might have some of their children coming in the business, but none of these people were working really hard.

After a lot of looking on our own, we contacted McKay Golf out of Michigan. They were a brokerage firm, and all they did was represent golf courses trying to sell. We also started to receive golf industry magazines and look for courses for sale in the back of the magazines. We got membership in the NGCOA *(National Golf Course Owners Association)* as potential golf course buyers, and we began to get information from NGCOA. We started to publish our own ads in golf industry magazines to describe the kind of buying situation we were interested in. We put out ads in major newspapers in the markets we were interested in. In 1990 after we sold our printing company, we were on the road for five years looking at golf courses.

While looking for a golf course, we bought rental homes at Eagle Ridge Resort in Galena, Illinois. We built some spec homes. So we kept our hand in different real estate ventures. After selling our printing business and our building, we had a pretty significant capital gains tax. We had to reinvest our money to save on capital gains taxes. We bought about 10 properties in the Galena area and decided to build our own house on one of the properties. Boom-boom-boom, I wrote the checks to buy, and we made a profit on each one of the houses that we built. I've always dabbled in real estate, but at the time, I didn't know what the hell I was going to do with those properties. It kept us busy while we were really looking for a golf course to buy. In the golf courses we were looking at, everybody was selling "blue sky" projects. They would say, "Here is a beautiful golf course. If you've got $3 million, we will sell it." At one point a woman in Wisconsin brought us a contract to buy a golf course and told us the price was right. They never even took us on a tour of the golf course. There was no way we would buy a golf course sight unseen. You wouldn't do it with a house; you sure wouldn't do it with a golf course.

Too many people seemed to be flying by the seat of their pants, so I ended up contacting Lee Merkel *(owner of Wisconsin courses The Golf Club at Camelot and West Bend Lakes, and at that time, president of the Wisconsin State Golf Association).* Lee knew everybody in the industry, so he became our consultant. I showed him we really had the money and were really interested in buying. So Lee started calling golf courses for us. He referred us to some courses, but we just didn't like them. Eventually he called the owners of a golf course in Menomonie, Wisconsin. The owners were a married couple like us. It was a nine-hole course at that time, and when we looked at a couple of the holes, I just wasn't interested. But after we looked at the wooded property that wasn't developed yet, I began to get interested. That was in June 1995. I said, "OK, let's do it." By July there was still no action on their part. If it wasn't for me pushing, he would have never sold. At the end of August, we bought the course. The deal should have been really clean. We had the money, but at the last minute the previous owners wanted to add in the costs of maintenance inventory and odds and ends. There wasn't even a computer. I had a tough lawyer from Milwaukee, and the deal got settled at the original price. Gina and I also bought two other adjoining tracts of land at that time. That brought us to 265 acres.

The previous owner was a PGA pro, and he and a local lawyer, who was an avid golfer, had already created a plan for an additional nine holes. They even had a contractor already lined up to build the extra holes. I told the contractor to get started, to build those holes. I wanted an 18-hole course by the next summer. So we started construction right away, the day after we closed on the purchase. Boom-boom-boom, that's how I do business. Even though Gina and I were clear on our values, our consultant Lee was from Milwaukee. He was really more connected with that urban market than the small community market like Menomonie. He advised us to raise green fees and membership rates right away, even though we were still under construction. He also told us we needed a pro, so he sent us a teaching pro. That guy was a great teacher, but he wasn't all that good at running a good golf business. He only lasted with us a couple months. At any rate, we moved too fast for the community. We expanded advertising, raised rates, and started rebuilding the clubhouse and practice range, too. Local folks began to wonder if their community course was now becoming a regional course. We made some mistakes moving too fast for the community. Lee was from Milwaukee and I was from Chicago. We really should have had more local advisors who knew the smaller community.

In construction, we had some costs that we hadn't anticipated. Fairways were too tight, there was hardly any drainage, and there were no cart paths. Lee recommended one of his buddies to consult with us on construction. He was a great older guy who ran dozers and moved earth and really had some skills and ideas for what was needed. We hired his son, at age 21, as our first superintendent. The construction crews worked right to Christmas Eve in 1995 and started again before the snow was gone the next spring. In August 1996, I decided to not open the course, even though we promised we would. We got complaints from customers. "You said it was going to be all 18 holes and it would be ready for play." By May 1997 the clubhouse was renovated and the course was really ready. Unfortunately we had a drought that spring and the course had no irrigation at that time, but we were in business.

We hired a chef from a local restaurant and opened a food service operation. We might have moved too fast on the food service, too. Food service is tough in this business. Winters are so long here, and it's really hard to have a quality chef on only a seasonal basis. Later we hired an Italian chef and tried to make the restaurant run with him. There was a lot of restaurant competition in the area, golfers don't always eat at the course, and lots of people in the community just weren't sure about eating here without having a golf membership. For a while we had Friday night fish fries, but the flow of customers just wasn't enough. Running the restaurant became a whole other job from running the course. We tried lots of ideas but eventually decided to just stay with a grill and a short-order menu.

**Gina:** Finding and keeping good personnel goes beyond the kitchen. The work is seasonal and the pay isn't great. In the summers we mostly hire college students. Most of them are just doing temporary work and don't commit to the business. When we need them the most on big weekends, they seem to have other plans and can't work. We try to overstaff to cover employee absences, but then there aren't enough hours for some who want the money. We are constantly training or retraining our staff. We try to get some older staff, but that's tough, too. One season we hired a clubhouse manager, a guy with some maturity and experience. That only lasted a few months. When people make decisions about money that isn't theirs, they get into trouble. A manager might want to order three years' worth of vodka to save some dollars per case, but then you end up with inventory you can't move in time.

**Rick:** When people handle money that isn't theirs, you give them a right to steal. For now, we are owners and operators. We're at the course every day. It's a lot of work, but it's our business.

**Gina:** We have had problems in the past with superintendents. Some were just nightmares, know-it-alls, lazy, undependable. Equipment would disappear. But we have a good one now. He's our fourth superintendent, and he's been with us for six years. He started as an assistant and after only one year became the head superintendent. Rick spent lots of time helping him at first because he was so young. He has a degree in turf from Rutgers, so he knows his stuff.

**Rick:** I have a hard time playing my own golf course. Every time I'm on the course, I'm taking notes about where to rope off wet areas, where repairs are needed. I just leave those notes for our super, and he takes care of them one by one without a complaint. I spent lots of time myself repairing ball marks on greens and patching up tee boxes. Now I don't spend as much time with him. He and Gina have a good rapport.

**Gina:** We communicate well. Communication is critical. He gives me a weekly report on the course. If there is anything urgent that comes up, he calls me immediately. When we're in Florida, where we spend our winters, he communicates with us by email every two weeks about what's been accomplished and what needs to be done next. He and I sit down for an annual report that's really comprehensive. He's basically a shy person, but he has learned how important it is for us to communicate.

For us the biggest challenge we have faced in owning and operating the course came during construction of the new nine holes. The construction company went bankrupt soon after we got started. We were under pressure to open, under pressure from the bank, and our construction company just disappeared off the face of the earth. Rick ended up in the emergency ward. He thought he was having a heart attack. I had to do the negotiations with our lawyer and I thought I would have a heart attack too. All of our plans were in place, but there was no one to do the work. We called in one of our earlier consultants and decided we needed to buy construction equipment we didn't have. We knew we would need it for maintenance, anyway. The budget got stretched right away. We needed a new tractor, a sand pro for leveling out bunkers and new tee boxes, and other stuff. The local banker was happy. He liked that we needed credit, and he liked our potential impact in the community. He said we were his largest client and we had just gotten here. He liked the fact that we had money to invest, and he gave us carte blanche with the bank. We hired the employees from the bankrupt construction company, got them rooms at a local motel, and got it going.

These guys were really interesting. They travel from one golf course site to the next doing green shaping and other skilled work. They were rugged people, rough around the edges, living on the road. I stayed away from those guys. Rick worked with them.

The most rewarding part of what we do is seeing the golf course grow and mature into the beautiful property it is today. It just takes your breath away. It's practically mystical. The course is so quiet, natural and full of wildlife. (*Chippewa Valley Golf Course is a heavily wooded parkland course, with no houses or real estate developments*). The reason we bought this course was because of the beauty of the property, and now it's even better.

**Rick:** I'm like Johnny Appleseed. I'm always planting new trees for the property around the house and for the course. I'm a tree guy.

**Gina:** Right now we are thinking about some real estate development on the property. We could see some nice homes, maybe condos, homes for people who want to get away and have nature in their back yards. It would definitely help our need to increase the golf course revenue.

**Rick:** We did not buy the course for that purpose, but as soon as we started course construction, a realtor called us and told us an adjoining 25 acres were going up for sale. I was going to have to pay to create access to that property for a new buyer. We did have first right of refusal, though. Well, I lost my cool. They backed me in a corner. Who knows what a different owner of that property might do with it. So I ended up buying the property to protect our golf course investment. We bought another small parcel next to the course at about the same time. In 1999 we looked at some plans for real estate development but didn't do anything about it. We have thought about building homes to create a golf community all along, though. People could drive golf carts to the course right from their driveways for low costs and convenience. We might have enough customers to reopen a restaurant in the clubhouse and have the clubhouse open year around. You could get drunk as a skunk and never have to drive on public roads. Security guards could be concerned with people getting home safely.

That's what I would like to have for myself, and I think others would love it, too. There's nothing around here like that. But I don't know. I'm 65. Maybe the next guys can do that project.

**Gina:** Originally some of our children were going to come up here and work with us. But now they have big jobs and are getting promotions, so it just never happened. That's affected how we look at things. Now we want to be closer to our family in Illinois. We have four children and seven grandkids. They don't come up here that much to visit, and we usually just can't get away. *(For the next 10 minutes, Rick and Gina proudly talked about their kids and grandkids.)*

The Menomonie community may not be large enough for our business to grow. There are a lot of other golf courses in this area. Like lots of other mom-and-pop owners, we have to manage our business skillfully. Those courses that don't manage themselves well will not likely survive. Also, we have to market more broadly to bring in new customers. People just don't have much discretionary money these days. If they don't have a course membership and they only play five times a year, they want their money's worth. You have to have great customer service and quality to encourage customers to come back.

**Rick:** You have to give people the idea they're getting a deal. People like their coupons. People always have their eyes open for discounts, coupons and special promotions. It's just the way things are done these days. The Internet pulls in new customers like nothing we've ever done before. We recently had a cross-country trucker pull in our parking lot, driving a full rig with tractor and trailer. He said he saw our monthly special online but didn't have a printer to print out the coupon. He was wondering if he could get the special rate without the printed coupon. Of course he could get the rate. He left the truck in the lot and went golfing. The Internet is a driving force for golf's future. Next year we might go with a new marketing company to make our website more interactive.

**Gina:** Even with coupons and discounts, you can't lower your price to the point that it takes away from money you put into maintenance and improvement. If you start to take a nose dive on course quality, you're done. Word travels so quickly. You can't give it away. People are willing to pay a little bit more for a quality golf experience.

**Rick:** I do wish our customers would take better care of the course. I'm always positioning ropes to keep people from driving carts right up to the greens. Nothing ever seems to work for too long. Why do people insist on ruining their own playground? Maybe that should be on the cover of your book.

**Gina:** Running a golf course is like a stage production. Our guests see what's on the stage, but they have no idea what goes on behind the curtain. Maybe that should be on the book jacket, too.

## Budingers' Lessons

- Acquiring a golf business in a new location requires due diligence. That process is more than examining finances. Advice from golf industry experts is helpful but may not be sufficient. Be sure to consider insightful local knowledge from the community where the property is located.

- Owning a golf course with a nice restaurant is a great idea. However, running a golf business and running a restaurant at the same time are two very different jobs. Be prepared to consider the kind of food service best suited for your market and available expertise.

- Seasonal businesses have many seasonal employees. Hiring, training and retraining practices will require special attention. Thorough communication between management and staff is a reciprocal process, but it is management's responsibility to communicate expectations, and provide training and feedback on performance.

- Murphy's Law states that if something can go wrong, it will. During construction and reconstruction projects, look out for Murphy.

- Protecting your golf course investment may mean acquisition of buffering properties to preserve the kind of golf course experience you intended to create.

- Customers love bargains. But you can't give it away. If revenues are not sufficient and as a result, course quality suffers, then word of disappointment will quickly spread, and business will be challenging to recover. Find the right price-point to satisfy customers and preserve quality.

- "Why do people insist on ruining their own playground?" Friendly but direct communications with guests about repairing damage and obeying course rules are appropriate.

- "Running a golf course is like a stage production. Our guests see what's on the stage, but they have no idea what goes on behind the curtain." That's OK.

# British Invasion

Michael Hatch, Owner of Birkdale Golf Club in Chesterfield, Virginia, and Brandermill Country Club in Midlothian, Virginia

∞   ∞

*I interviewed Mike Hatch on February 10, 2011, at the Golf Industry Show in Orlando, Florida. Mike's story is a bit different from others in this book. He is British, married to an American, and owner of two American golf courses as well as a golf management consulting company.*

*Birkdale Golf Club is an 18-hole semi-private golf club that permits daily-fee players to enjoy the course in addition to members. Designed by Dan Maples in 1990, Birkdale offers a traditional, tree-lined layout, a spacious practice facility, swimming pool, clay tennis courts and restaurant. Members at Birkdale also have access to the private Brandermill Country Club.*

*Brandermill Country Club is an 18-hole private club. The course was designed by Ron Kirby and golfing legend Gary Player in 1973. Brandermill Country Club's golf members also receive complimentary golf at Birkdale Golf Club, located within 5 miles. Members have access to practice facilities, a swimming pool, 18 clay tennis courts, a fitness center, and restaurant and banquet facilities.*

www.acumengolf.com/birkdale-golf-club

www.acumengolf.com/brandermill-country-club

*Additionally, Mike is director of operations and owner of Acumen Golf Consulting. At Acumen his executive team of owners and managers has experience operating golf courses, clubs, hotels and health suites in Florida, Virginia, Maryland, Indiana and Wisconsin, as well as private and public courses outside the United States. Acumen's consulting services include guidance on operations, financial restructuring, strategic planning, sales and marketing strategies and other club management challenges.*

www.acumengolf.com

∞   ∞

Back in England I was a pretty good football, or soccer, player, and I was a pretty good cricketer. I didn't play much golf when I was growing up, but I was pretty good at golf when I did play. I didn't have particularly good grades in school. I was too busy playing sports, chasing girls, and drinking at a young age, which isn't all that good, but it's a reality of life. But I fell into doing a higher national diploma, which led to a basic degree. During that last year of my degree, I was asked to help sell memberships at a golf club that was being set up on the outskirts of London. That was at a time when golf was just booming. So a little skinny guy who wasn't used to wearing a shirt and tie was suddenly put into the position of selling memberships at a nice golf club. We sold about 2 million pounds worth of memberships in a space of 18 months. The owner of that golf course got all the credit for it, which is fine, but then he was asked to set up American Golf Corporation when they were moving into the U.K. market. *(American Golf is one of the largest golf management corporations in the world, currently operating 110 public, private and resort golf properties across the United States.)* American Golf was the biggest player in the industry. They bought five properties in the U.K. American Golf offered me a job, so I came in as sales manager as soon as I had my degree, at 22 or 23 years of age. I'm 37 now, so that was about 15 years ago. The people at American Golf asked me if I fancied running one of these clubs. I told them I don't really know what I'm doing, but I'll give it a go. So at 23 I took on a nice private country club.

Country clubs in England are very different. A lot of them don't have pools, and they don't have tennis. It's just golf, golf and more golf, with food and beverages as an ancillary spend. When I started managing that club, I knew nothing aside from the fact I was passionate about golf and I was pretty good at golf. For nine months I worked open to close, finding out how people were stealing off me, and what I was doing right, what I was doing wrong. I was young, so I was still going out in the evenings. I still remember throwing up in a trashcan one morning before selling a $10,000 membership 10 minutes later. I was naïve. I was stupid. I was young. But I spent those nine months learning the business inside and out; every steal that was out there, every receipt that wasn't being given to the marshal, working out food and beverage, working out what inventories were wrong. That experience stood me in the most amazing position I was ever in. I was young and naïve, but by God I was willing and wanting to learn how this business works.

American Golf at the time was an amazing company, but we didn't really have much corporate involvement from America apart from some of the guys who were brought in to help us sort out some of the skills that we needed. We were really not as developed as golf management was in America. American Golf then asked me to manage another golf course, and soon they asked me to move to more and more distressed assets, or the assets that weren't performing. That's when for three or four years I moved from club to club to sort out what the issues were. They then asked me to become a regional manager. I was overseeing six of the clubs in London by the age of 26 or 27. It was pretty cool. I was pretty proud of it, but I was still learning, winging it as I was going along. David Price, who was the owner of American Golf, had started the company something like 30 years ago on the back of a dollar bill. He was passionate about England because his dad was English and he had fought in the war as a Spitfire guy. David would come to England and mentor the management group. It was stunning, stunning, stunning. He was the most beautiful, articulate, engaging person I have still ever met in the golf industry. I have so much respect for him that it's unbelievable. When it was booming, American Golf was full of so many talented people. Now that I'm in America, I still see so many of those talented American Golf people splattered all over the industry and still being successful. They were so well trained and had such good systems in place.

When I was making such good progress in golf management, I met a gorgeous South Carolina girl on a date in England. We got married, had a baby, and soon she wanted to move back to the United States. I went to my boss at the time, Geary Leathers, who was an amazing boss and is still my mentor 15 years later. I told him I wanted to move to the states. He said, "Why on earth do you want to do that?" I told him my wife wanted to go back to the States, and about two months later it was all agreed. We jumped on a plane on a Friday night and started work right off in Tallahassee at a golf country club and hotel. I had never run a hotel. I had never worked in America. They knew I was fairly good and fairly flexible, but they threw me into the deep end. Ten days after I landed on American soil, Geary got laid off. I hadn't been paid $14,000 in moving expenses, and I didn't have a contract, because I didn't think I needed it. American Golf was outstanding. They stepped up to the plate and paid all the bills. In the space of one year, the hotel, golf and country club had more success than it had ever had in the past 10 years. Well, I thought, OK. This is good! I'm off to a pretty good start.

American Golf then asked me if I would run one of their Hilton Head properties, or would I rather go to Naples and run the Lely Resort properties. They had a private golf course and a very busy public golf course. Lely Resort was stunning, absolutely stunning. My wife actually knew the markets better than I did, so I asked her whether we wanted to go to Hilton Head. It looked beautiful on paper. She told me it would be a retirement job, that I would be bored within six months. So we put Hilton Head out of the equation, and we went to look at the properties in Naples. The guy who offered me the job told me I would have to work 110 straight days in high season, and the rest of the year would be mine. That really didn't have any appeal to me.

At that time, Geary Leathers, who had brought me to the United States, had gone to work for Meadowbrook Golf Group, another corporate golf management company, and he wanted me to come and run some properties for him. So I left American Golf and went to work for Meadowbrook Golf, running four or five of their properties to begin with, as well as being their general manager in the mid-Atlantic region. Then they offered me 14 golf courses and the position of manager for the East Coast. Still being a little naïve, I didn't know what I was getting into. The east coast of England is about three hours top to bottom. I found out quickly that the way my company defined the East Coast in America is a little bigger. I was given four properties in Wisconsin and then picked up another with a management contract. I had some involvement in Philadelphia, Indiana, Maryland and Virginia, while my head office was in Orlando. I was involved in making the properties more profitable, and my region had great success. I brought in some great managers, turned some despondent people around, hired and fired and basically reshuffled it all.

Then the company told me they had too much debt and needed to sell a lot of properties. The last year I spent with them was really the toughest year I've had in the industry personally. I didn't lie to my managers, but I didn't tell them we were selling their properties. I would tell them we didn't know yet which properties were going to fall, that it would depend on price and interest in the properties. With people who had worked extremely hard and were extremely loyal to me for three or four years, I was working to sell their clubs with or without them knowing. It was very, very tough, because I'm extremely loyal and extremely passionate. My managers had worked so hard to make their clubs work and advance their careers, and now we were selling many of their properties. We sold golf courses in Wisconsin, Maryland and Virginia. I had a defining moment, and I said to my wife that I needed to go find a golf course for myself. I needed to stop traveling. I needed to get set up and make a real difference in the lives of people I worked with.

So I stopped working for Meadowbrook Golf, and we ended up buying the first of our two golf courses with two silent partners back in England. Our partners have only been to see my courses once in five years. They know they can't really impact my clubs from England, but they trust me and leave me alone. I pay them the investment return that we've agreed upon. The first club we bought was Birkdale Golf Club near Richmond, Virginia. We moved to Richmond into the community where the golf course is located. That was extremely good for the first couple of years. We grew membership and we grew bottom line. We went from breaking even to making about $400,000 profit in the first couple of years. We knew by then that we had a good strategy and could make it work. I worked from sunup to sundown, and I brought some people in who had worked for me before.

At about that time, other people I had worked with in the past started calling me to tell me they were struggling with their properties, or that their course had just been bought and the new owners were awful. They asked me what they could do to get sorted out. I spent a lot of time on the phone and doing emails, sending ideas about what I thought they could do to improve. Then it sort of clicked one day. I was doing all of this consulting for nothing. I was helping friends out, which was OK, but maybe I could charge for the help I was giving. So I set up a consulting company, Acumen Golf Management, and within a couple of years we had five clients. We had equity clubs with boards of directors, absentee owners and a couple of the former Meadowbrook properties that had been sold. The new owners of those properties called me to see if I could help advise their new staff on how to run their clubs.

One of those was back in Wisconsin again. I hadn't expected that, and I didn't really want to get back into an airplane again for my work. I didn't want to go back to Wisconsin in the winter. That's for sure. But I ended up managing a golf course in Pewaukee, which was outstanding. One day a bank called me up out of the blue about one of the Wisconsin golf courses I had done some work for while I was with Meadowbrook. The bank said they had a guy who was trying to build a golf course that could attract a U.S. Open, a high quality, championship course. They said he was having a tough time and asked if I would come out and meet with him. I did, and that's when I met the most loving, caring, talented person I had ever met in Bob Lang.

Bob is amazing, but unfortunately he was consumed by his dream. I formed a bond and a relationship with Bob that was second to none. We got involved with financially positioning the club to have success, even though it had a lot of debt. We also got involved with Bob's luxury hotel and his tavern in Delafield. I really immersed myself in Bob Lang's dream and what he was trying to do. For a while, I had more involvement with Bob's club than I did with my own club, which I depended upon for my family and my livelihood. I was just so consumed with seeing him struggle and not understand the business that it really became a passion for me to help him. I told Bob I was available to him 24/7 and he could phone me up at four in the morning or at 10 at night and we could talk for an hour. I told him he wasn't a client, that he was a friend. The rollercoaster of Bob Lang is another book in itself that maybe Bob will write. *(For 11 years, Bob Lang rode the rollercoaster of his Erin Hills Golf Course with the dream of hosting a U.S. Open. Erin Hills opened in 2006 and was remodeled more than once to achieve U.S. Open selection. Lang's investments in the course became such a financial burden that he had to sell his hotel, and eventually in 2009 he sold his golf course. Erin Hills will host the 2017 U.S. Open under its new owner.)* Working with people like Bob and others, I knew I had a gift for helping independent mom-and-pop operations.

The consulting side of the business is going well. I take lots of phone calls where people tell me, "Look, I own a golf course. I don't know how I ended up owning it. A deal went wrong and I got it back." Or I might hear, "I've owned my golf course for three or four years, and I don't know what I'm doing." So I get a lot of owners coming to me asking for my help. They've heard that I'm discreet, I'm to-the-point, I'm very affordable, and they think I could put them on the straight and narrow. It's exciting for me.

Then we looked at buying our second golf course just down the road from Birkdale. It was a private course that we knew was struggling. When we first asked about a potential purchase, we were told, "No." After a while, the private golf course came back on the market. I told my investors that we were in a great position. Our first course was doing well, and I wanted to buy the private course. We all went thirds again and we bought Brandermill Country Club, only four or five miles down the road from our first course. It was a nice country club, but the former owners had raped and pillaged it. They were members who played golf but didn't understand the business. They had put some money into it and then decided to sell 20 tennis courts to try to turn them into condos. Well, they ripped the golf club apart. Tennis members left the club, bought the tennis courts not to make them into condos, but for a tennis club. The golf club went from 350 members down to 200 members within six months. Those owners were almost forced out of ownership. We bought the club, invested new money, and re-created a relationship with the tennis members who had been in the club. Within 13 months of being open we were back to 300 members. We got the golf club back to breaking even in a down market, a recession, within two years. We got the dues line from $71,000 a month back up to nearly $100,000 a month in a space of about a year. It was outstanding. We created new marketing and I branded myself and the properties.

At Birkdale, which is semi-private, people can walk in the doors as public golfers, and great, we love them and they can pay their money. If they want to come back and play their next round for free, we ask them to sign up for our loyalty program. There's no cost to them, the next round is on us, and we email them notices of specials. They can be an affordable member at a great club, Birkdale, and they can still get access to the private Brandermill socially with the pool and the fitness room. If they pay $35 to $50 extra a month, they can play Brandermill offpeak. We picked up $6,000 a month in extra dues just from Birkdale members opting to pay additional amounts to get access to the private club. The private club was just booming. Old members came back, and they were so excited they went out and found new members through creative marketing programs.

To show you the passion we've had in the club, when Virginia went nonsmoking last January, all the card-playing, smoking gals and guys said, "This sucks. We want to build a smoking room." I told them that for every dollar they raised to create a smoking room, I would match it. We raised $52,000 in 10 days! What we have built is basically an English pub. I always wanted to bring the English pubs to my golf clubs. We'd already achieved that kind of atmosphere at Birkdale, where we tag it as "community golf at its best." That's what we are, community golf. There are no fancy frills. It's community golf that's affordable, and we give them a good time. We have programs for kids, programs for moms, free clinics for everybody, and all kinds of cool initiatives to get people out to the club. At the private club, we were breaking boundaries with these kinds of programs. I own the club, but if members wanted ownership, they could come up with some money to show how genuine they are. To get $52,000 in 10 days, I was like, "Oh my God!" So we built this fantastic smoking room, and it has been a huge success, a slam. I put a $6,000 pool table in there, a dart board in there, a bar, card tables and so on. Wednesday, Thursday and Friday nights are now so busy that we had to bring in a full-time bar person just to take care of that room. It's fantastic!

Now we're in a position where both clubs are running well. I've got good, talented teams in place. I brought in some raw talent that I've helped develop. The clubs are breaking even or making some money after all expenses. I wish they were both making another $100,000 so I could get my payrolls out of club revenues and then concentrate on the next levels for the clubs. I love my clubs, but it is hard work. I still open up and I still close them up. Twice a week I do "Club Night" where we become English pubs. I'm at those special nights to 9 p.m. Every Saturday and Sunday morning, I'm at the golf courses. Every day I try to visit both clubs and drive the golf courses when I can. My office is always open and my light is always on, or they see me on the golf course. The members love it that Mike is always here. That is one huge asset that we have as mom-and-pop, independent operations that the corporations just don't have.

Because I was involved in the corporate golf ownership and operation business, I have to be careful what I say here. Now I sit on the NGCOA national board, and there are lots of those big corporations on that board. But in my time at this conference, I find it amazing how mom-and-pop are scared by the corporations when they need to know that their biggest assets are themselves. In a mom-and-pop operation, the players or members can go and talk with the owners and they can have an impact on the club's life. In a corporate-owned golf course, you may see the regional manager once a month, which is how I used to do it. The clubs are corporate driven, and any initiatives come down from a corporate office. Although I am very concerned that the corporations are going to gobble up some of these clubs that are struggling, I also think that Mom and Pop have the best opportunity ever. They are not corporate America. They are independent, small owners who live in the community. They need community support but can give that support back to their communities, as well. These small owners need to come up with creative community initiatives to get people excited about coming back to their clubs.

For example, for the last couple years we've had a program called "Play Golf Chesterfield," where every Saturday afternoon in May for three hours any resident of Chesterfield County can show up for free golf and instruction. We do one hour of standing up and talking about the game, and then all of our staff and some volunteering local pros walk the line and watch guests hit balls. We spend time with the guests and tell them we need them to come play golf. The seminars and lessons are absolutely free. The volunteers don't get paid, but I always give them a thank you present at the end. We've created so much loyalty from that program. We obviously got play for the golf course, but we got new memberships, too. Last year we discovered that some of our current members were showing up for the Saturday instruction. They would be making the turn after the front nine, had to pass the driving range, and they would stop their rounds to come to listen to the seminar. It really took us off-guard. Calloway Golf and Bridgestone Golf got involved and gave two-ball packs to everybody who came. They did demo days to promote their products. We send business their way, and it comes back to benefit us. This coming year we will be doing the program on Sunday afternoons. Saturday afternoons were too busy to manage the regular golf course business and the Play Golf Chesterfield program at the same time. This next year we will be doing an hour and a half for the public and an hour and a half for members. The members are already excited about it.

Every Tuesday night in May and June we will be doing free clinics for the kids to try to get more kids playing golf. We're going to do a surprise twist on it so that when Mom comes with the kids, we are going to have someone set aside just to teach the moms, even when the moms don't expect it. We don't want the moms to come expecting they'll have to play golf and maybe make fools of themselves. So we will dedicate staff to teaching the moms, and they can have a go on the side.

I don't have PGA pros at my clubs, which is sometimes frowned upon, but I believe I have extremely talented people who have been in the golf business long enough that they can teach professionally and they can create programs and initiatives as good as any PGA pro. Their main job for me is driving revenue, getting golfers on the golf course, and giving them a unique experience. I don't think that with what I pay my staff, I could get a PGA pro who could do any better than these home-bred, talented people I have and I've trained. When I take these staff on, I tell them we have good programs in place, I don't need for them to re-create the wheel, I just want them to come with great personalities and commitment and put golfers on the courses. I want my staff to play golf, but I also want them on the first tee to greet people, to drive the golf courses on the weekend. If it's busy and we made a mistake like booking too many players, or something else goes wrong on the course, I don't want my staff to send out their assistants. I want them out there and available to help in person. I insist on it. They'll address a mistake by saying something like, "Sorry guys. We goofed up. Here's a six-pack. Here's couple sleeves of balls. We apologize. Let's make sure everybody is happy. We want you to come back." Some staff is still reluctant. They cower and run away, not quite sure of how to deal with problems. We know we're going to goof up. We're doing 32,000 rounds a year at one club, and we're going to sell 100 shitty burgers, 100 cokes that don't have enough ice, or whatever. We will sometimes mess up. Anybody who says they don't mess up is garbage. Don't believe it. We hope we don't have to use it very often, but we work hard on service recovery. We know it works very well for us.

I don't have excessive payrolls. I'm tight in how I run my clubs because I need to be. I know where the margins are. We know we're lean and we know we're mean, and we work to get better all the time. We are at a disadvantage compared to corporate courses where if you have 30 golf courses you can hire someone specifically to deal with social media, twitter, facebook or other initiatives. You can pay that specialist $30,000, but that works out to $1,000 per club, or $88 a month. It's just easier to swallow up in your budget. The independent owner may not be able to hire specialists.

At this conference, there is a lot of talk about the impact of social media, and it's apparent to me that we are behind at my clubs. Who knew? It's becoming so popular that I will probably have to spend maybe $20,000 to bring someone in to do social media. On the other hand, I have been listening to some of the corporations talking about what they are doing with social media, and I think a lot of it is rubbish. When I was in the corporate world, I said I did all of those things, too, but some of those big plans never get down to the club level. You can never get 16 or 30 managers to all buy into an initiative your way.

The mom-and-pop operations at the conference are probably thinking they wish they could do things the way the corporately owned courses do things, but they shouldn't be scared. The big guns talk a good game, but they don't always deliver the way they say. When the independent owners are present and involved intimately with their clubs, they can make things happen that day. When plans are regional or corporate, new plans may take three or four months to roll out. Don't get me wrong, some of the initiatives are fantastic. American Golf, 15 years ago, made every head of department shake the hands of three to five customers a day that they didn't know. To me, that was the best program I had ever rolled out. I made some loyal friends through that program. I needed a kick up the ass to go out and do it, but it was a good idea. I still have in my office a template that was called AGC 2000. Back in the 1990s we were preparing for 2000 and how golf was going. The template was all about your staff, what they expect from you and what you expect from them. I give that template to every one of my employees today. Have you been told what your job is? If you don't know what your job is, do you know who to contact to find out what to do? For department heads, have you truly followed up with your staff? Have you met with them 10 days after starting something new to see how they are doing? It was a great tool that reminds us every day that the staff is where it all happens. It's really not about the corporation or the owner; it's about the starter, the marshals out on the course, or the guys behind the counter. That's what excites me the most. I can drive the golf course with the marshal or the pro, and we do. It makes such a tremendous difference in our industry to get involved where the customer gets served.

I suppose I've become Mom and Pop. I'm not corporate golf anymore. With the consulting company, I'm trying to fight for Mom and Pop. It's not because I'm antsy with the corporations. I'm not. I have full admiration for them, but I view them as a huge threat to my business. I still believe Mom and Pop have an amazing opportunity, not to dominate the market, but to have a huge impact in the market. If I'm coming into your town and you say there's a great bar that Bill owns or there's an Applebees, where are we going to go? I still think most people are going to Bill's. You know who Bill is. Now Applebees is a great place, you know what you're going to get and it's good, but it's still a chain. I don't know if people are really resistant to corporate America, but we think Bill can offer a unique experience. Now Bill may be drunk at the bar, or Bill may buy you a drink at the bar. At Applebees you know what you're going to get, and they won't break any of their rules. So is it the excitement that you can break the rules, or is it the excitement that Mom and Pop are going to come over and say hello to you? Or would people rather go to corporate America or Applebees because they know what they will get and no one will bother them, which some prefer. It's so exciting to work out what the customers want, and as an independent owner, I can create that unique experience.

When I look at my Club Night at both of my clubs, we throw $50 in a pot as a club credit every week. If you are present and your name is pulled out of the membership database, you win $50. If no one wins that week, it's $100 the next week. On Club Night we were averaging 60 to 70 people a week. It was their one night out during the week and it didn't matter if it was $50 or $100 in the pot. Now the last four weeks, it's been at $1,000, the limit we set. So we're getting 130 to 140 people a week coming to the club. We've basically created a train wreck. But the golf managers are there, the golf pros are there, the superintendents are there, and the food and beverage managers are there. That's an opportunity to come and meet our staff and for our staff to meet our customers. We'll be there all week, but on Club Night you can see us all. Instead of working through an advisory board or getting annoying emails, come to see us. We're there! Come and talk with us. Don't let any issue build up for two or three weeks. Just come see us and talk with us at Club Night.

Club Night has been a tremendous asset in terms of the business bottom line, but also for relationships with our customers. In the past we've had a few winners, but now we are at $1,000. No one won last night, making it five weeks in a row without a winner. The customers think it's a fix and don't want me to draw the names now, so we let them draw names themselves. At Brandermill we've been up to $800 for the Club Night there. Then somebody won the pot, but 90-percent of the customers came back the next week, anyway, even though the pot was back to $50. That's loyalty! That's seeing the members and having them see the staff. That's what we want. Come see us and touch us. If you don't like us, just say so, we are here for you. Tell us the "goods" and the "bads," and we will use the input to improve.

Yeah, I'm nervous, but mostly I'm excited about the future. In the club we've had for five years, the rollercoaster ride of starting the operation is over. The honeymoon is over and we are down to business now. We sold so many memberships and we have so much repeat business. People appreciate that we put so much new money into the club to get it right, and it paid dividends. We don't need to put that kind of money into the club right now. We are at a place where we can get down to our core values. That is, we can really take care of our members by creating a unique experience for them by having a team of staff that's dedicated to making it work. There's no magic wand. People ask what's unique about us. All golf course owners say they have great customer service and they all say they have the best golf course. Well, they don't. Everyone is good out there. What I do think makes us stand out is that with the two courses, we have 36 holes of golf at one great price. I do have a lead on some of my competitors because of that. I think when you get to five or more golf courses, you become more corporate, less personalized and less unique.

The golf course we've had for five years started off as a tremendous success, but the last year or year and a half has been really tough. From all of the memberships we've sold, we've still lost 30 to 40 percent just because people are losing their jobs at companies that are downsizing. We've sold so many memberships that some of those people didn't get their value for their money. They jumped on for passion, the excitement and the buzz, but then later realized they may have spent $3,000 last year and only played golf 10 times. We've had some attrition that way, which is sad.

But I still say, last winter was the worst winter in Virginia history. We had the hottest summer ever this past summer. Now we're going through another awful winter. So I'm having a tough time saying, "What's Obama doing? What's the country doing? What's the recession doing to my business?" The weather is reducing play, and I'm losing members because of it. Also, some are leaving because they just can't afford it anymore. They are opening up and telling me. I'm losing some who tell me they just can't play golf 12 months a year like they thought they could. They don't mind the cost when they're playing, but when those membership bills come for three or four months in the winter and they aren't playing, then life is suddenly not as much fun. That's what weather can do in Virginia. I just don't see how anyone can make golf business work in Wisconsin with that weather.

Certainly, some beautiful golf properties are not making it. At one of the courses in my area, the owner has invested heavily in a new course, but he keeps hiring and firing staff. The turnover is amazing, and he is going to need some mighty deep pockets to keep the course going. But that's what is so unique and beautiful about our business. You've got the visionaries like Bob Lang at Erin Hills, you've got the egotistical guy that wants the hottest and horniest golf club out there but won't allow someone to run it professionally for them because they want to be hands-on, you've got some who have an OK idea about what they are doing, some who are mediocre, and some who are just amazing operators. Those really good operators have learned by trial and error, by managing on their feet. There is no textbook that says how to be successful, so there are so many levels of ownership. That's what makes it so much fun to me. That's what makes it so opportunistic. It is also why the corporations are probably licking their lips right now, because they can go out and pick up a bunch of gorgeous golf courses that are distressed assets. That's one of my biggest fears right now.

American Golf at one time managed 360 golf courses. Now they have 110 courses. That corporation, along with other corporations like Troon Golf Management and Billy Casper Golf are on missions to get up to 200 clubs each. If they dominate the market, the mom-and-pop operations are in real big trouble. At one time I was the bad corporate guy. At one time American Golf had 26 golf courses in England and members at one course were members at all of them. At Meadowbrook Golf we created cluster markets, and we picked on the little local clubs. Now it's come full circle and I am that local club. That's what terrifies me the most. If the big guns get together in your market, they can really hurt you. When that happens, you can only react by price. It's hard to react through service, because that should be as good as you can provide, anyway. When owners try to compete through lower prices, then it becomes a downward spiral for everybody. At my clubs we haven't gone to lower prices yet because we still have new product, but our competitors are going extremely low, and we may have to follow. We know the lower-priced competitors can't ride that strategy forever, but if they can make it for a couple of years, other owners will pay the pain eventually. The market is stagnant, and there are only so many golfers. We are all fighting for that same market share.

Most of us also have debt. Sometimes it's 10 percent or 15 percent. In the old days debt could have been as high as 80 or 90 percent, but those days are long gone. We just can't walk away from these properties. Golf courses are expensive. You can start off a restaurant for maybe $300,000 now-a-days. You wouldn't want to walk away from that kind of investment, but golf courses may be $3, $4 or $5 million, and you can't just walk away from that kind of investment. When I've done consulting, I tell people they can't sell if they only get 30 or 40 cents on a dollar. If they can live with that kind of loss, then sell. Otherwise, they need to have a plan that will get them through the next couple years, a plan that makes their financials look better. Then if they decide to sell in a couple years, their financials will look better on paper to help them get a fairer price. We definitely help owners develop exit strategies, but they usually aren't immediate exit strategies. They are more like three-, four- or five-year exit strategies. I just don't think it will get any better for two or three years. Certainly there are some owners who are millionaires, and selling below value may be tolerable, but for many of us our golf courses are our retirement plans. We don't have pensions coming. The properties are our retirement plans. That really worries me. If it all goes wrong for me, I could be 50 years old and have to start over from scratch. That's scary! For some very wealthy owners, they don't go to work every day to make ends meet. For me and many, many others, we do have to make ends meet for our families and the families of our staff. On the other hand, I think most owners are still passionate enough about their clubs, and there are enough smart people out there to make it work. For the Mom and Pops and the absentee owners, it's going to be really tough.

I was asked to be involved with the inaugural board of directors to set up the National Golf Course Owners Association in Virginia about a year ago. Mike Hughes, the chief executive officer of NGCOA, asked me to sit on the national board a year later. I am normally pretty low key. I'm not a great social being at networking, but I do a lot of talking to groups, particularly in my region, about succeeding in the golf business. I'm not a big razzmatazz kind of guy, but I do offer my opinions and I just like to get down to business. I'm willing to help anybody. I had a lot of great mentors helping me, and I want to share my experience.

At conferences like this one, you look around and see lots of guys in their 50s and 60s. They aren't at the end of their careers. They are still working really, really hard on their businesses. At my age, I'm really just starting my career compared to most golf course owners, but that's my choice. Very few golf course owners are under age 40, like me. But then again, how many people under 40 are stupid enough to want to own a golf course or have the opportunity to own a golf course? If I were starting over, I don't know if I would want to own a golf course in this current economic climate. That may be a bad thing to say. I'm glad about where I am and what I'm doing, but starting over, I might not want to do it again. It would have been easier to stay with a corporation, have a good paycheck and retirement benefits, get three weeks of vacation a year and let the corporation deal with the issues. Now if there is an audit from the wage-and-audit board, I have to deal with it. If the IRS is on my back, I have to deal with it. If I have property tax issues, I have to deal with it. With the corporation, I just worked with my managers and let the corporation handle all of those kinds of issues. Now I have to worry about a wrong checked box on an IRS form that can put you under scrutiny, or a manager who smacks a woman on her bottom and results in a lawsuit. It hasn't happened to me, but it could, and I would have to deal with it. If you don't budget $50,000 a year for attorney fees and something goes wrong and you have a sudden attorney expense, it can eat you alive. It could eat you up personally, eat your family up, and eat your business up. No one understands that about running a business. I think that's what is comforting about coming to trade shows like this one. We can huddle up and have a team hug and laugh at some of the stories. We all can identify because in some shape or form we have all been there.

I still have English citizenship. As an English citizen, my kids can study in Europe free of charge. If I become an American citizen, the kids will lose that opportunity. Once the kids are old enough and make their decisions, I will apply for American citizenship. It's the right thing to do. Some people frown on my nationality and would rather give their money to other Americans, but you don't come across many golf course owners like me. My nationality makes me somewhat unique. When people hear me talk at the golf course, they know straight away who I am and that's a good thing. Being English with an American business does make me stand out and help create my brand.

## Hatch's Lessons

- Having enough experience to be respected for the business advice you give others may develop into a revenue-producing consulting business, as it did with Hatch when he created Acumen Golf Management. The golf course business is tough. Some owners and operators may need help.

- Providing free golf clinics may generate new club memberships and customers and create increased loyalty with current customers. Incorporating demo days with equipment manufacturers during those clinics enables them to promote their products and increase customer participation, too.

- Sometimes mistakes are made that disappoint or upset customers. Focus on service recovery to assure apologies and amends are made to keep customers happy.

- "The mom-and-pop operations…are probably thinking they wish they could do things the way the corporately owned courses do things, but they shouldn't be scared. When the independent owners are present and involved intimately with their clubs, they can make things happen that day." Members and guests at a golf club appreciate knowing that the owner is present and approachable.

- "Your staff is where it all happens. It's really not about the corporation or the owner; it's about the starter, the marshals out on the course or the guys behind the counter. That's what excites me the most. It makes such a tremendous difference in our industry to get involved where the customer gets served."

- Be sure your staff understands what you expect from them, and you understand what they expect from you.

- "It's so exciting to work out what the customers want, and as an independent owner I can create that unique experience."

- Each week Hatch holds what he calls "Club Night" during which drawings for cash are held. Not only does the event create customer loyalty that helps the bottom line, but the golf managers are there, the golf pros are there, the superintendents are there, and the food and beverage managers are there. That's an opportunity to come and know the staff and for the staff to know the customers. Customer input can be used to improve services and quality.

- "If you don't budget...for attorney fees and something goes wrong and you have a sudden attorney expense, it can eat you alive. It could eat you up personally, eat your family up, and eat your business up. No one understands that about running a business."

# The PGA Pro

## Mike Malone, Owner and Operator of Ridges at Sand Creek in Jordan, Minnesota

ᔓ    ᔥ

*I interviewed Mike Malone at his course, Ridges at Sand Creek, in Jordan, Minnesota on April 6, 2011. Ridges at Sand Creek is an 18-hole public golf course with a year-around restaurant and banquet facility that opened in July 2000. The facility was rated #1 in the* Twin Cities Golf Guide *and was nominated as "Best New Course" by* Golf Digest *in 2001. Less than half an hour from Minneapolis, Ridges at Sand Creek continues to be voted as the "Best Value in Golf" in the Twin Cities of Minneapolis/St. Paul. In 2009 Ridges at Sand Creek was voted "Midwest Golf Course of the Year" by the National Golf Course Owners Association and was the only public facility in Minnesota ranked in the top 50 in* Golf World *magazine's "Readers' Choice Awards" for 2010.*

*With five sets of tees, large bentgrass greens and beautiful scenery, Ridges at Sand Creek has been host to many state, local and high school events in its short history. The course was designed by Joel Goldstrand.*

www.ridgesatsandcreek.com/

ᔓ    ᔥ

When I was in seventh grade, a good friend of mine and I decided to make a few dollars. I had never picked up a golf club, but we decided to go out to the golf course to try to caddie. We peddled our bikes about two-and-a-half miles out to the golf course, Faribault Country Club, and met the new pro at the course, Ken Gorg. He told us that sure, he would like to have some caddies available on Wednesday's Men's Day. So we went out on Wednesdays to caddie, and we met some of the gentlemen, the movers and shakers of our small community of Faribault, Minnesota. Ken soon told us that we had done a nice job and invited us to come back on the weekends, because lots of the men played on Saturday, too. So we caddied on the weekends, too. We'd caddie for $2. Maybe we'd get a dollar tip if we did a good job. We did that for a year, and then Ken told us, that we'd done a good job and the members liked us so he asked if we would come out to pick the driving range, too. So we started picking balls by hand on the driving range. We carried clubs with us, and we would chip the balls to the flags in the center of the range to make it easier to pick them up. That was really my first contact with actually playing golf.

Soon I started taking lessons and hitting lots of golf balls. Working at the club, I could hit all the balls I wanted to hit. I just kept hitting balls and hitting balls. Then I got playing rights to the golf course. The pro was great to me. He told me there was very little play on Tuesday afternoons so I could play then. My buddy and I played constantly. We'd play 36 to 54 holes in a day if we weren't caddying. Then Ken asked if I wanted to wash clubs for the members. When the men and women at the club came in from playing, they stored their clubs at the course, and their clubs needed to be washed before storing them. So we started washing clubs, too. By then I was growing a little taller, and Ken told me I could even watch the counter in the clubhouse once in a while, answer the phone and that sort of thing. Then he said that he was gone on Mondays and I could watch the counter on Mondays. I asked him what time that would be, and he told me they opened at 7a.m. and closed around 9 p.m. It was a bit intimidating, but I started doing that, too, and everything was working out well. Even during school I worked the shifts that I could and I kept playing more and more golf.

In high school at Bethlehem Academy, I won the conference championship, the DeSota Championship, for the small, private Catholic schools in the conference. I was the medalist for the conference in my sophomore and junior years and tied for medalist in my senior year. I had done very well in junior tournaments, too, so I thought that in college I wanted to play golf. I thought maybe there was a future for me in golf. One of the members at the club who was a good golfer had gone down to Ft. Lauderdale, Florida, to a junior college, Broward College. Being from Minnesota, going down to Ft. Lauderdale sounded like a really good idea. So I went to Broward College on a partial scholarship that took care of books and food. That seemed like a pretty good deal to me.

The golf coach at Broward took us to the golf course to meet the other players. We had the Florida state champion, all four players from the Florida state championship team, the Massachusetts state champion, the Indiana and Michigan champions, and me. That was intimidating enough, and then we started playing. I thought maybe something had happened to me driving down to Florida by myself. I was 30 yards short of those other guys on my tee shots. I thought maybe I was doing something wrong. Then I found out that these other guys were just so darned good. I was lucky to become the sixth man on their six-man team. I had been good in my local area back home. I won tournaments and I hit it the longest. Then you go to the next level, and like in all sports when you go to the next level, you find out that some guys are *really* good. In Florida there are lots of very strong players. The guys on my college team were longer than the players on the other teams we played. They were good guys and good players, and we came in second in the nation that year. Ft. Lauderdale was a very fun place.

In my second year at Broward, the pro at Faribault Country Club called me to say that his assistant pro was going to quit to go to another club. Ken asked me if I would come back to be his assistant pro. He said that even though I was only in my second year of college, I had a good record at Faribault, and I was his first choice for the job. I took a long walk on the beach with one of my golf buddies and asked if he thought I should do this. I was just playing golf and having fun, and I really hadn't spent that much time thinking about the future. Life was good. After a long walk, I was thinking I didn't really want to go back to Minnesota, but Ken is a really good guy. He was a Minnesota Hall of Famer, and he was at Faribault for 33 years. He was on the national PGA board and president of our local PGA section. He was a very good golf professional teacher. He taught me well and he was my mentor. He taught me how to run good tournament programs. He talked me into coming back to Minnesota to work for him. I finished my two-year degree in Minnesota while I was working. I didn't go for a four-year degree because I was busy working.

I worked for Ken for two years, and then I substituted out to do some teaching at Waseca Lakeside Club, where they had never had a golf pro. It was basically virgin territory for a pro over there, and I wanted to make some extra money giving lessons. I gave a lot of lessons, and the people at Waseca liked me, so the next winter they asked me if I would be their first golf pro. We all met over a nice dinner to discuss things. Ken Gorg came to the dinner, too. He told me it was a fair contract and he thought I was ready to be a head pro, even with only two years' experience under his supervision. I had really been in the business since seventh or eighth grade, and I had helped to do everything on a golf course. Ken had taught me to really peddle to go after golf customers. You can't just sit back; you have to work at getting customers and encourage their play. I still do lots of the things Ken taught me, like going out to the first tee to talk with guests. On the first tee you can really talk to people. They are relaxed and excited to go play golf. They haven't started their round yet, so everything is good. You can talk with them about all kinds of things. The clubhouse is just too busy. People want to pay in a hurry and go play. Getting to know the people on your course and giving them a chance to know you are really important for customer relations.

So at age 21, I set out on my own to be a head pro at Waseca Lakeside Club. I was one year away from finishing my PGA card that requires three years of working as a pro. If you aren't working for a head pro, it can take twice as long. If you are working for a pro, you get one credit per month toward your Class A card, and it takes 36 credits. After the first year at Waseca, I got my Class A card. There were no organized programs at the course when I took over, so I set up tournaments, outings and junior programs. We started a spring opener to get people mixed up with people they might not know. It's kind of a trick and part of my philosophy to get people to know others so they will be more comfortable. I believe that's part of what a pro needs to do. If I know a player likes to play golf a certain way, such as fast or slow, or by the rules only, early in the day or in the evenings, then I can introduce that player to others who like to play golf the same way. If I can find a good, comfortable game for a golfer, then I've got them committed and loyal. If a golfer can't find someone they enjoy playing with, then they keep looking and might go somewhere else. Golf is a very social activity and it should be fun. That means finding the right people to play with. Honestly, it really isn't so much the golf course that matters. Of course, the golf course has to be in good condition and the food has to be good, but most important are the people you are having fun with.

I worked at Waseca for three years—1977, '78 and '79. Waseca was an hour and a half from the Minneapolis metro area. Even though I had a house near the course, I was driving back and forth to the city, and it was starting to really get to me. I was young and trying to meet a lot of people and doing some dating. But I didn't want to date where I was working. Old pros will tell you, don't date members of the club or anyone in their families. That's a no-no. Driving back and forth to the metro was killing me so I started looking for a job closer to the city. I interviewed and got a job in Chaska at a semi-private course called Dahlgreen Golf Club in 1980. It was a similar scenario in that they had never had a head pro, either.

Dahlgreen was a very beautiful golf course, and there were really nice people there. When I took the job the course had only 12,000 rounds of golf that year. Within five or six years, we got the course to 48,000 rounds, which was our high point. Then we tried to stay around 45,000 rounds a year. For Minnesota golf with a limited season, we were really humming. We built a great membership of loyal players, and they brought their friends. We typically had 100 outings or tournaments a year, and we got lots of programs for golfers up and rolling. I had the pro shop concession, and I had the golf cart concession, which was financially beneficial to me.

Once the club got busier, they wanted to add onto the clubhouse. We needed more space. The club had owned the golf carts, but they needed some money for the additions, so I said I would buy the golf carts from the club. They had older Harley Davidson carts, and I offered $20,000 to buy them and have the cart concession. They took the deal and I went to my local banker and got the loan. I kept the cart concession for the next 15 years there. As rounds grew and more people started riding, the cart business became very profitable. I loved playing golf, but I loved the business side of golf, too.

My dad had been a car dealer in Faribault, Minnesota. He was always kind of mad that I didn't follow him into the car dealership. I was always out at the golf course. Dad retired and got into trucking for a while. He was even driving trucks. Then an E-Z-GO golf car dealership became available, so I told Dad, "Why don't we get into the golf car business? I know a lot of people in the golf business, and I understand how it works. You know how to run a dealership." So we bought the dealership and started our own business, called Versatile Vehicles. We had kind of missed that father-and-son working relationship when I was younger and he had the car dealership, so it was really fun being in business together. That dealership grew, and later Dad retired and has now passed on. I still have part ownership of Versatile Vehicles, which now is the second-largest golf car distributorship in the country. That small purchase of golf carts at Dahlgreen Golf Club turned out to be a pretty good investment.

When Dad was 72 years old, he decided to retire from our golf car dealership. We decided to sell Dad's part of the business to our controller, Gabriel (Gaby) Accad. Gaby is from Lebanon, and he was going to Bethel College on a student visa. He's a great guy and he had been doing our books. I had become friends with Gaby, and instead of putting Dad's half of the shares on the market, I wanted to sell them to Gaby. We helped Gaby get American citizenship. It's a tough process. We had to assure that Gaby's position in the company wouldn't take a job from an American. So we put an ad in the newspaper that made the job as complicated as we could make it sound. Surprisingly, we had 80 responses to the ad. To prove to the immigration people that those applicants weren't acceptable to get the job, we had to respond to each one of them by certified mail. It was a long process, but eventually he did get American citizenship and he did buy half of the golf car dealership. He's a great partner and he's done a wonderful job. If you call him to talk to him, you'd better schedule a lot of time. His name, Gaby, really suits him. He's a fabulous salesman and operator. With him now as president of the company, we do 20 times the business we used to do. It's a great personal story.

In the mid-'90s I helped to start another company called NHD (Newman, Herth and Durand) Property Management with two other guys. We were looking to acquire golf courses. The timing was good, and the market was great for acquisitions of new golf courses. They were property managers, and I was in charge of the golf end of the company. In 1993 we bought a golf course called Southern Hills in Farmington, Minnesota. That meant that I was running Southern Hills and golf operations at Dahlgreen Golf Club and the golf car company. At NHD I was really running everything. Oh, and I was raising a young family, too. We have four daughters. When we acquired Southern Hills, I was over the general manager and had to oversee food and beverage, everything. I was really busy, and we were still looking to acquire more golf courses. After a couple of years I decided that it was just too much, and I decided to sell my interest in NHD. I had to wait out the non-compete clause of my contract, and then I went for getting my own golf course. I knew the golf business, and I learned a lot about budgets and financial models working with NHD and those excellent property managers. I was ready to go on my own.

In 1999 I was called by a friend one night who told me he and his friends had just picked up an option on 400 acres in Jordan, Minnesota, and wanted to know if I would come take a look at the property. We met at the property and tramped around the 400 acres. It was beautiful wooded and hilly land, with a river running through it. They wanted to build homes on the property, and they could only build one per 10, or 40 home lots for the 400 acres. They also picked up an additional 40 acres from local property owners. With three-acre lots, there were 120 acres used out of the 400-plus acres that were left. They asked if I would like to build a golf course on the extra acreage to increase the amenity for the eventual homeowners. I was interested and there were some other bidders. I was actually the lowest bidder, but those guys had known me for a long time and knew I had a good track record with some of them. They decided to take a shot with a young guy, me. They decided to do the home development part of the project, and I would do the golf development separately.

In developing the golf course, there were some philosophies that I thought and still think are important. People don't like to hit shots out of bounds. Make the golf holes wide enough that people won't get penalized for hitting out of bounds. I wanted to make the game as easy as I could, with bounces toward the hole rather than away from the hole. At that time it seemed like everybody was making golf courses more difficult to play. The mantra at the time was "championship" golf courses and building difficult courses. I thought that was holding the game back. Courses were just too hard, and people were getting their brains beat in on the golf courses. If players don't have a good time, they just might not come back to play again.

I had spent a lot of time behind the counter at my golf courses, and I knew what the players wanted. I wanted a golf course that made players feel successful. I wanted players to make birdies. When golfers finish their round of golf, they love to talk about their birdies. They don't want to talk about their triples or holes that beat them up. I wanted some holes on the course that players could score well on. If you look at a scorecard on a Pete Dye (*noted golf course architect*) course and you see there is a par-4 hole that's only 300 yards long, you immediately know the length will be deceptive. There will be 4,000 bunkers, out-of-bounds left, out-of-bounds right, and players will not be likely to get a par. On the greens, don't make the slopes so difficult that players can't score and the difficulty slows play down. Nobody likes to 3-putt, especially on greens with big mounds in them. Make the greens so they can be putted with some success. Those were some of the philosophies that I wanted to build into the golf course. Make the bounces go the player's way. It's really unusual to hit out of bounds on my course. Sand Creek, which is really a small river, runs through the golf course. Visually, the river is always present on six holes, but the holes are designed so that the river doesn't really come into play. You really have to hit a terrible shot to hit into the water. Golf should be a setting to have a good time, not to destroy you and create a bad time. I think these philosophies have helped to make us successful.

I bought the property in 1999 and opened the course, Ridges at Sand Creek, in 2000. The course was designed by a friend of mine, Joel Goldstrand. I interviewed different architects around the country. I wanted to create a unique look for the course, something different from other courses in the area. I talked to architects in California, Kansas City and Texas. Their ideas were great, but they didn't know who the contractors were in Minnesota. Then I interviewed Joel Goldstrand, who is a local pro from Minnesota who had been on the PGA Tour for 18 years. He has designed about 60 courses in Minnesota. He's a friend of mine, and I saved his interview until the end of the process. After we talked, there was no question. He was the man for the job. He knew the contractors. He knew right away who we wanted to construct the course. It was a tough job. There is a lot of fall on the property, and there were lots of trees. Joel said he would be on site every week, maybe twice a week. The other architects I interviewed could not make that promise. He gave me a flat-price bid for the job. Regardless of what might come up, I knew what he would cost. He had previously designed a lot of par-3 courses and short courses, but I didn't think he had ever had the right property to work with to show his creativity. Also, I thought he had broader knowledge than the others I had interviewed. He's a fabulous architect.

To be honest, I had laid out some holes on the property. Joel's design used some of the same sites for holes that I liked, but his design ran the course the opposite direction from what I had been thinking. When I saw his design, I knew it made so much more sense than what I had been thinking. We both wanted to use the high ground on the property for tee placements, so the golfer sees the holes and can see their shots. There are no blind shots. Also, I wanted the back nine holes to have 3, 3 and 3. I think it's the most fun to have three par 5s, three par 4s and three par 3s. We wanted to stage the golf course so that people would enjoy it and have fun.

From the time I bought the property to the time we opened the course was only a year. I sent out bids to all of the local banks and they were all cooperative and sent me bids. I have a good track record with golf courses in the area and that helped. I'm not a plumber who decided he wanted a golf course. I had financial experience, and I had lots of experience running a golf course. I got the funding from a local bank. Fortunately, we were kind of at the end of a big construction era. We started building in 1999 with a construction crew from Ashland, Wisconsin, called Northern Clearing. They had two crews. One crew started right away, but their second crew was building a course in North Carolina. By July that year I had both crews working at Ridges. Then things started to move very fast. Money was important to me. I am not a wealthy individual, and I knew we had to open as quickly as we could to start making some revenue. We finished construction by that August. I had two superintendents, who happen to be brothers, one for each of the construction crews. By September we seeded the course, and we were thinking that by maybe the next August or September we could open the course. In the spring we saw that the seeding really took, and we had a great growing season. We fertilized like crazy. By the end of June, the course had just exploded with growth. From the first of that June to the end of that month, things really grew. The days start to get long, and it's unbelievable how quickly things can change. We just kept cutting grass. It was unbelievable, and by the first of July in 2000 we opened.

It was so fun that first day. My dad was around and helping. He'd be driving around in a cart, smoking his pipe, and keeping an eye on things. During early construction, I was still working at Dahlgreen Golf Club, 12 miles away, but Dad would be on-site at the Ridges and keeping in touch with me by cell phone. He'd let me know if I had to rush over to check something out. I knew what to expect. I knew the southwest metro area, the golfers and the competition. In some ways I didn't see my new course as a big gamble. But you never really know how the golfers will respond to your course. You think you've done your homework, and you think the golf course is good, but on opening day it's still scary. You don't know what the golfers will think. Then when you open and you hear the first golfers come in after playing and say, "Wow! This is really good! We had so much fun!" That's when you can take a breath.

When we opened, the clubhouse was in a trailer. We were watching the budget and thought it would be best to do clubhouse construction in the winter. The clubhouse was completed the next summer in 2001. After a year and a half, we decided we needed a bigger banquet space, so we doubled the banquet space. People in this area like to have big weddings. Three hundred wedding guests is not uncommon, so we created a banquet area for 400 people. That took us from four or five weddings a year to 40 a year. We're in a nice niche. There is a nearby facility that can handle 800 guests, and there are lots of places that handle about 100 people, but there was nobody else who did the most popular wedding size of 300. Also, the bigger clubhouse and banquet facility allows us to book charity outings where you need lots of tables to spread out auction items and that sort of thing. To be honest, I needed that extra space from the addition for cart storage, too. We had gotten so busy that I needed the room for more carts that we store in a big, fancy garage underneath the banquet facility.

We went right up to 35,000 rounds a year. That's right where we want to be. At first we crammed tee times close together and tried to get to 40,000 rounds, but it wasn't a fun experience for the golfers. So now we space the tee times a little farther apart so golfers don't feel packed in and their rounds won't take five or six hours. At first there just weren't many other golf course options in our area, and we knew the golfers would come to our course. Now there is competition with other courses and we want to be sure the golfers come to our course because it's the course they enjoy the most.

We've had some great recognition. With the golf shop I was "PGA Merchandiser of the Year" for three years. Ridges at Sand Creek was rated #1 in the *Twin Cities Golf Guide* and was nominated as "Best New Course" by *Golf Digest* in 2001, soon after we opened. We continue to be voted as the "Best Value in Golf" in the Twin Cities of Minneapolis/St. Paul. In 2009, we were voted "Golf Course of the Year" by the National Golf Course Owners Association. Maybe the recognition we are most proud of was for our hospitality as the only public facility in Minnesota ranked in the top 50 in *Golf World* magazine's "Reader Choice Awards" for 2010. We got ranked right next to Bethpage State Park, where their Black Course has been a site for two U.S. Open tournaments. We think our golf course is great, but it feels really great to get recognized for how people are having fun and enjoying being here.

The golf course has five sets of tees, so you can play it short or you can play it long at 7,000 yards. It's fun to play, but from the longer tee boxes it's challenging, too. The course record was set by PGA Tour pro Troy Merritt, who shot a 66. All that golfers really want is to have fun and hit some good shots. Our course has the flexibility to give golfers the chance to feel successful when they play from the tees that suit their game. I wish other courses weren't so difficult. For most golfers the really hard courses just don't encourage play. Golfers want to have a good time, and giving them a course that helps them have a good time is the key.

We do as much as we can to stay involved with our community. We have lots of fund-raising events at the course, and we work closely with the charity events to help assure their success. The golf course is really a community asset. That's how we look at it. We collect demographics from our players to see where they come from. The course is 20 to 30 minutes from the metro area, so we do draw business from the Twin Cities, but also from local communities in our area. One of our biggest draws is from Prior Lake, which is a pretty large town. Prior Lake has two very good golf courses, The Wilds and The Legends. Both of those are $100 courses. Our price-point at about $50 makes us very competitive. I'm more interested in getting players to come here regularly than I am in having them come just once in a while to check it out. Our price-point, the quality of our course and our service all encourage the player loyalty we want.

Being located in a smaller community helps me to select the kinds of employees I want. I look for team-oriented people who understand customer relations. If I have a position to fill, I can get lots of suggestions from our regular golfers about who in the area would be a good fit. The people I hire who say "Hi" to everybody and look the guests in the eye are the ones who get the most hours of work. Those employees who aren't comfortable with that kind of open hospitality just won't get the hours and won't stay.

Our restaurant is open year around. As much as possible we buy our food locally, and we make everything from scratch. We don't serve any pre-made food. In the winter the restaurant really isn't all that profitable, but we want it open, because it gives the community a place to go for a nice meal. For weddings and banquets, it's important to have a good chef. You have to have really good food when you bring in hundreds of guests at a time. Because the food service is year-around, the chefs are employed all year long, and that helps keep them here and gives us the quality and consistency we want. At the clubs where I worked before, it seemed like we had a new chef every year, and I saw how that didn't create the consistency I wanted. Our chef has been with us since 2002. She is a wonderful chef and just a pleasure to be around.

I suppose that one of the biggest challenges I've faced is the discounting of golf that has become so popular as too many courses try to compete for business. I decided that I would not do discounting and coupons. My philosophy has been to establish a fair price and stay with it. The *Twin Cities Golf Guide* in 2001 named us the "Best Value in the Twin Cities." Maybe I'm just not smart enough to do the new marketing. I'm more old-school. You set one fair price and stay with it. That's how we used to do it and I still do it. I think customers enjoy knowing what the price is going to be and that everybody who plays here will pretty much pay that same price. Loyal players can buy packages at reduced rates per round, and we also sell corporate rounds. When car dealerships were booming, we started selling corporate cards so that dealerships could buy 100 rounds of golf that they could give away or distribute as incentives to employees or customers however they wanted. Corporations can use the expense as tax deductions. The corporate business isn't as good as it once was. There is a lot of competition among golf courses for corporate business, and corporations are not investing in those entertainment or promotional practices as much during the recession, but we do still sell corporate cards and it helps us.

Our immediate goal is to increase play with our loyal golfers. The town of Jordan, where we are, is at a population of 10,000 now, but the projection is that the population should be 30,000 by 2025. The area is growing as the Twin Cities continue to spread out, and we want to be sure to bring that population growth to the course. The town has planned for that growth with an infrastructure to support more people, and there is a brand new school in town, but the recession has slowed down real estate development and the growth in people is slow. It will happen, though. When we built here, we planned for that growth, so we are ready. I don't think we will see any new courses being built in the area, and that will help us, too. I was always concerned that someone would build a new course between our location and the Twin Cities, but financing for a course is nearly impossible now, and property for a course is more and more scarce. With the supply of golfers, there really isn't a market for another course. That's good for me.

The residential development real estate on our property was sold out within the first three months. Forty-four home sites went in less than three months. All but about six lots have homes built on them now. The course itself is designed so that the homes on the property are mostly not even visible to the golfer. That helps create the kind of get-away experience I always wanted.

For the golf industry in general I believe we have to make better connections with the 25- to 45-year-old age group. In our area every other demographic is doing well. We have the seniors, the juniors and women playing golf. These groups are up, but it's the 25- to 45-year-old guy that is missing. I say "guy" because I think that's the demographic we need. These guys are active and should be spenders, but they have to work longer hours, may be mortgaged over their heads, don't have the deductions that some might have gotten in the past, have young families with children's activities, and they just don't have the recreational time that group used to have. Parenting alone is taking more time than ever. To be a good parent, Mom and Dad now have to go watch their kids play soccer, or whatever. There are a lot of constraints that have hit that age group really hard. That's the guy we're missing in the industry, and I am looking for ways to bring them back to golf. They like "techie" stuff, so we are trying to use new technologies to make contact with them. Maybe they would prefer short rounds of golf. I've done three holes of golf with a cart for women who want to play for only an hour. I might do something like that for the young men to see if that brings them back. The first time I ran an ad for women to come out for $10 for a short lesson, three holes of golf and a cart, I had 160 women show up. They swarmed us. The clubhouse was completely full. Since then, we've put a limit of the first 40 to register. You just can't fit too many on the course at a time. For the guys, I don't know how or what timing is best, but I am searching for the key, the secret to bringing them back to put some fun in their lives.

I always think that golf has a positive future. Golf is one of the few things that people can do outside, and that makes golf unique. There is no question that there are just too many golf courses right now. Some courses aren't that good or aren't located in the right spot. Some courses are just old, and like everything else, their time has come. Clubhouses need to be rebuilt; irrigation systems, greens, everything has a lifespan. Personally, I hope those kinds of courses will close and not be bought by someone who loves the game and tries to bring the courses back. It concerns me that people are buying those distressed courses very cheaply, and then they can reopen them with even lower fees for golfers. That kind of cycle of making golf cheaper and cheaper is not good for most people in the industry. We simply have too many courses for the supply of golfers, and some courses have to close for the health of the industry.

I was on the board of directors for the PGA for three or four terms. I've been president of the Midwest Golf Course Owners Association before, and now I am serving as president again. Right now I'm also on the Minnesota Golf Association board's management committee. It's important to me to be involved like that to promote golf and the golf industry. I've been a golf guy since the seventh grade. I love the game, and I will continue to do all I can to promote the industry and my golf business.

## Malone's Lessons

- You can't just sit back; you have to work at getting customers and encourage their play.
- Getting to know the people on your course and giving them a chance to know you are really important for customer relations.
- If a golfer can't find someone they enjoy playing with, then they keep looking and might go somewhere else. Golf is a very social activity and it should be fun. That means finding the right people to play with. Create opportunities for golfers to mix with each other through tournaments and outings, and introduce golfers to others with similar interests and playing preferences.
- If you know your business thoroughly, from the bottom up, then you recognize opportunities to develop. Because Mike had worked at every job imaginable on golf courses, beginning as a child, he knew that golf cart concessions could be profitable. His initial cart concession led to ownership of the second-largest golf car distributorship in the country. His understanding of golf led to partnership in a property management company involved with golf course acquisition and then to ownership of his own golf course.
- In designing a golf course, keep in mind that if players don't have a good time, they might not return. Reduce the likelihood of penalties, make bounces go the player's way, create opportunities for players to succeed. For most golfers, the really hard courses just don't encourage play. Golfers want to have a good time and giving them a course that helps them have a good time is the key.

- A clubhouse and banquet facility should be large enough to accommodate the kinds of business you wish to attract. At Ridges at Sand Creek, the facility was built to accommodate up to 400 guests, a perfect size for most weddings.

- Do as much as you can to stay involved with your community. Ridges hosts lots of fund-raising events at the course, and they work closely with charity events to help assure their success. The golf course is really a community asset.

- Create a price-point that is competitive and that encourages players to come to your course regularly, with loyalty, rather than once in a while to just check it out.

- Hire employees who say "Hi" to everybody and look the guests in the eye. Those employees who aren't comfortable with that kind of open hospitality just don't have what it takes in the golf industry.

- You have to have really good food when you bring in hundreds of guests at a time.

- One of the biggest challenges golf course owners face is the discounting of golf that has become so popular as too many courses try to compete for business. The philosophy at Ridges has been to establish a fair price and stay with it. "You set one fair price and stay with it. That's how we used to do it and I still do it. I think customers enjoy knowing what the price is going to be and that everybody who plays here will pretty much pay that same price."

- When you love the game of golf and you are in the golf industry, then it benefits you to stay involved in promoting the game and the industry locally and through regional and national trade associations.

# A Family Affair

Tom Brady and Family, Owners of Toad Valley Golf Course and Conference Center in Pleasant Hill, Iowa

               80     CR

*I interviewed the Brady family on September 31, 2011, at their Toad Valley Golf Course in Pleasant Hill, Iowa, just east of Des Moines. Participating in the interview were Tom Brady (owner and president), his wife, "Fred" Brady (The Kitchen Guru), and their daughter Allison George (The Wizard of Fun). Tending the snack bar in the clubhouse was Tom and Fred's son Jason (Gorilla). Jason's wife, Theresa (Queen of Clean), was in and out of the clubhouse. Allison's husband, Kelly George (Turf Jedi), was on the course working as superintendent. The Bradys and Georges are one big, happy family. The reader will see that this third-generation, family-owned business does things a bit differently from the traditional golf course business.*

*Toad Valley Golf Course is an 18-hole public golf course that opened in 1973. The course was largely designed by Tom and built by family patriarch Dale Brady, now deceased, and his sons, Dan, Tom and Steve when they decided to change the family farm into a golf course. Over three generations, 10 members of the family have participated in owning and operating Toad Valley.*

*In addition to the golf course, there is a conference center for hosting weddings, banquets and outings and a miniature golf course, called Field of Greens, which is particularly helpful for involving children and parents in family golf.*

www.toadvalleygolfcourse.com

               80     CR

**Tom:** My father, Dale Brady, was the founder of a local farm equipment manufacturing company, which oddly enough was called Brady Manufacturing. He started the business in 1945, the year I was born. He was more of an inventor than he was a manager. In 1950 he sold part of the company to get the financing he needed to expand his inventing interests. In 1959 he sold the rest of the business, but he continued to work for the company, still called Brady Manufacturing, until the early 1970s. He was their vice president in charge of development of equipment. The point of this story is that in 1959 he purchased this farm that we're sitting on right now. At that time it was a 260-acre farm. He never actually farmed the land, but it was used partially as a demonstration farm for the equipment manufacturing business that he was a part of since the '40s. It was the Brady Manufacturing Demonstration Farm.

My younger brother was a golfer in high school, and my older brother piddled around with golf, too. I had played golf a bit as a kid, but I really took it up at age 22. At that time I was a supervisor at the local Firestone tire plant. I remember my dad and I went to Walgreens and bought starter golf sets. We each bought clubs, bag and wheels for about 30 bucks. Dad and I went out to a local golf course to play and be joined by my two brothers, who actually knew something about playing golf. So my two brothers, Dad and I started playing golf together and taking vacations together. We really enjoyed playing and having the time with each other. One time we were all together, and we suggested to Dad that he change the farm into a golf course. We enjoyed it that much, and it seemed like a good idea at the time. My dad had plans already drawn up to change the farm into a camp ground, but he took the golf course idea and ran with it. Dad always had big toys to play with, and a golf course suited how he did things.

That's when I got involved with designing the golf course as an architect. We have always been self-sufficient, and we didn't want to pay for an architect. As I said, I was a supervisor at the tire plant, working nights, and I had the time during the day to work with an aerial view of the farm to lay out the golf course plans. Initially I laid it out on big pieces of paper as a nine-hole course, but we had enough land and decided to make it an 18-hole course. That was 1971 and 1972. Our family actually used those plans and built the course in 1972 and 1973, and then we opened the course in 1973. Things were much cheaper in those days, but we figured we still needed a couple of hundred thousand dollars. Dad cashed in all of his insurance, everything he had, and then borrowed the additional money to build it. As I recall we never owed more than $125,000.

We built it ourselves. My dad and I began by building the number-18 green, right by the pond. We watered it with a portable watering system, just to see if we could do it. When the green survived the winter, we knew we could build a course.

As an example of how we did things, most people today who want to install irrigation systems hire an irrigation contractor who will draw up the plan and give you the materials list for pipes and pumps and all that is needed. We got in touch with a trenching contractor who wanted $3,700, and they wanted to do the work in a day or two. It would have never worked for us to have all those open trenches on the property at the same time. So instead of contracting out for the work, Dad bought a used trencher for $2,300, and we did it ourselves 1,000 feet at a time.

When we started building the course, there was a crew building the paved road alongside the property. My dad flagged those guys down, and we used them to help move soil for greens, tee boxes and that sort of thing. We were using the plan I made, but we also hired a guy who had some experience building golf courses, Harold McCullough, who made some minor changes to my plan to guide the road contractors for the main soil movement. Then we installed the greens mix ourselves with some of the big toys my dad liked to have. Dad had a big, four-wheel-drive Steiger tractor that we used, probably even before John Deere was making them. We had a scraper behind the tractor, and Dad built a blade for the front of it. He had a road grader, too. Dad ran over his pickup truck with the grader. Jason, our son, who was riding with his grandpa that day, turned to him and said, "Grandpa, I think you just ran over your El Camino."

As a typical Iowa farm, there were hardly any trees anywhere when we started building the course. Every tree that we have now we have planted. I don't know if you could build a course like that today. I've probably planted 90 percent of the trees. The birds and the squirrels spread some seeds, and you have to give them their due too.

We named the course Toad Valley. We do have lots of toads on the property, because we have so many ponds that amphibians love, but that's not how we came up with the name. Dad, my two brothers, our four spouses and I decided that we would name the course by each of us submitting all the names that came to mind. We had some off-the-wall suggestions. The ones I remember that made it into final consideration were Irish Spring, which is a brand of soap, and it was too strange to name a golf course for a soap, even if the Bradys are Irish. We considered Stephandale because my younger brother's first name is Stephan and his middle name is Dale. I didn't vote for that one. We thought about Hill and Dale, using my dad's name of Dale. By that time we had bought a tree spade, and we were planting pine trees by the tee boxes so we thought about Pine Tees for a name. All together we had 64 names that we considered. When we all voted for our favorites, we eliminated every name but Toad Valley. The process may not have been all that interesting, but we do like the uniqueness of our name. Since the beginning of the course, all of our tee markers that I make are in the shape of a toad.

**Fred:** We liked the name Toad Valley. It's playful and it's different. Our family just never takes ourselves too seriously. Others must like the name, too. Logo balls with Toad Valley on them are one of the top sellers because the name is so unique.

**Tom:** It's turned out well for us. Elsewhere people might think Toad Valley is a funny name, but around here, where people know our course, the name comes out easily. I've looked at the names of every golf course in the United States. There is only one Toad Valley.

We didn't really do what people today would call market research to study the feasibility of opening a new golf course in the area. Our family had been playing golf at a local course a few miles away in Altoona. The founder of that course, Joe Riding, and my dad were friends. Dad asked Joe what he thought about us building another golf course in the area and Joe said, "The more the merrier." That course is now owned by the third generation of Ridings, and I'm not so sure the new generation would still feel that way, but at the time, there wasn't all that much concern about competition out here. Now it's a golfer's paradise, overbuilt with golf courses. Now we see local golf courses going broke or struggling to stay open. Times were different when we started.

I just don't know that anyone could open another course like Toad Valley in today's market, designing it and building it yourself. Typical golf courses today are built in forested areas, and trees are cleared to create the course. Here we had a few trees along the fence line, some along the creek bed and some willows in some low areas. That was it. We had to take the willows out to build a pond in that location, and some of the other existing trees were lost as we started shaping the course. Then we had to start planting every tree we have.

In some locations on the course, I've created what I cleverly call "no-mow" areas, where I've planted some of the more exotic trees. Even a bad golfer like me should never hit a golf ball into a no-mow area, because they are that far out of the way. With the squirrels and the wind spreading seeds, it's just amazing how quickly a forest can grow. I guess that without forest fires and development that takes trees out, maybe the whole state of Iowa would turn into a forest in a very short period of time.

In 1973 we opened all 18 holes at the same time. We only had five golf carts. Of course, the area has grown and the golf course has changed, too. We're only 15 minutes from downtown Des Moines with the new highway system. As the city spreads out our way, we miss the rural feel of the property, but at the same time, being accessible to more people is good for the business.

We've made a concerted effort to make the golf course reasonably quick to play. The course is like a park. We don't have undergrowth like you would have in a forested area, and the course is mowed right up to the trees. Even the evergreen trees are trimmed from the ground up to about four or five feet so golfers won't have to spend time looking for balls.

**Allison:** We host a lot of fund-raiser golf outings, and it's great that those groups can complete their play in four-and-a-half hours. Having the trees trimmed that way really helps keep the groups moving. It's a user-friendly golf course. I've played golf outings at other courses that take six-plus hours, and it takes away from the fun.

**Tom:** When we opened the clubhouse was pretty small. It was about 36 feet by 76 feet, but we made half of that space into living quarters. My brother Steve, his wife, and eventually three children lived in that space. Over time, we enlarged the clubhouse. Now it's about 150' long and we added a second story. Everything has grown. As we said earlier, we started with five golf carts. That was enough for a family outing for us. Now our fleet of carts has grown to 72.

**Fred:** Every Monday night we had a family golf outing for the eight of us at that time. Tom's brother Dan would create the teams and keep the statistics for everything. Tom and I would always ride together in the same cart, but we weren't always on the same team. Sometimes other golfers would have all the golf carts, but we never felt bad about it. It was our weekly family outing, and we just waited until carts came in, as the customer always comes first.

**Allison:** We have golfers here who have played the course since we first opened. It's not as common these days, but then, as well as now, they are allowed to bring their own carts to the course. Also, walking was more common then.

**Tom:** We quickly went to 10 carts within the first year, and as I've said, the numbers continued to grow. We think 72 carts is the right number.

**Fred:** Allison grew up on the golf course. The course was here before she was born. Tom's mom would pick up our children, Jason at first and then later Julene and Allison, from grade school to bring them out to the golf course to play. By the way, Tom's mom, Audrey, is 95 years old and lives on our property.

**Allison:** I've always played golf. I was seven years old when I competed in my first tournament. I was the youngest person then, and probably still, to compete in the Des Moines city golf tournament for youth. It was a nine-hole tournament, and I shot something like 111, 112 and 110 over the three-day tournament. I actually won the Good Sportsmanship Trophy.

Over the years we have somewhat accidentally developed our marketing for the course. We made some big remodeling changes in the clubhouse, and we hired a marketing firm to help us develop an identity. There are so many golf courses in the area, and we struggled with identity, trying to shove ourselves in a country club-like brand. That just wasn't our style at all. The marketing firm started gathering information about why people played one course or another, and at the end of the day she told us that people play Toad Valley because we are fun. She said our marketing scheme should be that we are fun. It was money well spent, because from that time on, we stopped trying to fit into a golf course "box" that just wasn't who we are. We are about having fun. That identity has helped us be very successful. The NGCOA (National Golf Course Owners Association) has featured Toad Valley a number of times. It's because we don't do things like so-called "normal" golf courses do.

We aren't stuffy people, and it isn't that important to us if stuffy golfers come here or not. There are far more fun golfers than stuffy golfers out there. So we market ourselves as a place for "average Joes" who want to have fun, for families and for kids who want to learn golf. It's a place for families to bond with each other. Our marketing reflects that playful attitude. When I write my email blasts, they are always funny. We don't even have regular titles for our positions at the course. I'm The Wizard of Fun. Mom is The Kitchen Guru (sometimes The Kitchen Nazi) and my brother Jason is Gorilla. All of that has enabled us to release our personalities. When we are free to be who we are, we attract those golfers who enjoy us. I'm sure there are some people who don't care for that style, but that's fine with me. It works for us as people, and we think it's good for our business.

I have many hats that I wear. My original title was general manager, but I hated being general manager because I'm really just part of the family. I'm the person who does all the background stuff. I do all of the marketing, the website, the event planning and so forth. I'm basically in charge of the fun that happens.

Growing up, I never thought I would be in the family business. I went to college with the plan to become a high school English teacher. Then about eight years ago, my uncle expressed some interest in retiring from the golf business and selling his portion of the business. He was just casually expressing his thoughts. It wasn't like a buyer was being actively sought. My husband Kelly and I had owned a lawn care business for several years. Our business had grown, and we were doing pretty well. I'm just a naturally ambitious person. I see some opportunity and I go after it. I'm not shy about it. Also, as you can see from what Dad has been saying, our family is naturally very close. We get along very well. Not all families could do what we do. At the end of the day we love each other, and even if at times we don't agree with each other, we can easily set aside those differences and move on. Anyway, the thought of driving past something that my dad and my grandpa and my uncles had built and thinking that someone else might own it really bothered me. Our family is like a "good cult." We all live on this side of the road. Dad calls it the "compound." There was a nostalgic motivation for me, and eight years ago I approached my brother, Jason, who was an air traffic controller in Chicago. He had always wanted to come back home to the golf course, but he had a good career going where he was. So I asked Jason if he was interested in us putting together some kind of package to buy Uncle Steve's share of the business. Jason was interested, and so his wife, Theresa, and my husband, Kelly, and I, with Mom and Dad's full financial support, bought out Uncle Steve's share of the business. When Dad and his brothers took over the golf course from Grandpa, no money exchanged hands. Dad wanted to return that favor for us. We kid that Mom and Dad bought the golf course from themselves, but by their actions, Toad Valley is now in its third generation.

As third generation owners and operators, we were younger and more energetic and brought new blood to the business. Our idea was to make the business a family-friendly, fun environment. The first thing we did was build the miniature golf course that we call Field of Greens. It's a really nice miniature golf course, and there wasn't really anything like it on this side of Des Moines. The second thing we did was started remodeling the clubhouse. Our philosophy was that first impressions were everything. The golf course itself always looked great, but the clubhouse needed improvement. We did about 60 percent of the remodeling ourselves, while keeping the clubhouse functioning all the while. It was kind of miraculous. People started coming out and telling us how amazing the golf course looked, when we hadn't done anything with the course itself, just the clubhouse. First impressions really do matter. Of course, we have also made improvements to the golf course, but not nearly as much as we have with the clubhouse.

Then about five years ago, we turned our maintenance facility that was attached to the clubhouse into a conference center. That has really unleashed us from the woes of trying to make the business successful based on golf alone. This year it rained nonstop from April through June, and then the heat came. We had a month of the hottest weather we've had in 22 years. You can't force people to play golf, and bad weather affects golf businesses. However, there are always anniversary parties, weddings, fund-raising events and that sort of thing that don't depend on the weather. The conference center has even helped us refine our philosophy, that we don't sell golf. We sell memories. Our goal is to make every memory that occurs here at the golf course a pleasant one. That goal drives us. We have grandparents bringing their grandchildren to the course. We recently had a soldier getting ready to go to Afghanistan spend his last day before going there, playing golf here, with his family. We have miniature golf birthday parties, weddings, anniversary parties, charity fund-raisers all taking place at the golf course. If people only have a few days of their year that they truly remember, we want one of those days to be a day they spent right here.

At a recent wedding we hosted, the photographer came up to me and said she just loved the way Toad Valley feels. She said, "It's almost like you guys are family owned." I started laughing and told her we are family owned. She told me that must be why we have the atmosphere she felt. In a corporation you can't really make your employees care, but we genuinely do care. When I pass my grandpa's picture on my way to my office every day, it resonates with me. It drives me.

**Tom:** When Allison was growing up, we hoped she would one day be a part of our business, but we didn't push it. I guess we are an unusual family, but I don't know why we are. I think we are the way things should be. We love each other, and we want to be near each other.

**Allison:** We are God fearing and active in our church. I really think that's a big part of what drives us. We understand that the business isn't what really matters. It's family that matters. We do our best to keep ourselves in check and remember where our treasures really are.

**Tom:** Keeping family close was why I wanted to get our son who was working in Chicago back here with us, where he really wanted to be. I mentioned earlier that I had two brothers. My older brother died in 2002, and that became part of the reason for my younger brother wanting to get out of the business. The business was a lot of work, and losing our brother was sad. With both brothers out of the business, it was up to our children to carry it into another generation. My brother Steve's children didn't have the desire to be in the business. We always wanted the family together and involved. Even our other daughter who is not in the business lives only three miles away, keeping us all close to each other. Fred and I have three children and each of them has three children.

**Allison:** I have three children, but I don't really see them continuing with the golf business into another generation. It's just too much work. I thoroughly enjoy the work, and maybe in 20 years I'll want my kids to be involved. We'll see.

**Tom:** It was unlikely to have three generations involved in the business. I don't expect the fourth generation to follow us, but we surely wouldn't hinder it.

**Fred:** When Allison took over operating the course and decided to change the maintenance facility into the conference center, she lined up contractors to help with the work. The building had been used for maintenance for 30 years and was full of 30 years of equipment, tools and maintenance supplies. We had three weeks to clear the facility and begin construction. Then the contractors told us that their other job was canceled and they wanted to start in 24 hours. Instead of three weeks, that gave us 24 hours to clear that facility. It was absolutely insane, but we pulled together and got it done. If something needs to get done, we do it.

**Tom:** We have the equipment and the talent and usually the energy to get our work done. For example, yesterday Allison had a to-do list for me. I worked on a couple of urinals that weren't flushing. Hopefully I fixed them. We had an unusually windy day, and three letters on our landscaped sign for the course actually blew off. So I got my Gorilla Glue and glued those back on yesterday. Duct tape and Gorilla Glue get lots of jobs done.

**Fred:** I worked outside for 15 years. I gave up my inside jobs for our oldest daughter, Julene, so that she could start working when she was old enough. When Allison came along, she started in the clubhouse but then came outside to work with me. We were dynamos and got lots of landscaping done. After 15 years of landscaping, and mowing tees, fairways and rough, I moved back inside to cooking and ordering beverages.

**Tom:** That takes her back to her youth. Her folks owned the Lakewood Ballroom in Lakeview, Iowa, where she worked as a teenager.

**Fred:** I graduated from nurse's training and worked at a local hospital for a year, but that was it. Then it was back to hospitality, just as I had done as a kid.

**Tom:** I don't work 12 or 14 hours a day like I used to, but you never, ever run out of work on a golf course. Right now I have about 200 species of trees planted on the property. That's pretty much what I do full time now. You must have self-discipline and measure the amount of energy you have to invest. If you can't get it done today, it will be there tomorrow. You tend to do the things you like, but you have to prioritize what needs to be done.

Fred's maiden name was Friedrichsen. People called her Freddie in high school. When I met her, I shortened that to Fred because I thought it sounded more feminine *(smiles)*. She likes it because it keeps her connection to her maiden name.

**Fred:** My dad never had boys, so I get to keep his name alive with my name Fred.

**Tom:** I'm a guy, so I don't have that identity loss that comes with changing your name when you get married. I'm a traditional person, and having hyphens in your last name seems offensive to me because it's a loss of tradition. On the other hand, I'm sensitive to losing your identity by changing your name. That's why my wife is Fred.

**Allison:** I named my oldest son Brady to keep those family traditions going. My kids are 14, 11 and seven. My boys come and help move carts. They've been doing that for years. My youngest son could hardly reach the cart peddles when he started. They fuel the carts and wash them, too. My daughter who is seven helps us to work banquets. She's been doing that since she was six. She's really good at it. She's in charge of water, children's meals and cake. She takes her job very seriously. When a pitcher of water is empty, she replaces it with a full pitcher. When it's time to assemble children's plates, she puts on her gloves and assembles all the children's plates and delivers them to the tables. She hates weddings that don't have children. After we cut the bride's cake, she delivers the cut cake to the table. She wears our uniform of white shirt and black pants and her nametag, and she is just as adorable as can be. She's very polite with the guests and works hard. She does what she calls "busting" the tables. She goes to the tables and asks guests if she may take their empty plates, and the people love it. I started working early in my life, too. I think it's why I'm so energetic. I helped Dad change the cups on the greens when I was only two years old.

**Tom:** It took a few years before it was actually easier to have her doing the work, but I never told her that.

**Allison:** I loved feeling important like that, and so I return that favor to my children.

There are six of us who are full time at Toad Valley. In total, there are 75 employees, obviously most part-time. Of those 75 there are about 10 who are family members, cousins, nephews and sometimes my sister. There are 12 people who maintain the outside, about 12 who do banquets and events, and the other 50 or so do the golf shop, the snack bar, or they are starters on the course, marshals and that sort of thing. Most of the people we hire work very part-time, maybe two or three days a week or even less. Most of them are retired, and then we have a handful of 30-something people who enjoy golf, and they work a couple nights a week in exchange for golfing privileges. Then we usually have high school and college kids who do the dirty work. I try not to hire too many of them. This year we had six 18-year-olds. That's really all I can handle, because typically you have to really supervise them so closely.

*(At this point in the interview, the Brady family served pizza and we took a break. As we ended the break, Jason popped out from a doorway wearing a gorilla mask. I think he said, "Boo!")*

**Tom:** Jason sometimes makes the kids cry and scares the girls, but it's all in fun. That's why Jason is The Gorilla. He has the full bodysuit, but it's too hot for most days in the summer for him to wear it. Most of the kids really love it.

As you know, golf is a highly competitive business. Here we are in an overbuilt market that limits what we can charge for golf. Right now we aren't charging as much as we need to, but we just can't if we want to stay competitive. Even from the beginning, we have had limited finances to make improvements, but we've had the time and the talent to do most of our own modernization. Back when we installed fairway irrigation and built a pond, we did most of it ourselves. That self-sufficiency still drives us. That particular project cost us about $125,000, but the city of Des Moines was doing it with their municipal courses for $300,000. With limited resources but with the equipment, the talent and the desire, this is what you have to do to survive in this business. If you don't put in that kind of work, then you'll go under. We see courses going under in this market every year.

My big beef, or challenge, is the way Iowa does their property tax. They tax you at your highest and best use. Rather than taking the property at its underlying value as farm ground, which for good reasons gets huge tax breaks in Iowa, we get taxed at the level of developed land or as a golf course. All of our improvements, such as irrigation, greens and tees, are considered as buildings for tax purposes. These high evaluations cause us problems. Our second-highest cost each year, behind salaries, is property taxes. Our feeling is that we are performing a public service for the green space, the recreation and entertainment we provide. We know we would be missed if we were gone. It's not consistent across the state how what is basically farm ground gets taxed. It's a great burden to our business.

**Allison:** In Iowa there are 99 counties. If I were governor, the first thing I would do is consolidate some of those counties. Each county has their own assessors, and it gets complicated to create consistency in tax practices. The state has the philosophy of creating tax laws that honor our heritage of farming and wants any tax law change to benefit people across the state. To us it seems like the Des Moines area, with its rapid development, suffers under those statewide philosophies.

**Tom:** To expand on the tax problems we face, golf is an industry that has to compete directly with government agencies. There are three municipal golf courses owned by Des Moines in our market. None of those courses pay a dime for property taxes. A rough calculation for us is that for every round of golf played at Toad Valley, the first three dollars goes to property taxes. The municipal courses may charge the same prices as we do, but they don't have that three-dollar burden.

**Allison:** Those municipal courses in Des Moines are really nice golf courses. One of them is considered to be the oldest public golf course west of the Mississippi River. In some markets, the municipal courses are not as nice as here and the privately owned courses may not feel as much competition as we do. In this economy and in this market, the competition from the municipal courses which do not have the same tax responsibilities makes it really tough for us.

As I think back on some of our greatest challenges, I think about the year the road that leads to our course closed for construction. That was brutal! The new high school was built, and the two-lane road was changed to a five-lane road to give efficient access to the school. The road closed at the end of May and didn't reopen until September. That was our golf season. We figured we lost about 10 percent of our business. There were detour signs posted to get to Toad Valley, but people had easier choices, and it really hurt us. Then we had to try to make up those loses in subsequent years. That made it tough.

Of course, the weather always plays a role in our success as a golf course. Because we have diversified and don't depend on golf alone for our business, it has helped us tremendously.

**Tom:** The conference center we built was a brilliant idea. It has been a lifesaver for us. It's probably our greatest triumph.

**Allison:** The conference center seats 225 people. This year we will have had 42 wedding receptions and 35 outdoor ceremonies. The average wedding brings in about 175 people.

**Tom:** Allison plans and manages those events by herself. She is really a wedding planner without compensation.

**Allison:** I am The Wizard of Fun, you know. I do enjoy it. It comes naturally to me, but also I've trained myself to pay attention to detail. We pride ourselves that there is no chipped paint, that all the screws in the switch plates are facing the same direction. For weddings, everything on the tables will be lined up perfectly. People photograph weddings, and we want those photos to show our attention to detail. If I see a wedding photo with a dead branch on a tree, I go to Dad right away to ask him to take care of it. I'm notorious for my project lists. I have project lists for everyone. Maybe the guests don't really pay attention to the detail, but they do get a certain feeling about how comfortable and pleasant their experience has been.

Marketing for weddings is done mostly by word of mouth. I only formally advertise our service and facility in one place, but at 42 weddings a year, between March and November, we are near capacity. Dad is always telling me there are some other weeks we could book, but he's mostly kidding.

The conference center has helped us book more golf outings, too. I work a lot with fund-raisers. I sit down with their planners and teach them how to design their golf outing to attract golfers and sponsors. I'll design their website for the outing. We are very, very good at helping people raise money. It means a lot of hands-on work for me, but I enjoy it. Last year we had 60 golf outings. This year we had 45 outings, probably because of the down economy. We lost 10 fairly big golf outings this year that we have hosted in the past. Those were corporate-based events that those organizations cut out of their annual budgets.

I enjoy planning the weddings and outings. With my experience and English degree, I've even thought about writing a book on how to plan those kinds of events, but I'm too busy to do that now. I've also thought about outsourcing wedding planning, but to be honest, I just haven't found anyone else who is good enough to meet my standards.

The golf course stays so busy that we don't run that many leagues for golfers. Some golf courses really go after league play, but we don't really need more. We have standard men's club and women's club leagues, as well as a couples league that's followed by a potluck dinner and offers babysitting for children.

We have our Tadpole Junior Golf Clinic for junior golfers ages 5 to 15, where we have about 100 kids participate each year. We provide instruction for four age groups, miniature golf, time to play on the golf course, watermelon-eating contests, and a big awards ceremony at the end of the three-week clinic. It's crazy, but I run all of that as The Wizard of Fun. I enjoy it. Actually, I have a love-hate relationship with it. It's a lot of work. I make personalized trophies for each kid with their names on them. I make the website so they can register online and pay online. I make the schedules, arrange the instructors, everything to make the experience organized and fun. I guess it's my least favorite job.

For the opening ceremony, there will be up to 300 people in the conference center. There will be 100 kids and at least one parent for each kid, plus sometimes siblings and others to boot. With all those people, it's an absolute zoo! The more chaotic it is, the better I perform. I know it's going to be crazy, but I don't get stressed out. I enjoy it. I just love that rush. It's addictive. In the opening ceremony, I always stand in front of the group and say, "This is my favorite night of the entire year!" Up until that night I keep saying, "I hate all the work with these Tadpoles. Please put me out of my misery. It's just too much work. Let's stop this program." Everyone in the family laughs at me. We take kids as young as five years old. They are there with their parents, and they are so excited. We are doing exactly what I think almost all other golf courses are missing the boat on. We are getting them to play golf when they are young. Kids play baseball when they are three. They play soccer when they are three. Golf courses want kids to play golf, but for many courses, not until they are 18 years old. We want the kids here. That's our philosophy. For the last day, we have a little tournament for the Tadpoles, and we'll have parents pushing their young kids in strollers watching their Tadpoles play. It may not be "normal" for a golf course to do it, but I just love that. A couple of years later ,that little kid who was in the stroller will be out here playing. They can't wait to get their hands on a golf club.

At the awards ceremony, each kid gets a trophy with their name on it. That truly is my favorite night of the year. The parents are so appreciative that their child gets that kind of attention. At our church we have a "Meet the Teen" program. Part of that experience asks the teens to recall their accomplishments, and we have seen former Tadpoles recall their golf clinic experiences and their trophy recognition. I just love that. Like I say, I have a love-hate relationship with our program. It takes so much work. You have to be hyper-organized, manage the crowds, and work so hard. I'm blessed that I am naturally good at that sort of thing, and I always feel so rewarded seeing how much fun it is for the kids and their parents.

Golf is a very expensive sport, and that makes it tough for kids to play. We provide clubs for kids to play with for free. They are lost-and-found clubs that we cut down to sizes for kids. That helps reduce the financial commitment for families. In the clinics, the lessons are an hour long, and that is a long time for a little kid, so we keep the actual lesson to 45 minutes. Then we have something silly for them, like watermelon-eating contests or water balloon tosses. The kids look forward to that kind of fun. Then on the final night, everyone plays miniature golf.

Another program that I designed for us is "Ladies Night Out." Golf is a very male-dominated sport. When I go to the National Golf Course Owners Conference, I am one of very few women owning and operating a golf course. People at the conference seem fascinated by me. I can totally talk golf and golf course management, and that makes me somewhat unusual at the conference. Knowing how male-dominated golf is, I designed Ladies Night Out as an experiment to see what interest there might be. We expected maybe 10 or 12 women would be interested, but the first year we had about 40 women.

I'm not necessarily against golf professionals, but I don't find that golf professional philosophies cover enough of the issues that golf should be considering. As a woman, I know how I play golf. I could care less what loft my club is. I could care less about what compression my ball is. That technical stuff doesn't matter to me. For a woman, I think that's normal. So, when we bring women to Ladies Night Out, we teach them how to feel comfortable at a golf course. This idea began at one of our golf outings. At our golf outings, prior to starting the event, we always have a moment of silence honoring our soldiers. Then we shoot an actual gun to begin the "shotgun" start, where groups start their round teeing off on different holes. It's a shotgun start, so we shoot a gun and the golfers love it. There will be maybe 144 golfers taking off from the clubhouse at once. Typically, 140 of them are men and four are women. It seems that invariably someone's bag would fall off the cart, and it was almost always a woman's bag. That is always embarrassing, particularly when everyone is watching. My heart would always be breaking for that woman. She is already feeling a bit out of place as one of very few women and now she is just humiliated. So I designed Ladies Night Out to help that woman.

Many women who play golf do so at charity golf outings. I've been playing golf since I could walk, but now I only play golf maybe seven times a year. Women like me are busy. I've got kids, and I'm driving them all over God's green earth, I'm cooking supper, and the list goes on. I'm too busy to play golf regularly, but I do have time to raise money for my favorite charity. So I designed the program to teach women how to hang at a golf course and not feel awkward. We teach them how to strap their bag to the cart, how to carry their clubs so it doesn't look like they are carrying their purse, how to mark their balls, how to make a tee time, how to check in at a golf course, and how to talk in golf lingo. We just want to help them be comfortable at the course. Once they feel comfortable, then they can focus on playing golf and get better at it. We give instruction on playing too, but our real focus is on helping them be comfortable and enjoying themselves.

Sometimes we're teaching the mom and we're teaching their kid, so pretty soon mom starts coming to the course with the kid. Then golf helps with my ultimate goal of creating a family bonding experience. The most I've ever had for Ladies Night Out is 75. The average number of participants is about 50. We divide the women into different groups, depending on their interest. Some really want to improve as golfers, and others are more interested in an evening out with friends and then learning a little golf, too. We have hors d'oeuvres, and that helps make it social. The program has become so popular that four other golf courses in our area have copied the idea for programs of their own.

**Fred:** One of the things Allison has discovered is that guys are closing a lot of deals on the golf course. More and more women are in business, and they can learn to use the golf course to their business advantage, too.

**Allison:** I have had at least three Ladies Night Out women thank me because they think they got promotions because they learned to play golf. Guys love having women on their teams for scramble events, because women have some real advantages on some holes with forward tees. If the women can drive the ball decently, they can really help the team. When the women play golf, they can soon be playing with their bosses, or their employees, in these charity events. That can be five or six hours with the boss or their employees on the golf course maybe a couple times a year. When the women learn how to not be awkward on the course and can play a little, then the golf experience can help them in their careers.

**Tom:** For our future we have room to develop further. We have 400 acres here, with the golf course being 130 to 140 of those acres. We want to get out of the debt load we have incurred by the improvements we've made. That load is very burdensome, particularly in this flagging economy. When finances permit, we are considering some golf course redesign, including additional water hazards. Also, we are looking at areas around the course for home construction. The main goal is to develop sufficiently to get rid of our debt. If we didn't have the debt, things would be so much better. Without the debt, we would not have to struggle so much with pinching our pennies, and hopefully we wouldn't have to work so hard. Some of us, I'm not saying who, may not be able to continue to work as hard as we have in the past.

**Allison:** We are big dreamers. Our ideas change, but personally I would like to put a practice green out by the driving range to make our lessons for golfers more user-friendly. I'd like to see that portion of the property like a golf academy for teaching and practice. We never run out of ideas.

**Tom:** For the future of the golf industry at large, I think there will continue to be some consolidation of courses. We want to be one of the survivors as independent owners, but there is ample evidence that golf is a tough business. What I see in heavily populated areas, say Florida, for example, is that golf courses are being built for say $20 million, those courses go broke and get sold for $12 million, that guy goes broke and sells for eight and then goes broke and sells for four. Finally, the investment by the last guy is appropriate for the kind of money the course can make to sustain itself. There's a lesson in there, I think. We see that trend here. Arguably the best course in greater Des Moines went broke a couple years ago and now is owned at about half of its original cost. That's a course that's used on the senior professional tour.

**Allison:** We are blessed that Des Moines has a huge population of golf lovers. The Senior Tour enjoys coming here because people come out to see them play. Their very first senior event in Des Moines had more spectators than any senior event that had ever been held. Golf is very affordable in this area. Partially it's affordable because there are so many courses that compete with price for customers. Even with that competition, we are a very busy golf course. We do about 32,000 to 33,000 rounds each year. For a Midwestern golf course that's good. Our tee sheet is booked.

**Fred:** We get pretty creative with our pricing structure. We reduce prices a couple times a day, at 3 p.m. for twilight golf and again at 6 p.m. for super twilight golf. After 6 p.m. each day, we give additional discounts for family golf. We want to encourage family play. Our golf course is busy until late in the day because of these policies.

**Allison:** We have this super twilight discount for families, because I know as a parent that there is no way I could spend $100 for the five of us to go play golf. I think golf courses as a rule only think about one golfer at a time. If you want to attract families, you have to think about how much five golfers might be willing to pay. When I take the family bowling, I can have a couple hours with them and bowl for $25-$30. If I take the family golfing, at some course other than here, it would cost

$100 or more for my three kids and me. That would mean my kids might not have the opportunity to learn golf. That family orientation drives us.

Our dress code is relaxed to help encourage all kinds of golfers, including children. Some of the "stuffy" golfers might not choose to play here, but that's all right with me. We do have stuffier golfers come to play, too, usually on the weekends. That's great, but what we really want is for the golf experience to be fun, to be in a family environment, to be affordable, and we want to create memories. It's working for us. We are busy, we have kids on the course, we have tee times being booked all the way to 7:30 p.m. during the summer. For Memorial Day weekend in 2010, we had three nice days in a row. We had a little over 700 rounds of golf here on those three days alone. It's not unusual for us to have over 200 rounds a day. That keeps us busy, but that is what is good for the business.

You know, going back to my bowling analogy, if it costs $30 to bowl I know that additionally the kids are going to want a bag of chips and a drink. The cost can quickly go to $50. That's true here on the golf course, too. Getting people here and out on the course creates revenue for food and beverage, too. We may do things a bit differently from most golf courses, but we stay true to our values and it's working for us.

*(Thinking the interview had come to a happy ending, I suggested that we stop.)*

**Tom:** Hold on there! We haven't had a thorough discussion about the trees. *(I thought he was kidding. He wasn't.)* When we started, there were no trees. In the last 20 years I have personally planted over 25,000 trees. Now we have about 200 species of trees here. I've planted every tree known to grow in the Northern Hemisphere. We have had cypress, sassafras, pecan, persimmon, jack pine, tulip, and the list goes on. The trees are all spaced apart, and the grass is mowed close to the trees so that it looks like a park. I've killed some of the trees by accident along the way, and even though they were all supposed to be disease free when we bought them, some have invented or imported diseases that have taken some from us. I know all about the diseases. When Allison was a child, I used to mow the course with her sitting on my lap. For a while I had her convinced that the worst disease was "mower blight." After a while she knew I was kidding, but she got pretty good at identifying the trees. For me the golf course is an instrument to allow me to play with the trees. It's my passion.

That's the Brady family!

## The Brady Family's Lessons

- Count your blessings. Know where your treasures lie.
- Be self-sufficient when you have the resources, talent and time to do so.
- Develop a unique brand. The name Toad Valley reflects playfulness and uniqueness. There is only one Toad Valley Golf Course.
- Develop marketing strategies and customer bases that reflect personal philosophies and personalities of owners and operators. For Toad Valley this means a fun, family-oriented environment. As a golf course that does things a bit differently from the traditional upscale or country club model, Toad Valley has achieved business success. When the general manager is The Wizard of Fun, customers understand that they should enjoy themselves.
- When possible, make the golf course user-friendly. By reducing undergrowth, trimming trees and mowing playable areas around trees, golfers can play quickly. Faster play attracts golf outings and enhances enjoyment.
- Customers' first impressions of a golf course cannot be undervalued. Remodeling the clubhouse at Toad Valley improved impressions of the entire golf course.
- Golf is a tough business, and succeeding on golf alone is challenging. To diversify their business, Toad Valley built a miniature golf course and a conference center that have attracted weddings, birthday and anniversary parties and charity golf outings. These events produce revenues far beyond greens fees.
- Duct tape and Gorilla Glue get lots of jobs done.
- You must have self-discipline and measure the amount of energy you have to invest. If you can't get a job done today, it will be there tomorrow. You tend to do the things you like, but you have to prioritize what needs to be done.

- When possible, involve children in the family business. Most of the Brady family started working when they were young, and creating work responsibilities for their next generation of children is seen as returning the favor. Work develops a sense of importance and contribution as well as enhancing family bonds.
- In golf, like in other businesses, taxes that seem unfair and competition with others, particularly those other businesses such as municipal courses that do not face tax burdens, are challenging realities that require planning and forbearance.
- Attend to details. Maybe the guests don't really pay specific attention to the details, but they do get a certain "feeling" about how comfortable and pleasant their experience has been because details were attended to. Those feelings lead to repeat business.
- Develop golf programs consistent with your business philosophy. At Toad Valley their Tadpole program for children five to 15 years old and their Ladies Night Out program make golf social, comfortable, fun and family oriented. As added bonuses, these programs produce revenue and create future golfers.
- Don't just sell golf. Sell memories.

# The Vagabonds

## Charlie and Betsie Scott, Owners of Gull Lake View Golf Club and Resort in Augusta, Michigan

℘    ℘

*I interviewed Charlie and Jane (Betsie) Scott at the Golf Industry Show in Las Vegas on March 1, 2012. Gull Lake View Golf Club and Resort is southwest Michigan's oldest and largest golf resort, featuring five championship courses, lodging and dining, event facilities and golf course real estate. The facility near Kalamazoo and Battle Creek, Michigan, has been owned and operated by the Scott family for over 40 years.*

*The five 18-hole golf courses create a total of 90 holes of golf. Gull Lake View West, designed and built by the Darl Scott (Charlie's father) family in 1963, is the original 18-hole championship course that started it all. Gull Lake View East was designed and built in 1973 by Darl, Charles and brother Jim Scott. The course has been rated as high as the 10th-best course in Michigan. Stonehedge South was designed in 1988 by Charles Scott. This course has been included in Golf Digest's list of the top 75 most affordable courses in the United States. Bedford Valley was designed in 1965 by William Mitchell and was purchased by the Scott family in 1988. This 18-hole facility is one of Michigan's most frequent championship sites. Bedford Valley has hosted the Michigan Open, the Michigan Senior Open, the Michigan Maxfli PGA Junior Championship, the Michigan Publinx State Match Play, and the NCAA Division III National Championship. Stonehedge North is the newest of the five Gull Lake View golf courses, designed in 1995 by Charles and son Jon Scott.*

*The resort side of the operation has 64 two-bedroom villas within walking distance of the golf courses and restaurants. The East Course has a full breakfast, lunch and dinner menu and is open seven days a week. Villa guests can enjoy "Foursome Fares to Go" for dinners delivered to villas by 4 p.m. the same day and left in the refrigerators for after rounds of golf.*

*Gull Lake View Golf Resort is home to three spacious meeting facilities. The Gull Lake View Golf Club can accommodate 300 people. The Bedford Valley Golf Club has a brand new clubhouse that accommodates up to 200 for a wedding, business meeting, holiday party, office party, graduation or other events. The Stonehedge Golf Club also accommodates 80 people and is available for small events. Food and beverage managers at each facility assist guests with all dining needs, from simple breakfast buffets to four-course dinners.*

*The Stonehedge Development Community at Crane's Pond is a 250-acre private gated community with upscale homes and building sites around a 140-acre open space and a 54-acre lake. The community has access to all five golf courses. Crane's Pond is certified by Audubon International as subscribing to the highest standards in sustainable development.*

www.gulllakeview.com

℘    ℘

**Charlie:** Our family has been in the golf course business at Gull Lake View since 1963. Before then, my father was the superintendent at Gull Lake Country Club, about six miles from where we are today in Michigan. Then Dad got drafted and served in the Pacific in World War II for about three years. After the war he came back to Gull Lake Country Club, and he stayed there for 25 years. That's where I grew up. After about 20 years at the country club, he decided he'd had enough of dealing with the members and decided to build his own golf course. He bought a piece of property at the south end of Gull Lake, and he built a motel and golf course on it in 1963. We call that course Gull Lake View West now.

Having grown up around a golf course and with Dad being a superintendent, I went to college at the University of Massachusetts for their Stockbridge School of Agriculture, which is a two-year program for turf maintenance. University of Mass. and Penn State were two of the very earliest turf programs in the country. After two years in the turf program, I transferred to Michigan State, because I had decided that I wanted to become a golf course architect. Landscape architecture at Michigan State was a five-year program, but I only stayed for two years. I just wanted to start building golf courses. That was about 1965, and that was when I met this young lady *(referring to Betsie)*.

I built a couple golf courses in our area in Michigan in the mid-'60s, and then I started work for a company called Wadsworth Golf Construction Company out of Plainfield, Illinois. Wadsworth was one of the most significant golf course contractors in the country back in the '60s. Today the company has built over 800 golf courses, and the Wadsworth Company is still very influential with their Wadsworth Foundations and philanthropic work. When I started with them, they focused on golf course construction in the Midwest. They told me they would probably stay within a 300-mile radius for building new courses. We built a couple golf courses in Illinois, then moved to Toledo, Ohio, to build a golf course, then went down to Middletown, Ohio, and finished another 18 holes in a 36-hole project. From there we went to Lake Lanier, outside of Atlanta. We built that golf course on an island on Lake Lanier. That was an interesting project. We used a lot of dynamite to clear all the rocks on the island. We were on the island for about a year building the golf course, while a marina and motel were also built for that state park. Obviously we were outside of that 300-mile radius by then. In fact, Wadsworth built Innisbrook Golf Resort in Florida and had expanded for work in Colorado. They were getting big.

As the construction superintendent for Wadsworth, it was my job to go into a completely undeveloped site, take the architect's plans, stake out the course, hire equipment operators and build it. Sometimes I stayed on the sites until the golf courses were seeded and grown in, but other times I went to different new jobs before the one I had been building was finished. Sometimes I was involved with the design of the courses, as well. I did whatever was needed. We built in swamps, in rocks, in concrete, in all kinds of conditions. One night I left a D-8 dozer stuck in the mud in a swamp. The next morning we used two dozers, two scrapers and a big crane hooked up to it and saved it from sinking. I thought it was gone. Every project had its challenges, and I was in charge.

I got to work with the best designers in the business. I worked with Arthur Hills, Larry Packard, Gary Player, so many skilled architects. I learned each of their styles and later put them to use in my own golf course design and construction. Next to my dad, Brent Wadsworth, who owned the Wadsworth Company, was a real mentor in my life. He was a great architect and businessman. We always knew we would have good, functional equipment to work with, and things would be organized. I learned a lot from him, and I have so much respect for him.

We had been traveling all over the place building golf courses. We had a 10-by-55 foot trailer we contracted to be hauled wherever we worked. That was all of our stuff. That was our home at each place we worked, sometimes for up to 13 months for a single job. It seemed that every time the trailer was moved to the next site, that something would happen to it. One time the truck driver hauling the trailer went under an underpass that didn't have enough clearance and took the roof off the trailer. Another time the driver bent the trailer tongue. Because it was our home, those accidents added to the challenges.

I used to get so anxious, even physically sick, when we moved that trailer to a new work site and we had to find the right location for the trailer, unpack and then pack again, and watch somebody else haul away your home, knowing it was completely out of your control. When we moved the first time to build a course in Davenport, Iowa, the trailer was there waiting for us, but there was no place to set it up. We had to chase down the land owner, a dentist who was always busy, so we had to make arrangements with his wife. I told her they had our money and were obligated to provide a trailer site. Eventually they provided the site and I had to set the trailer up myself for the first time. When I hooked up the electricity, I got a huge electrical shock, so I unplugged the electricity. That night it was really cold, and I'll never forget all of us, with the youngest kid only six months old, the dog, all of us in bed huddled up together trying to stay warm. We ended up moving into a motel for a couple days until the trailer got sorted out.

**Betsie:** We had a cat, too, but the cat just disappeared. The cat was gone. Cats are wily, though, and a couple days later, he showed up at the trailer.

**Charlie:** We usually had great places to stay. In Lake Lanier, down in Georgia, the trailer was set up right on the lake, and that was wonderful. It was fun. In New Lebanon, Ohio, our neighbors in that trailer park were house and barn painters, pipe layers, electrical installers for Bell Telephone, just working people. The painters and pipe guys were pretty wild transients, though. It seemed like every weekend the police and the fire department were called into the trailer park. All that moving was exciting, but it was stressful, too.

After that year at Lake Lanier in Georgia, we moved back to Illinois in 1972 for a project outside of Chicago. Brent Wadsworth told me then that he wanted to send us next out to Durango, Colorado, to build a golf course called Tamaron. I told Brent that Betsie and I just couldn't keep moving the kids all over the place and that we were going to quit working for him and return home. Brent told me that the company was starting another division in Florida and that I was entitled to a percentage ownership of the division. Even with that opportunity, I told him we had to go home. By that time we had built something like a dozen golf courses, living as vagabonds, moving ourselves and our children all over the place. Betsie and I had two children at that time, and they were getting ready to start school. It was time to settle down.

**Betsie:** People sometimes must have thought I was nuts moving with the kids in a trailer to all those places. To me it was exciting going to all of those new places. Also, in the Wadsworth Company we had a family. Everybody moved together and we knew them all. It wasn't like you moved to a new community and had to meet new friends. Your friends traveled with you. They all lived in trailers, just like us.

*(I joked that when they retire, they should get an RV and travel around.)*

**Betsie:** We talk about that! It would be fun to have a little RV and travel around the country. We could see the country from the road instead of from the sky.

**Charlie:** Around the time we moved back from Georgia to the home office in Illinois, my dad and his partner at the time, Tim Mullenberg, found another piece of property across the road from the original course they had built. Well, the partner didn't think the property was very good for a golf course, and he didn't want to be involved. Dad wanted to buy the land and build another course, so he sold the motel he had built to get the money to buy the land and build the new golf course without his partner. For Betsie and me, the timing was right.

So in 1973 we left Wadsworth and went back to Michigan and designed and built the East Course at Gull Lake View on the property my dad had purchased. Then we had two 18-hole courses that we operated in partnership with Dad and my brother Jim.

In 1977 we built two 12-unit apartment complexes that we rented as villas for the golf courses. Between 1977 and 1988, we built three more units that were eight-unit buildings. Now we were in the resort business. We became one the earliest resort businesses in Michigan focused on travel golf. We were getting lots of Detroit business and later lots of Chicago business. With the villas and guests coming from distances our 36-holes of golf were full. Business was really good and we needed to expand, so we decided to build another golf course. We looked at some local properties and were fortunate to find a very nice property that we bought for $500 an acre. It had been a farm, and all of the property boundaries were lined with stones, some of them really big. We cleared the land, which was pretty overgrown and still full of stones, and built the course we call Stonehedge.

We were up to 54 holes and we were still busy, so we built two more villas in 1988 and 1989, taking us to 64 villas. At about that same time, another golf course was for sale, about 15 miles away. Bill Mitchell had designed that golf course in 1963, and it was a really great course that had hosted the Michigan Open and other important events. The course had been family owned, but the son who inherited it wasn't interested in continuing in the golf industry. We bought that course, called Bedford Valley, in 1988.

Then in 1993 we bought some other property we had tried to buy previously. We built another 18 holes on that property so that we had golf course properties on both sides of the main road. My son Jon, who has a landscape architecture degree and a crop and soil science degree from Michigan State, came home and helped me build that new course we call Stonehedge North. That took us to 90 holes of golf. Each of the courses averages between 180 and 220 acres. We have other properties, too. On one of them we've been building houses, but with the economy right now, that project isn't doing as well as we hoped.

**Betsie:** In all of this history, as busy as we have been, I think the most excitement was on opening days for our new courses. Those were always such fun days. During the times we opened our new courses, golf was at its peak, and people just couldn't wait to get out on the new courses.

*(I was having a hard time keeping up with the pace of Charlie and Betsie's accomplishments. I asked what kept them so ambitious.)*

**Betsie:** Charlie's dad probably started it. He did not know the meaning of the word "No." For him there was always a way to get something done and move ahead. When he was a superintendent he didn't have any education in turf management. He learned the trade himself. He was actively involved in the Michigan Turfgrass Association back in the 1950s. Actually, he was one of the founders of the National Golf Course Owners Association.

**Charlie:** All of our growth and development was as a family. My dad was a real visionary. Before we built the motel or did any development, my dad bought property around the lake, divided it into parcels, and sold lots. He was the kind of guy who was always looking for the next project and a way to make some money. He was a depression child, and his dad didn't work very hard, but my dad and his three brothers always worked hard and kept the family going. Being a superintendent at a nice country club, my dad had a very good understanding of what golf was all about, what the golfer wanted. With our experience added to the start Dad gave us, the golf business has been very good for us.

We are out in the country, right between Battle Creek and Kalamazoo. Both of those communities have big industries and a good population base for us.

**Betsie:** We draw our customers locally, but also from bigger cities like Detroit, Chicago, the state of Ohio. Because we are a resort, we become a destination for people from pretty far away.

**Charlie:** We do all kinds of business. We do outings, leagues, we have golf members, open golf and resort guests. We have resort groups who have been coming to us for 20 years.

**Betsie:** We have one large group from Detroit that came for years and years. When the man who organized the group died, the rest of the group came to Gull Lake to hold a memorial ceremony. They threw his ashes in the pond on one of the holes, and they each threw a golf ball into the pond in memory of how many balls he had hit into that pond.

Even though we are more toward southern Michigan, we have a rural, northern Michigan feel to our properties. That really helps us attract guests from the cities who want a getaway to a natural Michigan setting. From the Illinois border we are less than 100 miles. It's just the perfect distance and location to feel like you really got away for vacation.

My role has been in human resources. I was the payroll person forever, *forever*. Recently we contracted out for payroll. It's a big job. We only pay 30 people in the winter, but in the summer it's over 200 people.

**Charlie:** My brother has been our inside guy at the golf courses, and I've always been the outside guy. That's my background with turf and dirt. Of course, design and construction of the courses has always been my responsibility. A year ago my brother decided that he wanted to get out of the golf business, so we bought him out. We have three children, and the middle son, Jon, is involved in the golf business. He's our general manager right now. He's kind of a nerd. He loves education. After the two degrees at Michigan State, he got a master's degree at Western Michigan, and right now he has about one year to go to finish his law degree.

**Betsie:** He's another driven Scott.

**Charlie:** Not completely a driven Scott, though. Betsie's dad was a school superintendent after he retired from the Air Force as a lieutenant colonel. Even after active duty he stayed in the reserves and recruited for the Air Force Academy. In his spare time, he was an athletic referee for high schools and small colleges. He's another depression child, and like my dad, he is a driven, motivated man.

**Betsie:** My dad is 92, and now he is really into computers. He's not afraid to jump right in.

**Charlie:** I see a lot of my dad in our son, Jon, but I see a lot of Betsie's dad in him, too.

We have different superintendents and different golf pros at each course and those people do the hiring of staff at each site. Jon and I supervise the entire operation, with Jon as GM. For us it has always been a family business, and it's hands on every day.

We work hard at marketing our golf and resort. We have a marketing person who does email blasts, and we travel quite often to golf shows in our region where we put up a booth to advertise our facilities. We have to work hard at marketing.

With the economy, some courses have not made it. There are a lot of golf courses in Michigan, and we have to be sure we do our best to bring customers.

In Michigan there has been a lot of blue-collar golf, particularly with the auto industry. In the 1970s, '80s and '90s, the economy was pretty good, property was relatively inexpensive, and a lot of golf courses were built. Around 1990 in the Flint and Saginaw areas, there were about 250,000 union employees in the auto industry. Now that number is down to about 25,000 auto employees. Those people had enough money to buy "toys," and golf is kind of like a toy. But now most of that population base has disappeared. That has really contributed to the economic struggles that Michigan and the golf industry are facing.

**Betsie:** That decline in the big industries has also hurt corporate golf outing revenues. There was a time when the big corporate golf outings just weren't there for us like they used to be. Even the outings we did host typically had fewer players. Corporate golf is starting to get better for us lately, though, and that's a good thing.

**Charlie:** Most of the development we did was financed through our cash flow, not financing. For a long time we were a business that didn't have any real debt. Not many can say that. That has changed now. For the next few years, our main mission is to make sure we can keep what we currently have and improve the facilities we have. Once facilities start to show wear then you have pay attention that the wear doesn't get gradually worse. Our focus is to try to assure that any trend toward showing wear just doesn't start.

Because we are in a family business, Betsie and I plan to always be involved, but our son, Jon, is the future for Gull Lake View. He's the third generation in our family to take the business on. He's taking on more and more responsibility with the facility. Our other two children aren't that interested in the golf industry. When my brother decided to leave the business a year or so ago, part of the reason was that his children just didn't have interest in being in the golf business, even though one of their sons is a very good player and competed for a while on the smaller tours.

My mom is 91 and living in Florida during the winters. For a long time she was our inside person at the golf courses, behind the counter and face to face with customers. People used to always joke that she could squeeze a penny out of anybody. When she's in Michigan, she likes to come into the clubhouse now and then to pass out her advice. The golf business was a big part of her life, too.

I don't really need to retire. I'm in a position now where if I need to take a few days off, I can do it. We feel like we are kind of semi-retired right now. In fact, Jon is joining us tomorrow, and we are all going to a place called Lee's Ferry to trout fish in the Colorado River. And we have a cottage about two-and-a-half hours north of us where we can get away. We can go for a day, spend a night or a few nights. It's just the right distance to create a real change of pace.

**Betsie:** Neither one of us is ready to just cash it in and stop working. We are fortunate that we don't have to do that.

**Charlie:** I started working on the golf course, mowing greens, when I was 13. I caddied even before that. I've always worked, and I'm not real good when I don't work. If I have something to do, I'm easily motivated. I'm just more comfortable when I'm working, so right now I don't want to retire.

As for the future of the golf industry, times are tough right now, but I'm pretty optimistic. There are a lot of very intelligent business people working in the golf industry. If they aren't successful, then the business is going to weed them out. I think the next three or four years are going to be interesting. If the economy doesn't flatten out or start to get better, then it's going to be hard on golf. The conditions that we're used to playing in are going to have to change. There are some golf courses we've worked on and visited that are absolutely beautiful and cost fortunes to create, but they are so expensive to play that they just don't generate much revenue. Sometimes people build with egos that are bigger than their billfolds. Some of those people have mighty big billfolds, too. There are courses here in Vegas that were created completely by sodding, not by growing in grass seed. We were just in Palm Springs, and it's just a fantasy land. The conditions of the courses are perfect. They overseed with rye grass, mow every day, and water as much as they need without getting rain to help. They cater to a richer clientele, but we just didn't see that many people playing the courses. The costs to maintain those kinds of golf courses may mean that we see course maintenance expenses start to go down. That could happen with lots of golf courses to save money and survive.

Some of the big changes in the golf industry are not just economically driven, they are socially driven. Young people and young couples have less time for recreation. They have to work. The kids are different. When I was a kid, all of the kids I grew up with went to the golf course and caddied. We hung around the golf course all day long. Now there are very few golf courses with caddies. Also, the kids don't have to look for things to do. Recreation is systematized so that kids are in organized basketball, football, soccer or whatever. Getting young people to spend time at a golf course is more challenging than ever.

**Betsie:** We have to find ways to make golf more fun for children. If you put a young kid on a golf tee and tell them they have to hit the ball only four times to go over 400 yards, they'll just break out in tears. We have to find ways to alter the game to make it fun for young people. Golf is a social sport, and kids like to do things together, so there should be ways to make the game so much fun that kids will want to hang out at the golf course.

Costs for kids or families to play golf need to encourage participation. I also think it's important to set aside certain times of the week when family golf is encouraged. Good players don't want to wait while kids and families ahead of them on the course are learning to play. And people just learning the game don't want to feel embarrassed or nervous with others waiting for them.

**Charlie:** Golf business has been wonderful for us. Now the industry is faced with a challenging economy, and all of us are looking for ways to increase participation and reduce expenses. We have to be creative and innovative, and I'm optimistic that we will be.

---

## Scotts' Lessons

- When conditions are right, grow and diversify your business. The Scott family grew to five golf courses, diversified into villas to create a large resort, and then developed a gated, private residential community. Their market is local and distant.

- With a "can-do" attitude, there is always a way to get something done and move ahead.

- For multigenerational family businesses, the assets that pass from one generation to the next include knowledge from experience, self-reliance, self-confidence, and abiding trust for your family partners.

- In times of economic struggle, marketing your product must be a priority. The golf industry in general has struggled with the downturn in the economy. In Michigan, in particular, the declines in major industries, such as the automobile industry, have compounded the economic problems. Hard work and creativity are required to keep a business viable.

- Facilities show wear over time. Assure that resources are invested to prevent the appearance of wear.

- "Sometimes people build with egos that are bigger than their billfolds."

- The conditions that we're used to playing in are going to have to change. Many golf courses may need to reduce course maintenance expenses to save money and survive. Not every golf course needs to overseed, water and mow every day, or be a fantasyland.

- "Some of the big changes in the golf industry are not just economically driven, they are socially driven. Young people and young couples have less time for recreation. They have to work. The kids are different. Recreation is systematized so that kids are in organized basketball, football, soccer or whatever. Getting young people to spend time at a golf course is more challenging than ever."

---

- "We have to find ways to alter the game to make it fun for young people. Golf is a social sport, and kids like to do things together, so there should be ways to make the game so much fun that kids will want to hang out at the golf course."

# Asses and Elbows

## Whitey O'Malley, Co-Owner of Saddleback Golf Club in Firestone, Colorado

ଛ   ଓ

*I interviewed Tom (Whitey) O'Malley on February 29, 2012, at the Golf Industry Show in Las Vegas. Saddleback Golf Club is an 18-hole public course designed by Colorado architect Andy Johnson and opened in 2001. The golf course is located in the populated prairie just east of the Rocky Mountains, about 30 miles north of Denver. In addition to the pro shop, practice facilities and golf lessons typical to many golf courses, Saddleback Golf Club operates an active wedding program with an on-site wedding planner and a pavilion separate from the clubhouse. Saddleback was Colorado Course of the Year in 2003 and co-hosted the Colorado Open in 2007.*

*Talking with Whitey and visiting Saddleback Golf Club's website make it very clear that having fun and sometimes using edgy humor are priorities.*

www.saddlebackgolf.com

ଛ   ଓ

My dad had 150 acres right outside of River Falls, Wisconsin, and he couldn't farm it. It was a crappy farm, so in 1990 he decided to convert it into a golf course. He's got a bad habit of starting something, doing it for two or three weeks, and then getting sick of it and dropping it. He started preparing to build the golf course. My brothers, Greg and Pat, and my wife, Lanna, and I were watching Dad, and we thought his idea might have some legs. So we put our feet in the water, too, and started getting involved with building this course. It eventually got to a point where we essentially took over building the course from Dad.

We went for financing to build the course. We were looking for $175,000, which at the time we thought was a ton of money. We couldn't imagine how it could cost more than that. We found out quickly that it took more. At the time, I was a pilot for Northwest Airlines flying commuter airplanes. I was working three days on and four days off. One of my brothers was also a pilot, and he had days in a row off, too, to start actually doing construction with me. My wife was taking care of our two small children, with another on the way, and doing the financial work for the golf course. It was asses and elbows, all hands on deck. We were determined that we were not going to fail. We had Gordy Emerson from Spring Valley, Wisconsin, design the golf course. It took us three years to build the course. We were just scrambling to make ends meet. Our bulldozer was so old, we thought Moses had made it. It was the biggest piece of crap you can imagine. We needed a second engine just to get the bulldozer engine started. I look back on those times, and I wonder how in the heck we did it. How could we build something like that without any real tools, or with very few real tools. It was a family operation and we got it done. We opened Kilkarney Hills Golf Course in 1994. My brother Pat now runs that course.

After we got the course open, my wife couldn't stand me being in the airline industry because I was away from home so much. That was what I knew, but I got out of flying and went into underground utilities and directional boring. I bought a directional bore machine and started going all over the country installing fiber optic lines from 1994 to 1998.

Then in 1998 I had an opportunity through my family to get involved with building another golf course, out in Firestone, Colorado. At that time, Lanna, the kids and I were in Florida. Lanna was point-man. She went out to Colorado to scout out the situation. She liked the property and the area, and she thought it was a good deal. We decided to move from Florida to Firestone on November 1, 1998. We were going to build ourselves a second golf course. With only one previous experience, I was supposed to have all the knowledge we needed. Looking back, it was scary. I did have a good understanding of what kinds of work to hire out and get done by somebody else. I knew the machinery we'd need, and I could get all the tools in place, get the money in place, and get the expertise in place. So we started in November 1998, and we opened the course, Saddleback Golf Club, in June, 2001.

We made some mistakes along the way. We had to move a lot of dirt. I went up to Canada and bought some big mining trucks that could haul something like 20 or 30 yards of dirt at a time. It was a tremendous amount that they could haul. We shipped them to Colorado, and then we discovered that they tipped over when they were on really slight inclines. I had one actually tip over. We ended up bagging out of those trucks. We sold them and happily didn't take too much of a hit. Obviously that was a big mistake.

We thought we had enough knowledge of what to do so we jumped in and started building the course. We found out soon that we didn't have the proper permits to build the course. We pretty much gave the town the "bird" and kept building anyhow. Sure enough, two weeks later, we got a cease and desist letter. We had to stop building and go for the proper permitting. That caused panic. By that time we already had our financing and we were building. We looked like total idiots to the bank. We had people hired. We really didn't know what the outcome might be. In the end it might have been a stroke of genius, because we were able to buzz through the whole permitting process in three months. Instead of being a process that could take years and hundreds of thousands of dollars, we got the process streamlined with the town. The town of Firestone was really small at the time, about 3,000 people, and they were really supportive about having our business come there. So we got right back to turning and burning.

I was supposed to be the partner who knew what to do. When I first pulled up to the property, I had the biggest butterflies in my stomach I'd ever had. I had cold sweats, wondering how the hell I was going to do it. Underneath, I knew I could do it, but it was just so overwhelming looking at this piece of ground and knowing that in a year or two it has to be beautiful and playable. There were a ton of things that had to happen. We just broke it down into little pieces. My wife was handling the business end of things. She did the business plan for the bank and got the loan. I was out buying equipment. My partner at Saddleback Golf Club who owned the land, Vern Hamilton, didn't know anything about golf. He'd never even played golf. He turned out to be a wonderful asset, just a fantastic partner.

When we put the deal together, we bought surrounding properties that we sold to pay for our bad habit of golf. Most people build a golf course and then try selling adjoining property for real estate or commercial development. We did it ass-backwards from what most people do. We sold that land first. That kind of development just wasn't what we wanted to do. It was a high-growth area, and with some other properties, we sold 15 acres to Safeway Grocery Store, and that kicked everything off. The Carbon Valley, where Firestone is one of three small towns, grew from maybe 9,000 people in 1998 to over 24,000 people now. The area is still growing exponentially. The growth is just crazy, and that has really helped us.

During construction we found that we could move earth faster than we originally thought, so we ended up working two shifts. One shift worked from seven in the morning for eight hours, and then another shift started at 3 p.m. and went to 11 at night. We rented lights to work at night. After the debacle with the mining trucks, we got a super good deal and rented some off-road trucks for $35 an hour to haul dirt. Anything over 40 hours, and the price for rental dropped by one half. So for $17.50 an hour for over 40 hours a week, we had a good deal and we just hammered those things. They ran 80 hours or more a week. We worked weekends moving dirt. Keeping everything organized with two crews was a maddening time, but we were moving fast.

Andy Johnson out of Vail designed the course. He was really instrumental in getting us through it. He spent a lot of time on the site orchestrating the design, staking out the holes, and he had a lot of really good ideas. The design was very well received when we were done. Each hole is different from the others. There was no cookie-cutter look to any of the holes. I'll never forget when we were putting in the cart paths. Most architects would start designing with a computer program, but he'd just come out and look at the layout and make decisions. I had a D-5 dozer, and I would be right behind him making trenches where he put the stakes for the paths. I was right on his heels, and he had to keep hustling. That was just how we worked. Then I found a really good deal on concrete, and I found a paver that I got from a guy up in the mountains.

The paver hooked up behind a concrete truck, and we poured the concrete ourselves. We had like 20 guys behind the concrete paver doing the finishing work, and we were pouring a mile a day. That was something like 40 trucks of mix for a mile. It was the hardest I ever worked, and it was fun as hell. Those were long, long days. Finally I took a day off and drove by the course and saw my partner, Vern, out there with his tractor, working the ground. I was dead-ass tired, and Verne was still going at it.

Those cart paths are valuable for more than aesthetics; they really help protect the turf. We could have gone to gravel paths cheaply, maybe $20,000. It cost us $167,000 for 4.2 miles of 8-foot-wide concrete cart paths. That was a lot of money, and I had to really battle to do the paths before opening. Typically, city-grade concrete is 3,000 psi and that's pretty strong. We put in 4,000 psi concrete with a fiberglass mesh for stability. Now, 12 years later it still looks almost like new.

It took about two-and-a-half years from start to finish building the course. We traveled to Texas and to Phoenix to buy dozers and a front-end loader. We got some pretty good deals on our equipment by traveling to auctions. Then we'd truck the equipment back to our site. It was scary spending so much money on that heavy equipment and not really knowing if it would be reliable and work. We'd kick the tires and light the fires and hope for the best. We found that if we asked the right people the right questions we could get great information. People are more than happy to tell you what they know. Actually we got some really good equipment for the work.

You have to be creative. Vern had a really great idea. We bought our fuel in bulk by the semitruck load, just the way he had done on his farm. We watched the stock futures, and when prices for gas were down we bought in bulk. We paid an average of 34 cents a gallon for our diesel fuel. That really saves money. Then we had an older, retired guy who came in at night and with our gas truck would go around and fuel up all of our equipment. We burned a lot of fuel, and the bulk buys saved us a bunch of money. Overall, we moved about 500,000 yards of dirt. That's a lot of dirt.

The property is lightly rolling high desert. We're right at the foot of the Rockies. Our first hole green is framed by two large mountains. We have just unbelievable views all over the course. At first the clubhouse was planned for a low-lying area, but I moved it up on a hill so that people having a beer on the deck could really see the views. We had such a great team for construction. Everybody had their responsibilities, and we worked so well together.

This is kind of hard to explain, but being married and having children could have been tough. I was gone from home all day and into the night every day, but my wife never got upset with me for being at work. She was working to get the pro shop ready, and everybody was just on the same page, pulling together. We fed on each other's hard work, and everybody tried to out-work the others.

We didn't do everything right. We made some mistakes. Some days were 100 degrees, really hot. When we were putting in the irrigation, some of the glue used to seal pipes didn't set up because of the heat, and we had some leaks, particularly around tee boxes. That had to be done again. Overall, though, we did a lot more right than we did wrong. It was a lot of work, but it was fun.

We were building so fast that we didn't have time to build a clubhouse, so we moved into a double-wide trailer as a temporary clubhouse. We are still using that double-wide as the clubhouse today. We built a great deck around the clubhouse, and we have it set a bit to the side so that I can build a permanent clubhouse as soon as I sell some residential property. Right now the economy is crap, so I'm just waiting for it to pick up so I can sell the residential property.

Water is king in Colorado, and we are in high desert where water can be a problem. But it just so happens that the golf course is near an irrigation ditch, and we have the second oldest diversion right in our area for water out of a local river. That water right was part of Vern's farm property, and we benefitted from it. It was just another one of those fortunate breaks that helped make it all possible for us.

Building the course was gut wrenching. There were lots and lots of sleepless nights. It was scary as hell, but once we got marching down the road and we started to work together so well, we just made it happen. Overall, it was a fun, fun project.

Actually Vern and I had two other partners in the project, but in 2008 we parted ways with them. That was a very low point in this whole process. In the end, it turned out extraordinarily well. I think it was the biggest challenge we have ever had with the golf course. One was an in-law, and that made it even harder. It was the last thing I'd think about before I went to sleep at night and the first thing I thought about each morning before I even got out of bed. We had a good attorney who kept us focused when accusations got really wild. It was an embarrassing and expensive lawsuit. It was a lot of time, money and heartache. During all of that, there was no way I could see a good ending, but in the end it just turned out perfectly. I'm not saying that I would never go into another partnership, but if I did, I would certainly be very adamant about understanding all of the features of the partnership before I did it.

Opening day at the course was a zoo. Quite honestly, it was a blur. It was June 1, 2001—on a Saturday—and we had a full tee sheet. We had so much work to do to get that door open and then at last we were open. The golfers came in from their rounds and really liked the course. That was a good feeling. We had found out that a lot of golf clubs open up before their courses are ready because they need the revenue. So we had a really long grow-in time. We let it grow in a full year. We had a good superintendent who knew his stuff. Our turf was well established. Some of the courses that open up too early have turf that isn't established, and it just gets hammered and doesn't recover for a long time. That can really hurt a reputation for a golf course. There are courses in my area that are still suffering 10 years later from opening before the course was really ready. I listened to a lot of people about when and how to open.

You do have to know who plays your golf course. We are midrange. We aren't a $90 course, and we're not the $20 course with a cart. We're right in the $40-$55 range. Who we are is what we evolved into. We kind of grew into our own skin. In 2001, I was being told what golf is, this is how you act, and this is what you should do. The more experience I have in the golf business, the more I think all that traditional advice is crap. The game has gotten to the point where it isn't much fun. You can go into pro shops and feel that people are looking down their noses at you. There are so many rules, so many things that people think they should not be doing on a golf course. It's almost like you have to know the secret handshake to get on the golf course. That's crap and it's going to kill this industry. So we took a turn, and now our main goal is that we want to have fun at everything we do. That philosophy starts with me and works its way on down to all our staff. I'm starting to find my own groove on this approach. It's fun, and I just don't see many other courses doing it.

This approach started with my marketing guy, Robbie Finley. He started putting out email blasts on discounts at the course, but in the "fine print" on restrictions, he got to be a smart-ass. He didn't think anyone would read that small print, but people started reading the fine print just to see what Robbie would come up with next. Actually I don't know how much I want to tell you and give away some of these marketing approaches. Believe me, he is so clever. Our email database is around 16,000 people, which is pretty good for an 18 hole course. When we send out email blasts, our email open rate is about 36 percent. People actually open up our emails because Robbie is funny as hell, and they want to see what he has to say. We think that people are used to being advertised to and not talked to. They enjoy it when somebody talks to them like they know them. That's what Robbie does and people like it.

Sometimes Robbie gets a bit out there on the edge with his marketing, and sometimes people get offended by it. I do get some phone calls from people who say they are offended. I just tell them that I understand their position, but we have a plan and don't want to change our ways, that they should unsubscribe to our database. Part of having fun is that sooner or later you might cross the line a bit. Like I said, I don't want to give away all of our strategies, but as an example, we recently sent out an email blast and the subject line for the email was, "We're not Dicks!" Once you open the email, you discover that we are talking about some of our pro shop prices for golf equipment being better than at Dick's Sporting Goods, a big-box store. Lots of people see an email from a business and they delete the email before they check it out. But when people see a subject line like ours, they start to wonder what the heck might come next, so they open the email. Our disclaimers in the fine print are brutally honest. If we put out an offer, but the offer, isn't really all that good of a deal, we tell you, "Hey, don't get so excited. This isn't all that good of a deal. It's only a hotdog and some chips, it doesn't even include a drink. We want to see you open that wallet and see the mothballs fly out of it."

We started another strategy and had no idea how it would turn out. Robbie put out an "Old Farts Offer." The disclaimer said that even if you don't print out the offer to bring it to the clubhouse, just come up to the counter at the pro shop and say you're an old fart and you want your deal. Guys will come up to the counter, slam their hands on it and say, "I want my deal! I'm an Old Fart!" It used to be that on a Tuesday we would get 30 to 40 golfers, but this last year we were averaging around 120. I'm telling you, people want to be talked to like they are humans, like they are your buddies. The more experience I get in this business, the more I think this is how to run a golf course. If the guy behind the counter isn't having fun at their job, then the customer won't have as much fun, either. We aren't the IRS doing audits. We exist so people can come out and have fun.

Take our yardage books for how to best play the course. Usually those books give advice on where to hit and how far to hit. We are smart-asses in our yardage books. We say things like, "Management recommends that you use a very expensive golf ball for this shot. They sell better in the pro shop when we recycle them." Now, that's a bit of a smackdown, but it is a lot of fun and people enjoy it. This kind of thing is exciting. It has reinvigorated me. That's our niche, our brand. That's who we are.

We want to use this kind of approach to bring more women into the game. I think there is a lot of opportunity there. As soon as I get back from this conference, I'm going to put this challenge to my team. What can we do to motivate a 50-year-old woman to come play golf at our course? Women are starting to outearn men now. We are missing the boat if we don't market to women in ways they understand and appreciate.

The clubhouse, the double-wide, does about $225,000 a year with our snack bar. We have great hotdogs, breakfast burritos and cold sandwiches, chips, beer and that sort of thing. There are a lot of golf courses that have built million-dollar-plus clubhouses with restaurants and then have to close the doors to the restaurant. Restaurants very rarely work. Unless your debt load is extremely low, it's just too hard to make enough revenue to pay for the cost of the restaurant. By not having more restaurant facilities, we do lose our golfers after their rounds, but for now what we do is working for us.

Tomorrow I'm going home for the grand opening of our tournament pavilion. It's a 2,000-square-foot lid supported by pillars, with open sides. We just bought doors for it; it's heated and has installed bathrooms. We're hoping for an additional $150,000 to $200,000 in revenue a year. We're looking for weddings, banquets, corporate outings, tournaments, birthday parties, you name it. Since 2008 when the economy turned to crap, we have to do everything we can think of to keep our revenue stream up. We've had to cut our expenses, just hang on, and keep moving forward somehow. The new pavilion is really exciting for us.

We do stay open all year around, but typically it's a six to seven month season. If the weather permits, we're open. Just last weekend—at the end of February we had 150 rounds of golf, but when the snow comes, it's a different story.

This summer three of my daughters will be working the beverage cart. They are 18, 18 and 20. It always has been a family operation, and that is the biggest perk for us. My wife and I work really well together. She does all the accounting, and then she fills in everywhere. She'll do merchandizing, special events, whatever and whenever. For example, I always wanted my own Saddleback custom-made flag to put up at the course. Verne already has three big flag poles. When I priced a flag, they wanted $1,500 a flag. With the wind and the weather, you would go through one or maybe two flags a year. We can get winds of 80 mph a few times each year. Well, my wife Lana made the flags. She projected the flag image on a wall, traced it out, cut the fabric, and made our 10-by-6-foot flags. There is nothing that woman can't do!

If you had told me when I was in high school that I would someday be running a golf course, I would have laughed at you. I was going to be an airline pilot from as far back as I can remember. There was never any doubt about that. Now I look back and think that the best decision I ever made was to get out of flying for a living. One thing about me, though, is I could be happy doing just about anything. If I'm having fun and find the work intriguing, then I could do just about anything. Knowing that about myself, I just don't know what might come up for me in the future. I'm not going to pigeonhole myself into anything. If an opportunity comes along that I don't even know about yet, I might go for it. One of my best friends was an engineer, then he got into dairy farming, and now he's doing other stuff, too. One possibility for me is to run additional golf courses. With the economy of scale, you can run multiple courses with a relatively small administrative or management team, so I think about that.

When I think about the future of the golf industry, I think that future will be like with movies, other entertainment, the ways people like to have fun. People are always going to want to have fun. Even during the Great Depression, movies and bars still did OK. People always want relief from the day-to-day madness. When the golf industry focuses on this interest of people more intently, I think it will be just fine. We might have different business models than we did five or 10 years ago. We will be leaner and meaner as they say. Obviously we are oversupplied with golf courses. There is no doubt about that. Eventually we'll have parity with supply and demand, and the industry will be just fine. The days of making money hand over fist may be gone for the next 10 years. In the meantime it's going to be those businesses that get back to or stick with the basics that will make it. Every dollar that goes out of the checkbook had better have an ROI *(return on investment)* attached to it. Those business basics and making golf fun are the keys to the industry's future. Our numbers were up last year and we're optimistic.

We were Colorado Course of the Year in 2003 and we co-hosted the Colorado Open in 2007. Last year we got an honorable mention for the best risk-reward hole in the state. That's the hole where we recommend you use a really expensive ball. It's a par-4 dogleg hole that you can play as a dogleg, or you can cut the corner and go for the green with your drive, over water all the way, with water around the green. That's a fun hole. One of the guys who plays our course has had three holes-in-one on that hole. Three! That guy is having fun!

## O'Malley's Lessons

- "Most people build a golf course and then try to sell adjoining property for real estate or commercial development. We did it ass-backwards from what most people do. We sold that land first to invest in our bad habit of golf."
- Building the golf course was the hardest I ever worked, and it was fun as hell.
- Cart paths are valuable for more than aesthetics; they really help protect the turf and keep maintenance costs down.
- If you ask the right people the right questions, you can get great information. People are more than happy to tell you what they know.
- Nobody will do everything right. Making some mistakes along the way is normal and instructive.
- "I'm not saying that I would never go into another partnership, but if I did I would certainly be very adamant about understanding all of the features of the partnership before I did it."
- Some courses open up too early with turf that isn't established, and the course gets hammered and doesn't recover for a long time. That can really hurt a reputation for a golf course. There are courses that are still suffering 10 years later from opening before the course was really ready. Be sure to think carefully about when and how to open.
- "You can go into pro shops and feel that people are looking down their noses at you. There are so many rules, so many things that people think they should not be doing on a golf course. It's almost like you have to know the secret handshake to get on the golf course. That's crap and it's going to kill this industry. So we took a turn, and now our main goal is that we want to have fun at everything we do."

- "We think that people are used to being advertised to and not talked to. They enjoy it when somebody talks to them through marketing like they know them."
- "If the guy behind the counter isn't having fun at their job, then the customer won't have as much fun, either. We aren't the IRS doing audits. We exist so people can come out and have fun."
- People are always going to want to have fun.
- Women are starting to out-earn men now. Course owners are missing the boat if they don't market to women in ways they understand and appreciate.
- Every dollar that goes out of your checkbook had better have an ROI *(return on investment)* attached to it. Those business basics and making golf fun are the keys to the industry's future.

# Postscript

My first encounters with golf industry leaders came during the planning for the B.S. in Golf Enterprise Management at University of Wisconsin-Stout. Initially I was invited by the dean of my college, John Wesolek, to meetings to discuss how the university might address preparation of graduates for entry-level golf business management positions, primarily at golf courses. I can't remember exactly how it was that I was invited. Maybe John valued my incisive mind, or maybe I begged and whined to be included. That conversation about creating a new model for golf course and golf business management started with Curt Walker, who was involved with founding the NGCOA, is the executive director of the Midwest Golf Course Owners Association, and was familiar with UW-Stout. Curt had connections with leaders throughout the golf industry, and he played a critical role in getting us engaged in planning our curriculum and networked in the industry. The industry leaders we met encouraged us to develop an academic program focused on the business of golf, that did not include any instruction on playing golf or teaching golf techniques. They wanted a comprehensive and rigorous four-year degree that would have a different focus from the 17 professional golf management (PGM) university programs that were endorsed and guided by the PGA of America. We weren't to develop golf professionals like the PGM schools; we were to develop businessmen and business women who knew how to make profits in golf businesses. In their words, "The last thing we need in the industry is another pretty swing. We need managers who know how to make businesses profitable." We were to think about eventual general managers, not eventual head pros.

Our planning team included representatives from the National Golf Course Owners Association, the PGA, the LPGA, Golf Course Superintendents of America Association, American Society of Golf Course Architects, Toro Corporation, Kohler Company, a small group of regional golf course owners, and financial consultants within the industry. Before I knew what I was getting into, I was surrounded by some of the most experienced and knowledgeable people in the industry. My roles in the planning evolved from timidly reporting that I was pretty much a bogey golfer who played a fade to having the responsibility for co-writing the planning documents for the UW system for our new academic degree and presenting the proposal to the UW Board of Regents. My involvement included writing the curriculum for the first three courses of instruction in the degree program and managing the program and its students for three years. I knew academia and I had a reputation for getting things done. At the end of my career, I spent more time developing a golf business program than I did with psychology, my discipline. It was fun!

However, this "Postscript" isn't about me; it's about the people I've met on this journey. I knew at the outset that the golf industry is enormous and that its impact on our culture is extraordinary. I knew that my aging hippie persona, with a shaggy haircut and a too-long red beard, didn't look like "the face of golf." I assumed that my leaning-to-the-left politics would be different from the people in the industry with whom I would be working. I worried about my acceptance into the inner circles of business geniuses and multimillionaires. I had so much to learn.

In the planning stages for the academic program, I met some of the most impressive people I have ever known, whose assistance with this book has been invaluable. I have to acknowledge the leadership in the NGCOA. Mike Hughes, the chief executive officer, embodies sophistication and intellect. He is the voice of the association who advocates for the best interests of golf course owners and managers in the United States and around the world. This is a big job that demands exceptional leadership. What a treat to watch him deliver.

Mike Tinkey, deputy chief executive officer of NGCOA, is second in command. This southern gentleman nourishes the network of golf course owners, operators, suppliers and others with his interpersonal skills. He seems to know thousands of people personally. He smiles. He touches. He connects people. I think he likes me.

On that planning team I want to mention two others in particular. Stephen Johnston at that time was the national director of KPMG Golf Industry Practice. Now he is president and partner in Global Golf Advisors, his own company. These golf industry consulting companies conduct feasibility studies and develop business plans for all types of golf properties. His experience with over 2,000 golf courses around the world and his native intelligence make him one of the smartest people I know in the industry. He does statistical calculations in his head that would take me hours to work out. And, oh yeah, he has over 50 holes-in-one. At first he really intimidated me. Then he broke the ice in our relationship. After a planning meeting for the new academic program and a round of golf with the planners, we all met in the clubhouse and had a couple of beers. I was still wondering how or if I fit in when Stephen came over to me, put his arm around my shoulder, and said, "Tommy *(he instinctively knew that using my nickname would melt me)*, have you ever played Augusta National, site of the Masters?" Of course, the answer was, "No." He said, "I tell you what, I have connections. How about I fly down from Toronto to Minneapolis, pick you up, and we go down to Augusta and play the course for a few days. You won't need any money. Just bring your sticks. I'll take care of everything." By this time, a small crowd had gathered around us in the clubhouse. I was beginning to feel like I had won the lottery. Then Stephen said, "Just one condition. *(Long pause)* You'll have to shave." The last time I shaved was 1970 after the Army. The laughter broke out among our small audience before the reality hit me. I got "punk'd." To his credit, he kept his arm around my shoulder and helped me ride out the joke. He got me good and I loved it. He brought me, the shaggy psychology guy, into the inner circle.

Also on our planning team was Henry DeLozier, who at that time managed the golf course portfolio for Pulte Homes, the nation's largest homebuilder and community developer. Henry was named by Crittenden's *Golf Inc.* magazine as one of the 10 most influential people in the golf industry, and he served as president of the NGCOA. Now he is a partner in Global Golf Advisors with Stephen Johnston. He is widely recognized as one of the most knowledgeable people in the industry on all areas related to golf business. In college he was an all-American golfer, but now he rarely plays. His focus is business. Henry seems to know everybody in the industry, and on several occasions I have had to stand in a line just to say hello to him. The consummate professional, he is soft-spoken, articulate and tireless. The man sleeps only two or three hours a day! Being introduced to the industry by people like Henry has been a blessing.

Since the initial discussions about our academic program, I began to consider the nature of golf course owners. I knew some were born into the business, but I also knew there were many others who took enormous financial and personal risks to build or buy golf courses. Whether they had been in other businesses prior to golf ownership or evolved from positions within the industry such as golf course pros or superintendents, a time came when, in the words of Bill Aragona, they went "All In." They each had written the checks, usually for millions of dollars, to chase their dreams. They were entrepreneurs in an admittedly appealing business, but a business with many, many variables beyond their control. They may have understood the climate in the region they were located, but they had no control over the seasonal weather that directly influenced their revenue. Rain alone can wreak havoc on profitability, but earthquakes, floods, hurricanes, mudslides and other natural catastrophes can ruin a golf business. Initially they may have known the competition in the market where their property was located, but competing businesses can be developed to directly affect their market shares. Tax codes, zoning regulations, environmental policies and other governmental factors change. Economies change and have far-reaching consequences for business success. Even at the beginning of my education about golf course ownership, I admired the courage of those who took the risks to chase their dreams in the face of extreme uncertainty.

As I met one owner after another, primarily at Golf Industry Shows on both coasts, the idea for this book emerged. I observed that there was no hardcover literature on golf course ownership or operation in the "bookstore" sections of these huge events. With as many as 20,000 people attending the shows, with up to 1,000 people specifically associated with the NGCOA, it amazed me that there was little to no literature on ownership and operation of golf properties. When I watched golf events on television, I started to notice that it was extremely rare that the commentators made mention of who owned the golf courses where the major golf tours competed. Sure, if Arnold Palmer owned the golf course, he was usually credited. Stories about Herb Kohler, the plumbing magnate from Wisconsin who built Whistling Straits and other courses, typically got some mention on television. If Donald Trump built the course where an event was held, the only way he would likely get credit was when "Trump" was in the name of the golf course. Golf on TV more often gave credit to the designers, the superintendents or the head professionals at the famous courses of the world than it did to the owners. These observations fed my curiosity.

In addition to my perception that owners were somewhat ignored in the media, I became fascinated by the ones I met. From the owners of upscale resorts, residential golf communities, and multicourse properties, to private clubs or to public daily-fee courses, I found them fascinating. I understood the business risks they had taken, but more than that, they were really interesting people. Many had engaging personalities and the "gift of gab," talking about golf and describing their ownership stories. Occasionally there were some who just wanted to hear themselves talk, loudly. I'll never forget one of my first national golf conferences and meeting a residential golf community owner from the East Coast who wore an orange sport coat with purple trousers and a pink tie. I'm not making this up. His clothes were loud, and he could be heard across the room at a cocktail party. He's not in this book. Even though there is great diversity among golf course owners, he is not typical. The majority of the owners I have met understand they are in the business of hospitality and behave accordingly. Their stories in this book attest to this conclusion.

As I approached retirement and pitched my idea for a book on golf ownership stories to the people I knew in the industry, I was roundly encouraged. People agreed this was a good idea. Once I started recruiting owners for participation, however, some unanticipated realities became apparent. About one in 10 owners whom I approached for participation actually did participate. The reasons are varied. Certainly, these are busy people, and a couple hours of their time are valuable. Some are satisfied that they already have sufficient attention brought to their golf businesses through trade magazine publications and local media. At a deeper level, there is secrecy in the industry, as I suspect there is secrecy within any industry. Some just don't want to share their secrets, strategies or plans with the competition. Others who declined interviews mentioned that they had financial challenges, impending sales or changes in their properties they didn't want to discuss publicly. One owner who initially agreed to an interview later changed his mind. A collapsed business partnership during a stressful financial time with his golf course had meant the loss of his friendship with his partner. He told me that he just couldn't relive that painful time in his life. For a variety of reasons, some of which were typical in any industry and some of which were none of my business, more owners declined to participate than accepted.

Even though the golf property owners recounted their stories in their own words and better than anybody else ever could, I want to share some of the "behind-the-interview" experiences that I believe reflect who these people are.

Throughout the process of interviewing, I was amazed by the emotions shared with me. Rick and Gina Budinger were the only owners I previously knew. They own the course where I am a member. Rick has a reputation for using street language. I grew up on a Navy base and that's how I talk, too. You know what they say about talking like sailors. I think of him as a pretty tough guy. In the middle of the interview, Rick got choked up, really choked up, recalling a split with his partner and friend in their Chicago printing business. He asked Gina for half a glass of wine to settle him for the remainder of the interview. Collapsed partnerships can hurt deeply. Some wounds heal very slowly.

At a Golf Industry Show I approached Frank Jemsek and introduced myself. Frank was aware of our academic program and had previously noticed me in the crowd of conference participants, but we had never met. Since he's 6 foot 8 inches tall, I had noticed him, too. He is a towering figure in the industry, both literally and figuratively. I told him about the book project and asked him, if I were to drive to Chicago for an interview, whether he would be interested. He said he would love to participate, and within seconds he surged with emotion.

His eyes got red and misty. He quickly asked, "Could I talk about my dad, Joe?" *(His father, Joe, had built the Cog Hill dynasty.)* Honestly, the way I remember it, we were still shaking hands in our introduction and he showed me his heart. He showed me that family legacy comes with great responsibility for family. Business is second in importance. Now I've met Frank's daughters and son, Cog Hill's future. They understand the family legacy. Prior to meeting the Jemsek family, multigenerational ownership implied privilege for me. The real meanings of multigenerational ownership are so much deeper. With Frank's guidance, the Jemsek family is surely blessed.

During a conference lunch at a Golf Industry Show, I met Joe Lightkep and arranged for a breakfast meeting and interview the following morning. As we got to know each other during breakfast, I mentioned that my son John has had a spinal cancer since age 17 and has had several serious surgeries and other cancer treatments. I always get choked up talking about this, but as soon as I had spoken of my sad tale, Joe began to gently weep. Joe has had back surgeries and was facing a shoulder surgery soon after the conference. He said that unless you have experienced nerve pain, you could never understand its torture. His empathy for John overwhelmed me. After some nose-blowing and mopping up, we got back to our breakfasts and conversation about golf. His golf ownership story is remarkable. Joe, the person, is extraordinary.

Many of the golf course owners in this book, like Joe, grew up on a golf course. They picked up sticks, raked bunkers, washed golf cars, picked up range balls, and washed dishes. They learned their eventual businesses from the bottom up, and they nurtured their passions for the game from childhood. As children, some owners were from families just scraping by, and some came from more privileged beginnings. When he was a child, golf professional Mike Malone hit practice shots to the center of a driving range to make picking up the balls easier. One time golf professional George Kelley hit bunker shots and fairway woods to the first green at the famous Pebble Beach Golf Links, where he and his family lived. Their circumstances may have been different, but their joy from watching a ball in the sky after a well-hit golf shot and building their lives around that joy are similar.

Not all of the passion associated with golf has to do with playing the game. Playing in the dirt and making things grow have motivated many in the golf business. Well over one-half of the stories in this book recount this passion. Some owners grew up on farms, and those roots run deep. Some found satisfaction in cutting grass as kids and still do. Tom Brady couldn't stop talking about his love of trees. Moving dirt with heavy equipment to shape the earth into a vision was a source of satisfaction for many. Mike Rogers was compelled to work the ground at night after his construction crews went home. Roger Evans in Alaska must continually reshape his course to contend with freezing and thawing in the permafrost. Attorney James Oliff found diversion from his law practice in working the land. Some pursued advanced educational degrees to cultivate their agronomy and horticultural skills and then later focused on the business side of their facilities. Dick Shulz helped to invent a new turfgrass. George Kelley built a company specializing in environmentally friendly golf course maintenance. The "green" side of the golf industry is not only about cutting-edge science and technology, but also about the passions of those who love dirt and things that grow. Owning and operating a golf course isn't only about pencil pushing and the bottom line. Getting your hands literally dirty is not demeaning, it is joyful.

As passionate as many are about playing the game or playing in the dirt, business acumen is the singular requirement for thriving in golf businesses, just as it is with entrepreneurs in other businesses. Each of the owners whose stories are recounted in this book took financial risks that most people may find difficult to imagine. Finding ways to generate revenue and manage expenses while improving facilities and services, successfully competing with others for market share, using creativity to attract new customers and retain loyal ones, maintaining a committed workforce, managing debt and meeting demands of taxation, human resource regulations, safety standards, and other day-to-day business challenges are common for all of these golf course owners. Many of the conditions affecting golf business success, such as economies, government regulations and taxes, are variable. Other conditions affecting success are unpredictable. Weather alone can make or break a golf business. Catastrophic weather such as Hurricane Katrina destroyed golf businesses in the Gulf region. Too much rain, too much heat, too much cold, too much wind are all conditions that cannot be predicted and keep golfers away. And don't forget that most of the golf course businesses in the United States are seasonal. They have to make their "hay" while the sun shines. Roger and Melinda Evans in Fairbanks are the perfect example of the effect of climate on business. Of course, they stay open 22 hours a day during their season to make their "hay."

This short list of golf business challenges is probably terrifying to people in most businesses. Nevertheless, for golf course owners, their passion for what they do, their business acumen, their creativity, and their hard work enable them to meet the challenges. Of the stories in this book, consider the skill and courage of people like Mike and Linda Rogers, who in a very short time went from near poverty operating a bar in a depressed area to owning five restaurants, then a golf course and a custom home building business, not to mention a leadership position in the golf industry.

Consider the skills and "can-do" attitude of Richard Hampton, CEO of the New Orleans Fire Fighters Pension and Relief Fund, at Lakewood Golf Club in New Orleans. Following extensive damage caused by Hurricane Katrina, the Lakewood golf course is in the first phase of a multimillion dollar resort plan for the property that includes a hotel, four-story clubhouse, conference center, golf villas, condominiums, retirement center, office suites, restaurants and specialty retail businesses. The Lakewood story, like the New Orleans story, is truly inspirational.

For a short course on what it takes to succeed as an entrepreneur in golf business, go back and reread Frank Romano's story. Frank is a business genius who understands hard work, how to close a deal, how to build a brand and then market that brand, how to hire and then create opportunities and benefits for employees. There is a textbook in that story, and my head was spinning after our interview.

I love Tom Brady's comment that you go to work with a roll of duct tape and a tube of Gorilla Glue to get the job done. I am awed by the creative genius of Roger Evans, who attends trade shows on the newest golf course technologies so that he can return home to Alaska and then build that technology himself.

Consider the talents and career trajectory of Michael Hatch, who at age 23 started managing a private golf club in London and was managing six of them by age 26. After moving to the United States he managed 14 golf courses. Now in his 30s, he owns two American golf clubs as well as his own Acumen Golf Consulting business that offers guidance on operations, financial restructuring, strategic planning, sales and marketing strategies, and other club management challenges around the world. OK, it's obvious this is a bright and ambitious guy. For me, it's his eye-to-eye engaging charm that gets it done.

The collection of personal experiences and attributes exhibited by the golf course owners in this book demonstrates variety. Self-confidence, intelligence, diligence, imagination and passion are their common entrepreneurial qualities.

One of the trends in golf course ownership that currently generates a great deal of debate is the proportion of courses owned and operated by corporations. There are some large corporations that own and operate over 100 courses each. At the other end of the continuum are the independent, small business owners, or what the golf industry calls "mom-and-pop" businesses. My intention here is not to engage in the debate, but rather to point out some of my observations about the independent golf course owners in this book.

Independent owners operate within communities, and many of the stories in this book testify to the importance those owners place on contributing to their communities. Their contributions are economic in the forms of taxes, employment and generation of revenues for complimentary businesses such as restaurants and hotels. The contributions also include creation of social, recreational, educational, familial and environmental assets that might not otherwise exist. Golf courses create green spaces in communities, preserve wildlife, and instruct others in conservation. Golf courses become the venues for business transactions for small and large groups. A corporate golf outing can enhance socialization and even refine a corporate culture. Golf courses host banquets, birthday parties and weddings that bring people together for carefree fun and socialization. Golf courses can be the center of educational experiences. Jay Miller owns a golf course so that his foundation has a venue to teach golf, academic skills and life skills lessons to children. Golf instruction alone can introduce people to a sport for a lifetime. As many of the owners in this book are doing, bringing women, children and families to the golf course creates socialization opportunities that bond people and bring fun to their lives. The Brady family golf course even has a miniature golf course just outside the clubhouse to attract youth and their families to golf. Because Bill Aragona's golf course had an electrical generator and a satellite dish, Boulder Creek became "Emergency Central" following a major California earthquake. His course became their link to the outside world and a place for food and shelter. The theme of "giving back" to their communities resonates throughout the stories in this book.

Independent golf course owners tend to be focused on family. A majority of the stories in this book began with comments about the roles parents played in their lives. Siblings, children, aunts and uncles are central to many of the stories.

Jeff Hoag recalled being at home at Sunday dinner, overlooking the golf course, watching a car coming up the dusty gravel road, and either his mom or dad going down to check in a golfer. They would come back home to finish dinner and then get back to the course again to serve a hotdog or a pop. That's where Jeff learned what you need to do. George Kelley started his story as a California pioneer family going back five generations. Frank Jemsek inherited a golf family legacy beginning with his father, Joe, his mother and other family members. Now Frank works to assure that golf remains part of his family for generations to come.

Mike and Linda Rogers had their daughter, Michelle, in their very early 20s. Michelle, Mike and Linda say they all grew up together in a variety of businesses, including a golf course where Michelle is general manager.

Jay Miller, Jeff Hoag, Roger Evans, George Kelley, Joe Lightkep, Charlie Scott, Whitey O'Malley and others can be witnessed drifting back to the precious moments of their childhoods, remembering playing golf with their parents. They caught the golf "bug" early in connection with the love within their families.

In the Toad Valley interview were Tom Brady (owner and president), his wife, "Fred" Brady (The Kitchen Guru), and their daughter Allison George (The Wizard of Fun). Tending the snack bar in the clubhouse was Tom and Fred's son Jason (Gorilla). Jason's wife, Theresa (Queen of Clean), was in and out of the clubhouse. Allison's husband, Kelly George (Turf Jedi), was on the course working as superintendent. The Bradys and Georges are one big, happy family. The reader will see that this third-generation, family-owned business does things a bit differently from the traditional golf course business.

Family interviews were conducted with the Brady family, Mike, Linda and Michelle Rogers, Rick and Gina Budinger, Charlie and Betsie Scott, and Dick and Nancy Schultz. It was wonderful to witness the dynamics of family relationships as sentences begun by one person were completed by another, as they laughed with each others' stories and filled in missing pieces of their histories together. Mike and Linda Rogers and Rick and Gina Budinger demonstrated the yin and yang, the left brain and right brain, of relationships. As partners they created wholes greater than the sum of their parts. Dick and Nancy Shulz sat shoulder to shoulder, often touching, during their interview. They often complimented each others' strengths and clearly showed a loving bond as partners. And, of course, who would not be impressed by the strength of family in Charlie and Betsie Scott's story. Imagine traveling the country building golf courses while living in a trailer with two small children, a dog and a cat.

Jay Miller and Whitey O'Malley were interviewed by themselves, but they made continual references to their wives. Jay said, "She is a very intelligent, beautiful lady, and funny as hell. I just love that woman!" Whitey said, "That woman can do anything!" These stories about families give us all hope.

These are the stories told about immediate family. Most of the owners also talked about their employees becoming "family." Job creators build extended families. Many of the golf course owners spoke about employees who have worked for them for decades. At Cog Hill there have only been two head superintendents since 1927 when it was opened. Ken Lapp, Frank Jemsek's head superintendent, worked for Frank's dad beginning in 1949. Frank's head waitress has been with Cog Hill for 50 years. That is some extended family! Consider Bill Aragona and his Hispanic employees who teased him for his attempts to speak Spanish and fed him roasted pig and carnitas. Mike and Linda Rogers speak of employees as sons and daughters, and they have even made me a member of their "family." The golf industry employs hundreds of thousands people. One can only be impressed by the livelihoods created by these positions. These stories remind us of the depth of relationships these positions make possible.

As a business, golf course ownership is demanding and rewarding. Establishing one's brand as "a category of one," assuring that all staff represent the philosophies of the brand, creating an atmosphere of fun, meeting or exceeding guests' expectations for every service provided, are consistent themes within this hospitality industry. Whether it's Allison Brady assuring that all the screws in the electrical circuit plates are aligned or Jay Miller personally greeting golfers on the first tee, these owners focus on meeting or exceeding guests' expectations. For me, I love how this philosophy was described by Fire Chief Bud Carrouché in New Orleans. In his Cajun accent, Bud told how everyone at Lakewood is delivering lagniappe. He said, "Lagniappe is something like a baker's dozen that you may have heard of in other parts of the country. It's a French word for something that's a little extra. It's like when people go to the store to buy some beans and they get a little rice, too, as lagniappe." Providing your guests an unexpected bonus is lagniappe. Give a little extra, and benefits for your business will follow. I think that lagniappe is the mantra for the golf industry.

This book was written during an economic recession that has demonstrated that the golf industry is not recession-proof. Throughout the industry the recession has hurt. However, I believe that the golf industry really is "too big to fail." Those who enjoy the game and spend time on a golf course understand the timeless joy of hitting a round object with a stick to propel it toward some distant target. Watching that round object soar through the sky is joyful. The golf course is a place to have fun with friends and family. The golf course is a business center, a sanctuary from worries, a playground, a monastery for meditation, a test of athleticism and imagination, a place to appreciate nature, wildlife and fresh air, a sport for a lifetime, a place for celebration, a classroom for life lessons, and so much more. The golf course nurtures body, mind and spirit. We will always want what golf courses offer.

Lastly, in case you're wondering, there really never was a "Mooch Tour." Most of the interviews were done at conference settings rather than golf courses. My buddies interested in mooching understand. My putting woes were cured. Now I shank a lot! It's always something.

Ever hear the old saying, "I keep remembering the things I told myself I would never forget"? I learned that lesson again and again as I met the gracious people in the golf industry, particularly golf course owners, who time and time again showed me the naiveté of my preconceived notions of others who are different in some way. I also learned that even guys with long red beards are "The Face of Golf." Ain't life grand!

# Appendix A: Top Lessons Themes

## Customer Service

There are many beautiful golf courses, but service is how you distinguish yourself. Do your best to exceed customers' expectations in every service or product you provide. Treat every customer like it's their first visit.

Make sure your customers know how much you appreciate them. When possible, demonstrate your appreciation by knowing their names and their preferences.

Every customer's experience at the course is based on their interaction with somebody who works at the course. Distinguish yourself from your competitors by making sure that everyone on your staff adopts a philosophy that they are going to do everything they can to make sure the customer's enjoyment of the facility is their foremost priority.

Deliver "lagniappe," an unexpected bonus or something extra. It will pay dividends in recruiting and retaining customers.

## Managing Staff

Thorough communication between management and staff is a reciprocal process, but it is management's responsibility to maintain a positive organizational culture, communicate expectations, and provide training and feedback on performance. Management must assure that each and every employee takes pride and has a sense of ownership in their work and understands that creating a quality golf experience makes people happy. It's really not about the corporation or the owner. Your staff is where it all happens.

Treat employees with honesty and respect to create trust, commitment, loyalty and pride. Hire employees who understand hospitality and discharge those who do not understand your values.

Learning your business from the ground up, by doing all the different jobs that are needed, enables you to manage your business effectively.

## Community Asset

A golf course is an integral component of the community in which it is located. The course is a source of fun, recreation, social interaction and employment for the community. It also has the value-added qualities of serving its community with economic benefits and green spaces for quality of life and environmental assets.

The community is the source of revenue for the course. Hosting charity events, golf outings, weddings, banquets, and birthday parties enhances course revenues and perceptions of the integral nature of the course to the community. Do as much as you can to stay involved with your community and continually promote the fact that your golf course is their community asset.

## Partnership

Golf courses are expensive. Sole ownership may not always be possible. Consequently, limited partnership, limited liability partnership or corporate ownership decisions may be required. Each legal structure has advantages and disadvantages that must be considered.

Partnerships can make or break just about any business, as well as the relationships with those involved.

Good partnerships can produce sound investments with thorough understanding of business risks and potentials. Good partnerships create a sense of teamwork and provide a broader range of talents and experiences for operating a business.

However, when partnerships fail, the results can be personally and professionally devastating. When partnerships fail, best friends can be lost and family bonds can be broken, even if the business survives.

Enter any business partnership with a thoroughly considered contract that outlines the financial, managerial and tax responsibilities of each partner, as well as legally binding stipulations for possible negligent acts of partners. This kind of thorough planning may not be comfortable but could prevent disaster.

## Emerging Trends

Golf has always been a game based on traditions, typically played by men. There will always be a market for traditional "championship" golf courses and USGA by-the-rules competitive golfer purists. However, golf is a difficult sport to play well, it's expensive, and it consumes large amounts of time. Time and money are precious, particularly during times of economic recession. Consequently, there are emerging trends in the industry to alter traditional rules of golf, marketing strategies and even course designs in order to recruit new players and new revenues.

As several of the owners in this book remind us, "Fun is good!" Make the game more fun. Develop ways to appeal to your customers who just want to have fun. Whether they like the camaraderie, the fellowship, just being outdoors, or whatever, we should cater to them. The more fun you make the game, the more people will play.

*Alternative Golf* uses strategies such as playing from the forward tees to make holes shorter, permitting mulligans, and using equipment to make balls go farther, to make the game more fun. A new organization called the Alternative Golf Association (AGA) was formed in 2010 to alter rules and equipment to enable more people to have success at the game and to have more fun. The AGA *Project Flogton* ("Not Golf" spelled backward) was initiated in 2011. *SortaGolf* and *TeeGolf* are other emerging alternative golf games.

*Tee It Forward* is a new initiative designed to help golfers have more fun on the course and enhance their overall experience by playing from the set of tees best suited to their abilities.

*Get Golf Ready* is an ambitious adult player development initiative being implemented at facilities nationwide. The program is designed to teach everything golfers need to know to play golf in just a few lessons. PGA and LPGA professionals demonstrate that there are lots of ways to play by combining fun, friends and fitness.

Find ways to alter the game to make it fun for young people. Golf is a social sport, and kids like to do things together, so there should be ways to make the game so much fun that kids will want to hang out at the golf course. At some courses this means creating golf teams for young people and even designing a beginning set of holes to learn the game. (*The First Tee* and other initiatives are oriented to recruiting the next generation of golfers.)

Golf is a family game. Create opportunities to back up that philosophy by marketing to women and children. *Take Your Daughter to the Course Week was developed by the National Golf Course Owners Association and is part of Play Golf America, an industry-wide effort to grow the game. Women's Golf Month is part of the PGA of America's Play Golf America initiative.*

## Guests' Perceptions of Quality

Developing a unique brand and focusing on customer service are essential to distinguish your business. Your reputation is based on your guests' perceptions of the quality of their experiences. Below are some specific examples to create the kinds of perceptions that lead to repeat business.

When you open your door for guests, be ready. First impressions are powerful. The original course opening sets the tone to establish your course's reputation. When the facility is completely ready, turf is grown-in, cart paths and clubhouse are completed, you create the perceptions you intended. This means you may not generate revenue as quickly as you would like, but the positive impressions you create build the reputation that will soon pay dividends. Some courses open up too early with turf that isn't established, and the course gets abused and doesn't recover for a long time. That can really hurt a reputation for a golf course. The same principles apply to annual course openings.

One of the biggest challenges golf course owners face is discounting, which has become popular as too many courses try to compete for business. If you charge less for the same services, you risk not only your financial status but also customer perceptions. If it is possible, establish a fair price and stay with it. Customers appreciate knowing what the price is going to be and that everybody will pay that same price.

Attend to details. Maybe the guests don't really pay specific attention to the details, but they do get a certain "feeling" about how comfortable and pleasant their experience has been because details were attended to. Those feelings lead to repeat business.

## Seek Advice

Ask for advice. None of us knows everything, and others are usually willing to share what they know. Golf industry experts are available for help (See the Resources Appendix for suggestions). Additionally, consider insightful local knowledge from the community where the property is located, particularly when acquiring a golf business in a new location.

## Make Mistakes

Take some risks to be innovative and experiment with new practices to grow your business. You may be rewarded for your creativity. Remember, though, that nobody will do everything right. Making some mistakes along the way is normal and instructive. Be prepared to make some mistakes and then learn from them and move on.

If you aren't making some mistakes, then you just aren't trying hard enough.

# Appendix B: Golf Industry Resource Directory

The global golf industry is extensive. The number of private businesses that manufacture and sell equipment, shoes and clothing for playing the game, that develop and maintain golf courses, and that equip restaurants are too many to enumerate. Add to that list the thousands of suppliers for golf point-of-sale technologies, food and beverage, golf course development, construction and maintenance, media companies, marketing services, tournament services, and on and on.

In addition to the many private businesses connected to the golf industry, there is a variety of trade associations and foundations that represent the golf industry. These organizations create the umbrellas that coordinate, support and provide authority for the primary segments of the industry. Understanding the functions of these organizations provides the best insights into the golf industry.

Listed below in alphabetical order are the primary trade associations and foundations advocating for various golf industry interests in America.

## American Junior Golf Association (AJGA)

The American Junior Golf Association is a 501(c)(3) nonprofit organization dedicated to the overall growth and development of young men and women who aspire to earn college golf scholarships through competitive junior golf.

## American Society of Golf Course Architects (ASGCA)

Founded in 1946, the American Society of Golf Course Architects is the oldest professional organization of golf course designers in America. These architects have designed, renovated and remodeled many of the most famous and storied courses in golf. They are active in current projects not only in the United States and Canada, but also in Europe, Asia and beyond. All ASGCA members have completed a minimum of five major golf course projects and are peer reviewed by the ASGCA membership. This ensures that all ASGCA members are qualified and well seasoned in golf course design, with a trained eye for both functional and aesthetic excellence. ASGCA is actively involved in promoting environmentally responsible golf course designs.

## Club Managers Association of America (CMAA)

The Club Managers Association of America advances the profession of club management by fulfilling the educational and related needs of its members. CMAA provides its members with the expertise to deliver an exceptional club experience that fulfills the unexpressed needs and desires of its members and guests consistent with their lifestyles. This mission is accomplished through providing state-of-the-art educational programs, representing the members to allied associations, club members and a broader public, and providing unique information and resources that increase member performance and career potential.

## Golf Course Builders Association of America (GCBAA)

The Golf Course Builders Association of America is a nonprofit trade association of the world's foremost golf course builders and leading suppliers to the golf course construction industry. It was founded in the early 1970s, and its members represent all segments of the golf course construction industry. It is the only organization in the world organized by and for golf course builders, and the only organization that represents the interests of the golf course construction industry.

## Golf Course Superintendents Association of America (GCSAA)

The Golf Course Superintendents Association of America is the professional association for the men and women who manage and maintain the game's most valuable resource — the golf course. Since 1926, GCSAA has been the top professional association for the men and women who manage golf courses in the United States and worldwide. From its headquarters in Lawrence, Kansas, the association provides education, information and representation to more than 19,000 members in more than 72 countries. GCSAA's mission is to serve its members, advance their profession, and enhance the enjoyment, growth and vitality of the game of golf.

The Environmental Institute for Golf, the philanthropic organization of the GCSAA, is a collaborative effort of the environmental and golf communities, dedicated to strengthening the compatibility of golf with the natural environment. The Institute concentrates on delivering programs and services involving research, education and outreach that communicate the best management practices of environmental stewardship on the golf course.

## Ladies Professional Golf Association (LPGA)

The Ladies Professional Golf Association is one of the longest-running women's professional sports associations in the world. Founded in 1950, the organization has grown from its roots as a playing tour into a nonprofit organization involved in every facet of golf. The LPGA Tour and the LPGA Teaching & Club Professionals (T&CP) comprise the backbone of what has become the premier women's professional sports organization in the world today. The LPGA maintains a strong focus on charity through: its tournaments; its grassroots junior and women's programs; its affiliation with Susan G. Komen for the Cure; and the formation of the LPGA Foundation. The LPGA is under the guidance of Commissioner Michael Whan and is headquartered in Daytona Beach, Florida.

## National Golf Course Owners Association (NGCOA)

Established in 1979 and headquartered in Charleston, South Carolina, the NGCOA is the leading authority on the business of golf course ownership and management. The association represents the industry's key decision makers with ultimate responsibility for golf courses throughout the world. The not-for-profit organization is the only trade association dedicated exclusively to golf course owners and operators. Membership of the NGCOA includes owners and operators of daily-fee, semi-private, private and resort courses. While diverse in its makeup, the association serves as a resource to meet a critical need shared by all owners and operators in today's ever-changing golf industry: information and inspiration on how to operate their facilities as efficiently and profitably as possible.

## National Golf Foundation (NGF)

The National Golf Foundation, founded in 1936 and based in Jupiter, Florida, is the industry's knowledge leader on the U.S. golf economy. NGF is an objective and independent information resource dedicated to supporting all the people, companies, facilities and associations that earn their living in the golf business. NGF delivers market intelligence, insights and trends to fulfill its mission: to keep golf businesses ahead of the game. Four thousand member courses, clubs, associations, media and myriad golf-related businesses rely on NGF research and resources to support their best decisions.

## Professional Golfers' Association of America (PGA)

The PGA of America is the world's largest working sports organization, comprised of 27,000 men and women golf professionals who are the recognized experts in growing, teaching and managing the game of golf, while serving millions of people throughout its 41 PGA sections nationwide. Since its founding in 1916, the PGA of America has enhanced its leadership position by growing the game of golf through its premier spectator events, world-class education and training programs, significant philanthropic outreach initiatives, and award-winning golf promotions.

## United States Golf Association (USGA)

The USGA is golf's governing body that preserves its past, fosters its future, and champions its best interests for everyone who enjoys the game. The USGA conducts 13 national championships each year, writes and interprets the Rules of Golf, regulates and tests all golf equipment for conformance to the Rules of Golf, maintains the handicap and course rating systems, provides research-based turf management expertise, and generally celebrates the history of the game.

## World Golf Foundation (WGF)

World Golf Foundation focuses on a variety of initiatives to grow and celebrate the game of golf around the world. Through *The First Tee*, the World Golf Foundation focuses on positively impacting the lives of young people. Under the banner of the World Golf Hall of Fame, it recognizes and celebrates golf's greatest players and contributors and serves as an inspiration to golfers and fans worldwide. The World Golf Foundation's GOLF 20/20 initiative pursues programs to ensure golf's continued growth and vitality. All World Golf Foundation initiatives work together to support the growth of the game among youth, women and minorities, while also fostering diversity within the golf industry. The World Golf Foundation also supports the golf industry in a variety of other roles, including acting as a centralized vehicle for communicating the industry's initiatives to the media, initiating research projects to demonstrate the game's scope and impact, and providing a unified approach to the anti-doping policies being implemented by the major global professional tours.